Modula-2

Modula-2

John Beidler
Paul Jackowitz

UNIVERSITY OF SCRANTON

PWS COMPUTER SCIENCE

Boston

PWS PUBLISHERS

Prindle, Weber & Schmidt • ♣ • Duxbury Press • ♠ • PWS Engineering • ⚏ • Breton Publishers • ☸
20 Park Plaza • Boston, Massachusetts 02116

The following is a list of companies or institutions and their trademarked products mentioned in this text:

Apple Computer, Inc.: Apple
Control Data Corporation: CDC
Digital Equipment Corporation: PDP, VAX
Honeywell Information Systems, Inc.: Honeywell
International Business Machines Corporation: IBM
Regents of the University of California: UCSD Pascal, UCSD Pascal p-system
U.S. Department of Defense: Ada

PWS Publishers is a division of Wadsworth, Inc.

Library of Congress Cataloging in Publication Data

Beidler, John,
   Modula-2.

   Includes index.
   1. Modula-2 (Computer program language)
I. Jackowitz, Paul, 1955–   II. Title.
QA76.73.M63B45   1986   001.64′24   85–6298
ISBN 0–87150–912–1

ISBN 0-87150-912-1

Printed in the United States of America

   86 87 88 89 — 10 9 8 7 6 5 4 3 2

Production Coordinator: Ellie Connolly. Manuscript Editor: Ian List. Interior and Cover Design: Ellie Connolly. Cover Photo: Computer graphic image by Tom Norton. Interior Illustration: Horvath & Cuthbertson Illustrations. Typesetting: Beacon Graphics Corporation. Cover Printing: Phoenix Color Corporation. Printing and Binding: Halliday Lithograph.

For Pat and the sailboat fund

jb

To Jo Ann and for my parents and family

pmj

Preface

This book was written, with textlike organization and exercises, as a comprehensive reference for the programming language Modula-2. As such, readers with advanced knowledge of Modula-2, or some other high-level programming language, might find the earlier chapters somewhat lengthy. Readers with very little programming experience and background might find some of the later chapters overwhelming. This text is structured to serve the needs of a wide audience. Therefore advanced readers should feel free to peruse the text as their needs demand. Other readers should feel confident in knowing that as their knowledge of programming methodology expands, the corresponding language dependent material to support this knowledge is in the text. For reference, this text contains several appendixes and an extensive index. We hope readers find these references valuable.

In anticipation of colleges and universities making extensive use of Modula-2 in their computing curriculum, we have written this text to serve students as a reference to Modula-2 throughout their college education. We hope that instructors will then be able to concentrate their efforts on the selection of appropriate texts dealing with the specific subject matter of particular courses. We see this text as a complement to courses using the programming language Modula-2.

When students take courses in the computing sciences, the text must frequently serve two roles. First, the text must introduce students to the primary subject matter of the course. Second, students need an appropriate reference to the particular programming language being utilized. This second requirement tends to be the more difficult of the two. Since the primary purpose of a course text is to present the course material, usually only those features within the programming language that support the course material are presented. When students take other courses utilizing the same programming language, often the text is no longer appropriate because it was not intended as a complete reference for the language. We see this text as a reference for Modula-2 and we see it as offering considerable utility in supporting the programming language aspects of many courses within a computer science curriculum. Specifically, this text may be used in courses beginning with CS2 as defined in the ACM's curriculum '78, and continuing with courses in data structures, systems programming, operating systems, computer graphics, and potentially other upper-division courses.

This text is partitioned into four major parts:

1. Chapters 1 through 4: Language fundamentals and basic language features. The emphasis here is on syntax.

2. Chapters 5 and 6: Transitional material introducing structured data types and procedures.

3. Chapter 7: A reference to typical standard procedures and modules.

4. Chapters 8 through 10: Advanced programming supported through the use of library modules (Chapter 8), dynamic storage allocation (Chapter 9), and low-level programming (Chapter 10).

Pascal has had an important impact on computer science course and curriculum development. However, there have been a number of criticisms of ISO standard Pascal and its lack of features to support certain desirable programming capabilities. Perhaps the best-known set of criticisms are those voiced by Brian Kernighan in his paper, "Why Pascal Is Not My Favorite Programming Language."

We do not share Kernighan's feelings about Pascal; however, his criticisms are valid. Different implementations of Pascal have different extensions that allow programmers to obtain efficient file access, obtain direct access to systems software and hardware features, and so forth. However, Niklaus Wirth, the inventor of Pascal, has a better plan. The implementation of this plan is the programming language called Modula-2.

Modula-2 is a Pascal-like programming language that supports good programming practices and provides a standard method of extension. With Modula-2, programmers can gain efficient low-level access to machine features within the structure of a good high-level programming language.

This text presents the original definition of Modula-2 along with the later revision. The original definition appears in **Programming in Modula-2**, 2nd Corrected Edition, by Niklaus Wirth. The revised definition of Modula-2 appears in "Revisions and Amendments to Modula-2," also by Wirth. Where appropriate in the text, the term "revised definition" is used to present those restrictions, clarifications, changes, and extensions to the language.

The current implementations of Modula-2 on the PDP-11, VAX, Apple, and IBM PC are excellent. Given the similarity between Modula-2 and Pascal, schools with these types of computers should find the transition to Modula-2 easy and worthwhile. Modula-2 compilers are becoming available for most timesharing systems, in particular, the IBM 360/370, 30xx, 43xx family of computers, CDC, and Honeywell systems.

But what about Ada? We cannot ignore Ada because of the backing it receives from the U.S. Defense Department. Even here, Modula-2 fits. Modula-2 satisfies most of the requirements that led to the definition of Ada. Doubts have been raised about whether efficient implementation of Ada will become available on a variety of computers, especially microcomputers. Except for some of the most esoteric features, Modula-2 is an excellent and efficiently implemented stepping stone between Pascal and Ada. In fact, we are aware of several companies performing software development by using Modula-2 for their development work, then automatically translating their final product into the Ada syntax.

As the product of two authors, this text contains many compromises. One compromise was the formatting convention used to present programs. Since every programmer has their own method of indenting and formatting programs, the method we use is itself an agreed-upon compromise. The indenting should provide visual clues to program structure rather than just indicate the nesting of structure. We have adopted the following indentation conventions:

1. The contents of a procedure are indented three spaces more than the procedure declaration line.

2. The contents of every loop are indented three spaces.

3. In IF statements the ELSE and ELSIF clauses are indented two spaces and the statement sequences are indented four spaces.

4. All END statements are indented to align with the initial reserved word of the statement involved.

To make the programs more compact, we use very few comments. Explanations of the programs appear in the text in lieu of program comments. Comments are very helpful, and we encourage students to place meaningful comments at appropriate positions in their source code.

We are very fortunate to have received many excellent critical reviews of our work by our colleagues at the University of Scranton, who supported us (and put up with us) throughout the development of this text. They provided many suggestions while working with earlier drafts of this material in our CS2, data structures, operating systems, and programming languages courses. Many thanks to Mary Bahruth, Ruth Cicilioni, Ashok Kumar, John Meinke, Rosemary Schmalz, Dick Sidbury, and Charles Taylor for their tolerance and suggestions.

Our thanks, as well, go to the many students who suffered through earlier versions of parts of this manuscript and provided us with very thorough tests of the various Modula-2 compilers that were available to us. Special thanks to Cindy Cuffman, Joe Fabiano, Jim Fox, Paul Haggerty, Carl Sobeski, and Joe Touch.

Many thanks to Karen Ellison, our Editor, for her support of this project. She believed us before many people had heard about Modula-2 and provided us with many excellent reviewers. Not all of the reviewers agreed with our approach in this book, but whether they agreed with us or not, they provided us with many helpful suggestions, some of which we incorporated. Our deepest thanks go to Lyle Bingham, Ariel Frank, Jerud Mead, Richard Pattis, Adarshpal Sethi, Allen Tucker, and others.

Our special thanks goes to those who put the final touches on the book. We would like to thank Bill Bokermann and Ellie Connolly for ushering the book to completion and Ian List, who did an outstanding job copy editing the text. We also would like to thank the folks at Beacon Graphics Corporation. They performed "their magic" in transforming our IBM PC-based WordStar disks into the final product. Without this support, this text might still be a dream.

Contents

Chapter 1
Introduction   1
    1:1 Programming Practices   1
    1:2 Pascal   2
    1:3 Modula-2   4
    1:4 Modula-2 and Ada   6

Chapter 2
Language Fundamentals   7
    2:1 Program Syntax and Example Program   7
    2:2 Lexical Symbols   10
        2:2:1 Reserved Words   13
        2:2:2 Identifiers   13
        2:2:3 Literals   16
    2:3 Expressions   20
    2:4 Operators   22
        2:4:1 Assignment Operator   22
        2:4:2 Arithmetic Operators   23
        2:4:3 Boolean Operators   24
        2:4:4 Relational Operators   25
        2:4:5 Set Operators   26
        2:4:6 Dereferencing Operator   27
        2:4:7 Precedence Among Operators   27
    2:5 Delimiters and Comments   28

Chapter 3
Data Fundamentals   31
    3:1 Data Objects   31
        3:1:1 Constants and the CONST Statement   32
        3:1:2 Variables and the VAR Statement   34

3:2 Elementary Data Types   36
    3:2:1 INTEGER and CARDINAL Data Types   36
    3:2:2 REAL Data Type   38
    3:2:3 BOOLEAN Data Type   41
    3:2:4 CHAR Data Type   44
    3:2:5 BITSET Data Type   47
3:3 Unstructured Data Types   51
    3:3:1 Enumeration Types   51
    3:3:2 Subranges   53

Chapter 4
Program Structure   56

4:1 Overview   56
4:2 Importing and Procedure Calls   58
4:3 Decision Statements   63
    4:3:1 The IF Statement   63
    4:3:2 The CASE Statement   67
4:4 Looping Statements   71
    4:4:1 The WHILE Statement   72
    4:4:2 The REPEAT Statement   74
    4:4:3 The FOR Statement   76
    4:4:4 The LOOP and EXIT Statements   78

Chapter 5
Structured Data Types   82

5:1 Arrays   82
5:2 Records   94
    5:2:1 Records Without Variants   94
    5:2:2 Variant Record Structures   99
5:3 Sets   104
5:4 Multidimensional Arrays and Other Combinations
    of Structured Types   112

Chapter 6
Procedures   117

6:1 Overview   117
6:2 Variables and Parameters   125
6:3 Functions   133
6:4 Recursion   137
6:5 Using Procedures   143
6:6 Procedure Types   154

Chapter 7
Standard Procedures and Modules   158

7:1 Standard Procedures   158
    7:1:1 Basic Operations   158
    7:1:2 Type Transfer and Type Conversion   163
    7:1:3 Arithmetic Manipulation   164
7:2 The MODULE Concept   166
7:3 The Module InOut   170
7:4 Additional Standard Modules for I/O   173
7:5 The Module MathLib0   175
7:6 The Module SYSTEM   177
7:7 Other Modules   178

Chapter 8
Module Structure   180

8:1 Overview   180
8:2 Local Modules   187
8:3 Library Modules   192
    8:3:1 Definition Modules   193
    8:3:2 Implementation Modules   196
8:4 Data Abstraction   199

Chapter 9
Dynamic Data Objects   203

9:1 Dynamic Storage Allocation   203
9:2 Lists   210
9:3 Stacks   220
9:4 Queues   228
9:5 Trees   236
9:6 Directed Graphs   246
9:7 Variant Records in Dynamic Allocation   253

Chapter 10
Advanced Features   262

10:1 Low-Level Programming   262
10:2 Generics   273
10:3 Nontext Stream I/O   279
10:4 Coroutines   283

Appendix A
Modula-2 EBNF   293

Appendix B
Modula-2 Syntax Diagrams   297

Appendix C
ASCII Character Set   314

Appendix D
Standard Modules   316

D:1 Files   316
    D:1:1 Types   316
    D:1:2 Procedures   317
D:2 FileSystem   318
    D:2:1 Types   318
    D:2:2 Procedures   318
    D:2:3 Variations   320
D:3 InOut   320
    D:3:1 Constants   320
    D:3:2 Variables   320
    D:3:3 Procedures   321
    D:3:4 Variations   322
D:4 MathLib0   323
    D:4:1 Procedures   323
D:5 Processes   324
    D:5:1 Types   324
    D:5:2 Procedures   324
D:6 RealInOut   325
    D:6:1 Variables   325
    D:6:2 Procedures   325
D:7 Storage   325
    D:7:1 Procedures   325
    D:7:2 Variations   326
D:8 SYSTEM   326
    D:8:1 Types   326
    D:8:2 Procedures   327
    D:8:3 Variations   327
D:9 Terminal   328
    D:9:1 Procedures   328
D:10 TextIO   329
    D:10:1 Constants   329
    D:10:2 Types   329
    D:10:3 Variables   330
    D:10:4 Procedures   330
    D:10:5 Variations   332

Appendix E
Modula-2 Error Messages   333

References   337

Index   340

Modula-2

1 Introduction

1:1 Programming Practices

The term **programming** is used in this chapter in a general sense to describe the entire programming life cycle—the collection of tasks performed when designing, building, and maintaining software systems. Programming is not just coding. It describes the software-related aspects in a **system's life cycle**. One approach to decomposing the system's life cycle is to break it into the following four components:

1. Analysis Phase: Understand the problem to be solved by analyzing the problem and formulating the systems requirements.

2. Design Phase: Given the systems requirements, determine the appropriate structure of the system, including the structure of the design of the system's software at both a high and low level.

3. Implementation Phase: Following the structure from the design phase, build the system.

4. System Evolution Phase: If a system is good, it affects the environment that contains it. People using the system obtain new information, which leads to new ideas. Therefore the system evolves either to correct errors that have been found or to provide support for new ideas.

Once this broad view of programming is accepted by the reader, several items become very important. For example, programmers (systems analysts, programmer analysts, and so forth) must follow good programming practices. These practices include analyzing the problem

1

thoroughly; developing a detailed solution design; and following sound, structured programming practices. To succeed, the programmer must be supplied with good programming tools and, in addition, must make good use of these tools. Among those tools must be a programming language that supports the development and maintenance of complex software systems.

The role of the programming language may be critical to the success of any programming endeavor. New approaches to software development demand a programming language that is effective throughout the system's life cycle. The language must effectively and efficiently provide high-level solution design support as well as access to low-level machine features.

Modula-2 is a programming language that satisfies these requirements. It has its roots in Pascal, a programming language that continues to play an important role in computer science education and that has gained broad acceptance as a programming tool. Although Pascal has been criticized because of certain language limitations, it has had a very positive effect on the programming community. It supports good programming practices through its excellent support of strong data typing and control structures. As the programming community gained experience with Pascal in the development of large, complex programming systems, several limitations of the language became apparent. To compensate for these limitations, implementors of Pascal have developed many fine compilers for the language that contain extensions that overcome some of the limitations. UCSD Pascal™ is one example of an implementation that contains some interesting and important language extensions. From another viewpoint, it is this lack of standards and variety of language extensions that has lead to some of the criticisms of Pascal as an implementation tool for large computer systems.

1:2 Pascal

Although Niklaus Wirth is best known as the creator of Pascal, he had been involved in the development of other programming languages before Pascal. Students in some of the first computer science programs developed in the mid-sixties speak fondly of two programming languages available on IBM System/360 computers: PL/360 and ALGOL-W. PL/360 is best described as a structured assembly language. ALGOL-W, developed jointly by Wirth and Charles Hoare, built upon their experiences with the programming language ALGOL-60. In 1966, after several years of developing ALGOL-W, they published its description. Most of the computer scientists who had experience with ALGOL-W were satisfied with the features of this language, which supported the direct and explicit statement of problem solutions.

Two years later the ALGOL-68 report was published. It is interesting to compare ALGOL-W with ALGOL-68. ALGOL-W is basically the product of two people, Wirth and Hoare, who were interested in designing a clean and useful programming language. ALGOL-68, being the product of a committee, contains numerous compromises and biases. Wirth was involved with both projects, and the lessons he learned from them are apparent in his design of Pascal.

The first implementation of Pascal occurred in 1970. Over the next decade Pascal became the preferred language for introductory courses in computing. The implementation of the UCSD Pascal p-system™ by Ken Bowles extended this language into the burgeoning microcomputer marketplace and made this excellent software development tool available to this growing segment of the computing community.

Although Pascal's success far exceeded its original 1969 to 1970 design considerations, it has received a variety of criticisms. The most complete statement of these criticisms appears in the paper "Why Pascal Is Not My Favorite Language" by Brian Kernighan. Briefly stated, these criticisms include the following items:

1. Array sizes are fixed in Pascal. Because of strong data typing, programmers cannot write a single sorting procedure that sorts all arrays of a particular type (for example, all arrays of type INTEGER regardless of the predefined size of the array). This limitation means that separate, but basically identical, statement sequences must be written to sort arrays composed of data of the same base type.

2. Pascal has a predefined order of declarations, constants, types, variables, and then procedures. Because of this predefined order, identifiers cannot be grouped to indicate interrelationships. A more severe implication of this rigid order is that when a new type is declared, constants cannot be declared for that type.

3. The order of evaluation of boolean expressions is not defined in Pascal. More precisely, the boolean operations indicated by AND and OR are not defined as sequential operations. For example, assume that the array A is subscripted over the range 1 .. N for some constant N. The compound expression

(J < 1) OR (A [J] > A [J+1])

might be intended to express a programmer's desire that a condition become true if either the array subscript is out of range or a certain relationship holds between two elements in the array. In Pascal the evaluation of this expression could result in a run time error if the value of J is less than 1 and A [J] is referenced. Thus in Pascal the programmer is forced to write this compound expression as a boolean function, which complicates a simple situation. This problem is referred to as the **sequential logic problem**.

4. When a procedure is called in Pascal, its local variables are allocated; when a procedure terminates, the local variables are deallocated. Because of this feature, the only way a procedure may store information between calls is through global variables, which is undesirable because global variables might be inadvertently referenced and modified elsewhere in the program. It would be worthwhile, therefore, for procedures to be able to declare **own variables**. An own variable is a variable that may only be accessed by a specific procedure or collection of procedures so that information may be stored from one procedure call to the next.

5. Although various implementations of Pascal have facilities for separate compilation, most notably UCSD Pascal™, no standard approach exists for the development of libraries of identifiers. Therefore a Pascal implementation of a large, complex system tends to become a single, very large source file, which must be completely recompiled every time a modification is made. Not only does this recompilation consume time but it also eliminates the possibility of effectively hiding details and makes data abstraction incomplete.

6. Pascal does not support a standard low-level access to machine capabilities. For example, a bit pattern stored in a variable of one type cannot be conveniently and directly transferred to a variable of another type.

7. Pascal cannot be extended. This deficiency is most apparent in the limited definition of its I/O capabilities.

Various implementations of Pascal address many of these criticisms. For example, UCSD Pascal™ supports a separate compilation capability. Through this capability, programmers may build separate libraries of identifiers for procedures, types, constants, and variables. The separate compilation capability supports own variables and, to some extent, it supports the hiding of details and data abstraction.

1:3 Modula-2

Modula-2 is a product of the Lilith project, the goal of which was the development of a powerful personal workstation. The Lilith computer is a personal workstation based upon a powerful processor. The system uses a bit-mapped graphics display and was built with the requirements of a high-level programming language kept as a major consideration. As Wirth states in an article that appeared in **Byte Magazine**, "The History and Goals of Modula-2," the Lilith project had three fixed constraints:

1. A single programming language.

2. A single user operating system.

3. A single processor.

This combination of constraints influences the design of the programming language. In particular, the language must be used to implement the operating system. Hence the language must be capable of efficient access to low-level machine capabilities within the framework of a high-level programming language.

This goal led to the definition of Modula-2 in 1978 and its implementation in 1979. Modula-2 was first implemented on a PDP-11, then on the Lilith computer. In 1980 the first Modula-2 compiler was released, and interest in the language has been growing rapidly.

Although Modula-2 appears to be, on the surface, simply a modification of Pascal, the programming languages Simula, Mesa, and Modula have all made some contribution to its features. Perhaps the most striking feature in Modula-2 is its module structure, which is alluded to throughout this text and described completely in Chapter 8. Many of the criticisms made of Pascal are eliminated with Modula-2's library module capability. Hiding details, data abstraction, separate compilation, language extensions, low-level access to machine features, own variables, and I/O capabilities are all supported through modules.

Open array sizes, sequential logic, and the ability to mix the order of occurrence of declarations are all supported through the definition of Modula-2. For example, the compound expression presented in Section 1:2, as an illustration of the sequential logic problem in Pascal, does not need to be implemented with a boolean function in Modula-2. It may be expressed simply as the compound expression

$$(\ J \ < \ 1 \ ) \ OR \ (\ A \ [J] \ > \ A \ [J+1] \ )$$

because the boolean operator OR is defined sequentially, as

$$p \ OR \ q \ = \ TRUE, \text{ if } p \text{ is } TRUE$$
$$= \ q, \text{ otherwise}$$

Thus when $J < 1$, the first condition evaluates to TRUE; the second condition, $A [J] > A [J+1]$, is not evaluated, thus avoiding the range error.

1:4 Modula-2 and Ada

Ada™ is the programming language sponsored and developed by the United States Department of Defense. This language also has its roots in Pascal, with excellent support of strong data typing and good control structures. In many respects Modula-2 satisfies the requirements set forth in the documents that led to the definition of Ada™. Effective and efficient Modula-2 compilers exist for a large number of computer systems. An individual with experience in either of these two languages may easily learn the other.

In addition to being an important programming language in itself, Modula-2 is also a bridge between Pascal and Ada™. Modula-2 does not support all of the features supported by Ada. However, what it does support, it supports well, with efficient compilers generating efficient code. Many programming tasks do not need the entire gambit of support provided through Ada. Ada is a good language, but it is very complex with rather heavy systems requirements. Because of this complexity, it is questionable whether full, efficient Ada compilers can be built for microcomputers.

Language Fundamentals

2:1 Program Syntax and Example Program

In Modula-2, as in many other programming languages, a source program is prepared by the programmer. This source program, which is written in a well-defined language, must be translated into a form that may then be directly executed by a computer. This source program contains data declaration statements and executable statements, which represent an algorithm and specify the work to be performed by the computer. The exact form that the source program must take is described by the syntax of the programming language.

Syntax diagrams are one method of describing the syntax of a programming language. A **syntax diagram** describes a single language construct through the use of rectangular and oval boxes connected by lines and arrows. Oval boxes contain characters that must appear exactly as specified, whereas rectangular boxes contain the names of other language constructs. Lines and arrows show the exact order in which these constructs must be combined. A syntax diagram precisely describes the structure of a language construct.

Consider the syntax diagrams in Figure 2-1. They do not describe any of the syntax of Modula-2, but are presented here to provide an illustration of the use of syntax diagrams. These particular diagrams describe a syntax that might be used to form people's names.

The first diagram indicates the syntax of what is called *Full Name*. Syntactically, a *Full Name* consists of a *Title* followed by a *Name*, optionally followed by a *Letter* and a period. Another occurrence of *Name* com-

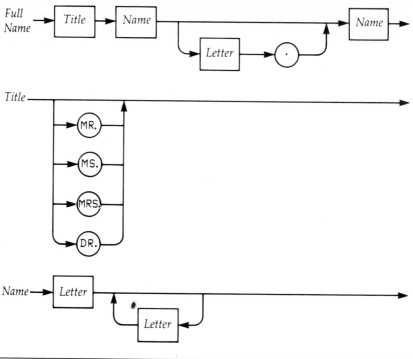

Figure 2-1   Illustrative Syntax Diagrams

pletes this syntax. Thus both of the following sequences are valid examples of *Full Name*:

    Title   Name   Name
    Title   Name   Letter   .   Name

The syntax of *Title*, *Name*, and *Letter* must also be determined, since they are constructs in the definition of *Full Name*. The second diagram in Figure 2-1 indicates that *Title* is either empty or one of the following four alternatives: MR., MS., MRS., or DR.. Each of these alternatives, like the period present in the first diagram, is enclosed in an oval box because it represents a sequence of characters that must appear exactly as specified. Thus each of the following sequences is also valid for *Full Name*:

    MR.   *Name   Name*
    MR.   *Name   Letter   .   Name*
    MRS. *Name   Name*
    Name   Name
    DR.   *Name   Letter   .   Name*

The third diagram in Figure 2-1 illustrates that a *Name* is any sequence of one or more *Letter*s. Although the syntax diagram for *Letter* is required to complete this definition, it is not shown in the figure because it is easy to visualize and would require too much space. Informally, a *Letter* may be any one of the 26 letters of the alphabet. Thus each of the following sequences is valid for *Full Name*:

```
MR.  JOHN  SMITH
JOHN  H  .  SMITH
HARRY  JONES
DR.  A  B  .  SEAY
MS.  X  T
```

In Modula-2 a source program is referred to as a **compilation unit.** Figure 2-2 contains the syntax diagram for a *Compilation Unit*. If we follow the lines and arrows in this syntax diagram, we see that a *Compilation Unit* is either a *Definition Module*, an *Implementation Module*, or a *Program Module*. As the syntax diagrams indicate, the construct *Implementation Module* is the reserved word IMPLEMENTATION followed by a *Program Module*. Definition modules, implementation modules, and their corresponding language constructs are discussed in detail in Chapter 8.

A *Program Module*, described by the syntax diagram in Figure 2-3, is what most programmers regard as a main program. A *Program Module* **must** contain the word MODULE and the delimiters " ; " and " . ", as well as the constructs *Identifier* and *Block*. As illustrated in Figure 2-3, the constructs *Priority* and *Import* are optional. *Priority* may occur only once, but *Import* may be repeated any number of times. Obviously, this description is not complete. The syntax diagrams for *Identifier*, *Priority*, *Import*, and *Block* are not given here but are discussed in later sections. Where appropriate, syntax diagrams appear in this text to describe the syntax of Modula-2 constructs. In addition, a complete collection of syntax diagrams for Modula-2 appears in Appendix B.

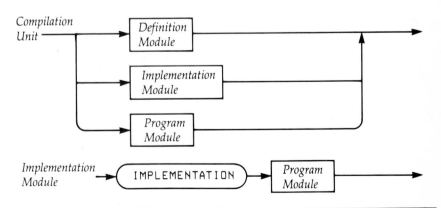

Figure 2-2   Syntax Diagram for *Compilation Unit*

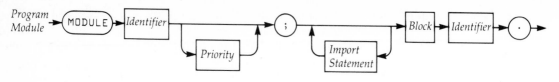

Figure 2-3   Syntax Diagram for *Program Module*

Consider the example Modula-2 *Program Module* shown in Figure 2-4. This complete *Program Module*, identified as TimesTable, computes and prints a multiplication table. Figure 2-5 shows a dialog obtained while executing this program. The *Program Module* presented in Figure 2-4 is valid because it satisfies the syntax indicated by the diagrams in Figures 2-2 and 2-3. At this stage you might not understand exactly why this example is syntactically correct because there is still more to discuss. When the Program Module TimesTable is revisited in Chapter 4, the syntax will be clarified. The fundamental syntax details of Modula-2 are described in this chapter and Chapters 3 and 4.

2:2 Lexical Symbols

The constructs that comprise Modula-2 are ultimately defined in terms of lexical symbols. A **lexical symbol** is a sequence of one or more characters that represents an element in the language. Certain words have a special meaning in Modula-2 and are called **reserved words** because they may not be used for any other purpose. All of the reserved words are lexical symbols. Figure 2-6 lists the reserved words along with other lexical symbols. As you can see, lexical symbols represent arithmetic, set, relational, boolean, and assignment operators. They also serve as delimiters. In addition, programmer-defined identifiers and literals may also be considered lexical symbols. Most of Modula-2's lexical symbols are familiar to Pascal programmers. This similarity does not mean that the lexical symbols appearing in both Pascal and Modula-2 have the same interpretation. There are some significant differences.

Syntax diagrams appear throughout this text wherever the syntax of a particular construct or statement is introduced. When reading these diagrams, note that whatever appears in an oval box is a lexical symbol and is therefore listed in Figure 2-6. Each individual alphabetic and numeric character may serve as a lexical symbol in its own right. Figures 2-8 and 2-11 indicate the roles of lexical symbols in defining *Identifier*s and *Literal*s. These roles are discussed in Sections 2:2:2 and 2:2:3. Any language construct used in the rectangular boxes of a syntax diagram and not defined in that same figure may be found in Appendix B.

```
 1 MODULE  TimesTable;
 2
 3 FROM InOut IMPORT ReadCard, WriteCard, WriteString, WriteLn;
 4
 5 CONST  Limit = 12;              (* Maximum allowed size of table *)
 6
 7 VAR    Size, I, Row, Column, Entry : CARDINAL;
 8
 9 BEGIN
10
11 (*  User interaction to accept desired table size  *)
12 WriteString ('Enter Size?');  ReadCard (Size);  WriteLn;
13 WriteLn;
14
15 IF Size > Limit THEN            (*  Test for valid user input  *)
16     WriteString ('---ERROR: Size exceeds the Limit of ');
17     WriteCard (Limit, 2); WriteLn
18   ELSE      (*  Write the heading across the top of the page  *)
19     WriteString ('    !');
20     FOR I := 1 TO Size BY 1 DO    (* Write the column headings *)
21         WriteCard (I, 5)
22     END;
23     WriteLn;
24     WriteString (' ---!');
25     FOR I := 1 TO Size DO
26         WriteString ('-----')
27     END;
28     WriteLn;
29                              (* Once for each row in the table *)
30     FOR Row := 1 TO Size BY 1 DO
31         WriteCard (Row, 3);
32         WriteString (' !');
33
34         FOR Column := 1 TO Size BY 1 DO (* Once for each column *)
35             Entry := Row * Column;
36             WriteCard (Entry, 5)
37         END;
38         WriteLn              (* Terminate the output line  *)
39
40     END
41 END
42
43 END TimesTable.
```

Figure 2-4   Example of a Modula-2 Program Module

`EnterSize?12`

	1	2	3	4	5	6	7	8	9	10	11	12
1	1	2	3	4	5	6	7	8	9	10	11	12
2	2	4	6	8	10	12	14	16	18	20	22	24
3	3	6	9	12	15	18	21	24	27	30	33	36
4	4	8	12	16	20	24	28	32	36	40	44	48
5	5	10	15	20	25	30	35	40	45	50	55	60
6	6	12	18	24	30	36	42	48	54	60	66	72
7	7	14	21	28	35	42	49	56	63	70	77	84
8	8	16	24	32	40	48	56	64	72	80	88	96
9	9	18	27	36	45	54	63	72	81	90	99	108
10	10	20	30	40	50	60	70	80	90	100	110	120
11	11	22	33	44	55	66	77	88	99	110	121	132
12	12	24	36	48	60	72	84	96	108	120	132	144

Figure 2-5   Example of a Dialog with the Program Module `TimesTable`

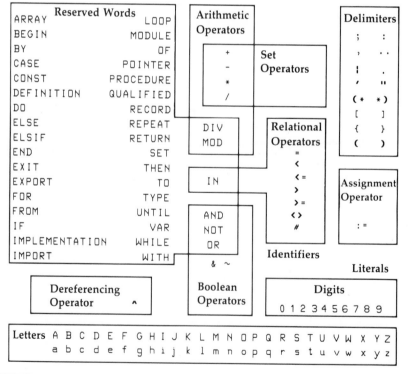

Figure 2-6   Lexical Symbols

2:2:1 Reserved Words

The 40 reserved words of Modula-2 may be used only for their intended purpose and may not be redefined by the programmer. Therefore we classify these lexical symbols according to their use in programs. As Figure 2-6 shows, the reserved words DIV, MOD, IN, AND, NOT, and OR serve as operators. DIV and MOD are arithmetic operators; IN is a relational operator; and AND, NOT, and OR are boolean operators. These operations are discussed in Sections 2:4:2, 2:4:4, and 2:4:3, respectively. Figure 2-7 shows the remaining 34 reserved words, classified according to their use in programs.

2:2:2 Identifiers

Identifiers are sequences of characters used by programmers to name modules, constants, variables, procedures, and other programmer-definable items. Figure 2-8 shows the syntax diagrams for identifiers. The first diagram in Figure 2-8 is the syntax diagram for an *Identifier*. This diagram shows that programmers may compose identifiers of any length using the 52 uppercase and lowercase letters of the alphabet and the digits. One constraint, conveyed by the syntax diagram, is that each *Identifier* must begin with a letter. A second constraint, not conveyed by the syntax diagram, is that none of the reserved words may be used as *Identifiers*. Thus each of the following items is a distinct example of a valid *Identifier*:

I, J7, VanHorn, MAXIMUM, x, Limit, Not, aRRAY, total

Likewise, each of the following items is an example of an invalid *Identifier*:

1984TOTAL, Gross-Pay, x$current, NOT, NET_PAY

Compilation Units	Data Definition	Decision Statements	Looping Statements	Miscellaneous Functions
MODULE	CONST	IF	FOR	BEGIN
DEFINITION	TYPE	THEN	BY	END
IMPLEMENTATION	VAR	ELSE	WHILE	DO
FROM	ARRAY	ELSIF	REPEAT	OF
IMPORT	RECORD	CASE	UNTIL	TO
EXPORT	SET		LOOP	WITH
QUALIFIED	POINTER		EXIT	RETURN
PROCEDURE				

Figure 2-7   Classification of Reserved Words

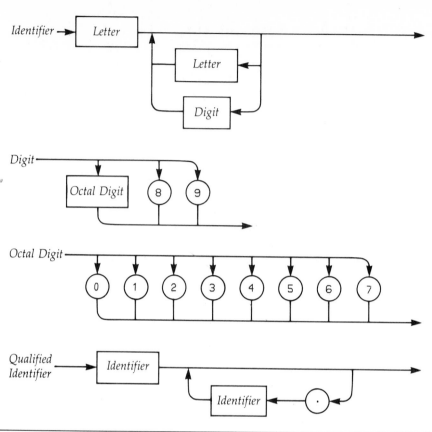

Figure 2-8   Syntax Diagrams for *Identifier*

Figure 2-8 also indicates that a *Qualified Identifier* may be two *Identifiers* separated by a period. A *Qualified Identifier* is not needed in most programming situations, but this construct allows *Identifiers* declared in one module to be referenced in another module. The first *Identifier* names the module in which the item was defined, and the second identifies the item. The syntax diagram in Figure 2-8 indicates that a single *Identifier* is also a *Qualified Identifier*. *Qualified Identifiers* are discussed in Chapters 5, 7, and 8.

In Modula-2 all *Identifiers* must be declared before they may be used. A collection of standard identifiers is predefined in the language and available for use by programmers. Figure 2-9 lists these standard identifiers in alphabetical order. Because these standard identifiers serve distinct purposes, they have been grouped according to their use in the language and listed as a reference in Figure 2-10. Data types are discussed later in this chapter and in Chapter 3, as are the data values TRUE and FALSE. The

```
ABS            DEC            INC            ORD
BITSET         DISPOSE        INCL           PROC
BOOLEAN        EXCL           INTEGER        REAL
CAP            FALSE          NEW            TRUE
CARDINAL       FLOAT          NIL            TRUNC
CHAR           HALT           ODD            VAL
CHR            HIGH
```

Figure 2-9   Standard Identifiers in Alphabetic Order

Standard Procedures		Data Types	Data Values
ABS	HIGH	BITSET	TRUE
CAP	INC	BOOLEAN	FALSE
CHR	INCL	CARDINAL	NIL
DEC	ODD	CHAR	**Dynamic**
EXCL	ORD	INTEGER	**Allocation**
FLOAT	TRUNC	PROC	NEW
HALT	VAL	REAL	DISPOSE

Figure 2-10   Standard Identifiers Grouped According to Use

value NIL and the procedures NEW and DISPOSE deal with dynamic allocation and are discussed in Chapter 9. The remaining standard identifiers correspond to standard procedures and are discussed in Chapter 7.

The revised definition of Modula-2, published in early 1984, additionally allows LONGCARD, LONGINT, and LONGREAL as optional standard identifiers. They represent data types in addition to CARDINAL, INTEGER, and REAL and provide for the representation of values in extended ranges. Because of the differences in computer hardware, these data types may not be available on all implementations. In addition, implementors are free to declare other standard identifiers to suit the needs or features of a particular computer system. Thus Figures 2-9 and 2-10 specify the standard identifiers that must be declared.

An important use of identifiers is in the naming of data objects. A **data object** is a programmer-defined container for values of a particular data type. In most cases a data object is declared by associating an *Identifier* with it. Data objects declared in this way are classified either as constants or variables. A **constant** is a data object that is permanently associated to a fixed value. A **variable** is a data object that stores values that may change as the program executes. In Modula-2 the value of a constant is specified in a declaration statement and associated prior to program execution. Values are stored in variables during program execution.

2:2:3 Literals

A **literal** is a data object that corresponds to a single, unchanging value during program execution. The literal itself directly represents the value that corresponds to it. Literals are not named by identifiers; instead the value of a literal and its written representation are equivalent. In Modula-2, literals may represent numbers, characters, strings, sets, and programmer-defined enumerated data values. Figure 2-11 shows the pertinent syntax diagrams. Sets, which are introduced in Chapter 5, are not discussed in this section. The syntax diagram for *Set* is in Appendix B.

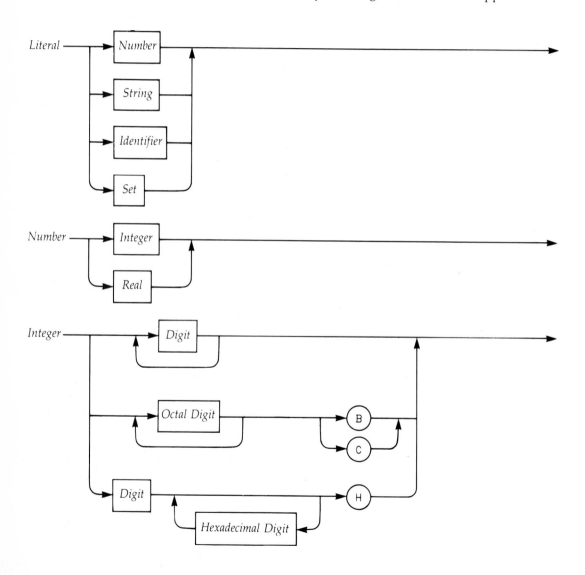

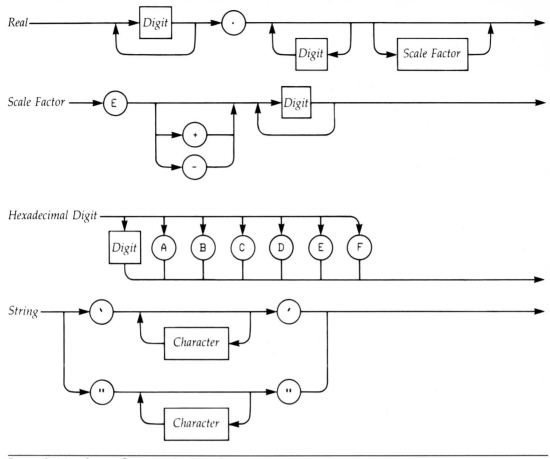

Figure 2-11   Syntax Diagram for *Literal*

The identifiers INTEGER, CARDINAL, and REAL are standard identifiers for three commonly used data types. The data type INTEGER represents the equivalent of the mathematical concept of integers, but with a restriction imposed by the limited capacity of computer memory locations. Because of this limited capacity, only a finite set of integer values may be efficiently represented and stored in a memory location.

Syntactically, an *Integer* is a sequence of digits. If this sequence is terminated by the letter "H", then this literal is regarded as a hexadecimal representation of a number, a number written in base 16. If the sequence is terminated by the letter "B", it is regarded as an octal representation, in base 8. If it is terminated by the letter "C", it is regarded as the ordinal octal representation corresponding to a character value. All other representations of integers are regarded as decimal numbers, in base 10. The following items are all examples of valid *Integer*s:

100, 32767, 20H, 175B, 7FFFH, 41C, 0077B

Note that the *Literal* 41C corresponds to the character "!". This association may be seen by referencing the ASCII chart in Appendix C. Characters are discussed in more detail in Section 3:2:4.

The data type CARDINAL is intended for the representation of non-negative integers. As with integers, only a finite set of cardinal values may be represented. The relationship between the syntax of CARDINAL and INTEGER literals is important. The syntax diagrams do not distinguish between these two data types, and for this reason all literals of type CARDINAL must follow the syntax rules indicated for *Integer*. Thus all non-negative integral literals are valid literals of types CARDINAL and INTEGER. Literals representing negative numbers are valid INTEGER literals, but not valid CARDINAL literals.

The data type REAL represents real numbers — numbers that consist of an integral and a decimal part. A *Real* is a sequence of digits in which one decimal point appears anywhere after the first digit in the sequence. Optionally, this sequence may be immediately followed by a *Scale Factor*, consisting of the letter "E", an optional "+" or "−" sign, and a sequence of digits. The following numbers are all examples of valid *Real*s:

3.14, 0.9854, 0.0001, 26.72E-4, 1.0E+7

The *Scale Factor* describes how the decimal point must be repositioned to correctly represent the number. A "+" in the scale factor means that the decimal point must be moved to the right; a "−" indicates that the decimal point must be moved to the left. The number in the *Scale Factor* designates how many positions the decimal point must be moved. For example, the literal

26.72E-4

represents the real value 0.002672.

A character literal is represented by a single character enclosed within quotation marks. Either single or double quotes may be used as long as they are consistently used in the literal. Strings are represented in the same way as character literals, with the exception that a string is a sequence of characters enclosed within quotation marks. Examples of literals are

'p', "I", '12.357', "Now is the time"

Also,

```
'She said, "hello".'
```

is a literal because it is surrounded by single quotation marks. Although the choice of which quotation mark to use is somewhat arbitrary, it is important to note that the chosen symbol may not appear as a character literal or within a string literal.

Exercises

1. Using the sample source program given in Figure 2-4, identify and classify as many of the lexical symbols as you can.

2. Classify each of the following words as either a reserved word, a standard identifier, or an identifier.

```
module
PROC
VARIABLE
NULL
Else
Module
sum
SET
Number
```

3. Indicate whether or not each of the following words is a valid *Identifier*. If it is not valid, give the reason why.

```
Totals
CARDINAL
Integer
Weeks-per-year
23skiDoo
```

4. Indicate whether or not each of the following is a valid *Real*. If it is not valid, give the reason why.

```
34.67e-05
419.8765375765
917.
0.7845.91
.314
```

5. The syntax diagrams given in this chapter imply that the length of an *Identifier* has no limit. However, implementations of Modula-2 may impose a limit on the significant length of *Identifier*s. Investigate this possibility by referring to the manuals for the particular implementation of Modula-2 you are using.

6. Assume that binary (base 2) numbers are allowed as valid *Literal*s. Since decimal, hexadecimal, octal, and character octal numbers are allowed, use the suffix character 'T' to signify a binary literal and then modify the syntax diagrams given in Figures 2-8 and 2-11 to reflect this change.

2:3 Expressions

An expression consists of references to one or more data objects along with operators that evaluate to a single value of a specific data type. Although the syntactical description of an *Expression* given by the syntax diagrams in Figure 2-12 is quite long and complex, the intuitive definition of an expression, especially an arithmetic expression, should be sufficient for most programming situations.

For example, a single *Literal* or a single *Identifier* qualifies as a valid *Expression*. More complex *Expression*s may be formed by combining *Literal*s and *Identifier*s with operators consistent with the type of data involved. Section 2:4 introduces the different operations available in Modula-2. Only after you understand these operations will you fully ap-

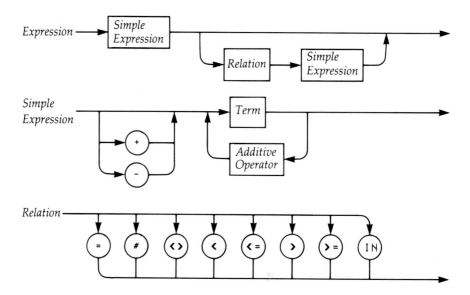

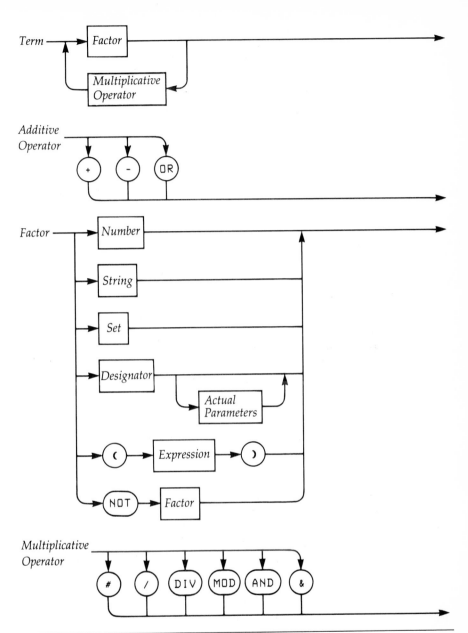

Figure 2-12   Syntax Diagram for *Expression*

preciate the wide range of valid *Expression*s. Thus examples of expressions are presented in the following sections as the various operations are discussed. The syntax diagrams provide a reference while their component constructs are being presented.

2:4 Operators

2:4:1 Assignment Operator

In Modula-2 the lexical symbol ":=" is the assignment operator. The assignment operator causes the value of the expression following the operator to be assigned to the data object immediately preceding the operator. Figure 2-13 shows the syntax of the *Assignment Statement*. For example, in the statement

```
Sum  :=  Total
```

the current value of Total is assigned to Sum. After execution of this statement, the data objects Total and Sum are both storing the same value.

Similarly, the value represented by a *Literal* may be assigned to a data object, as in the statement

```
Result  :=  9
```

which results in the decimal value 9 being stored in the data object Result. In every case where the assignment operator is used, the symbol ":=" must be preceded by the identification of a single data object whose value is changed. The *Expression* that follows the ":=" symbol may be any expression that computes a result compatible with this data object. Thus

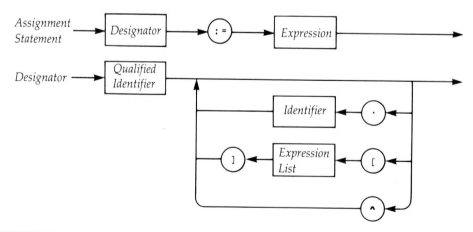

Figure 2-13   Syntax Diagram for *Assignment Statement*

the statement

        Count := 19.07

is valid only when the *Identifier* Count is REAL.

As an introduction to the next section, consider the *Assignment Statement*

        Result := (3 * 2) - 9

which evaluates the *Expression* following the assignment operator and assigns the value of the expression to Result. After execution of this statement, Result contains the value -3.

2:4:2 Arithmetic Operators

In Modula-2 the lexical symbols "+", "-", and "*" designate the arithmetic operations of addition, subtraction, and multiplication, respectively. Two division operators are designated by the lexical symbols "DIV" and "/". "DIV" is used only with operands of type INTEGER or CARDINAL, since it always computes an integral result. Thus in the statement

        WeeksPerYear := 365 DIV 7

WeeksPerYear must identify a data object of type INTEGER or CARDINAL because the expression computes the decimal value 52. "/" must only be used with operands of type REAL, since it always computes a real value as its result. "+", "-", and "*" may be used with operands of type INTEGER, CARDINAL, or REAL. Expressions involving operands of different types are invalid. Figure 2-14 presents a number of examples of valid and invalid expressions using these operators.

The reserved word MOD designates the modulus operation. This operator is valid only with operands of type INTEGER or CARDINAL and computes, as its result, the integer value representing the remainder obtained from the division of the first operand by the second. For example, the statement

        LeftOver := 11 MOD 4

assigns the integer value 3 to the variable LeftOver. The MOD operator may be better understood in terms of the DIV division operator. Consider

Valid Arithmetic Expression	Computed Result
(3 * 2) - 9	-3
10 DIV 3	3
1 DIV 5	0
3.14 * 2.0	6.28
(1.0 / 3.0) + 10.00	10.33333
2 + 3 * 4	14
(2 + 3) * 4	20
10.50 / 2.0 + 1.0 * 2.0	7.25
10.50 / 2.0 + 1.0 + 3.5 * 2.0	13.25
2 + 13 MOD 5	5
31 DIV 2 + 31 MOD 2	16

Invalid Arithmetic Expression	Explanation
14 + 7.0	Type incompatibility
(3 * 2.0) - 9	Type incompatibility
10 / 3	Inappropriate operator
1.0 DIV 5.0	Inappropriate operator

Figure 2-14   Examples of Arithmetic Expressions

the statements

```
Whole := 31;
Whole := (Whole DIV 2) + (Whole MOD 2);
```

in which Whole is assigned the value 16. This value represents the sum of 15 and 1, the quotient and remainder obtained when dividing 31 by 2.

When forming arithmetic expressions, we must be aware of the inherent precedence of the operators. In *Expressions* involving more than one operation, the multiplicative operators, "*", DIV, "/", and MOD, are applied first, left to right, followed by the additive operators, "+" and "-", also applied left to right. Matching left and right parentheses modifies or clarifies the precedence of operations in expressions. Several examples illustrating parentheses and precedence appear in Figure 2-14.

2:4:3 Boolean Operators

In addition to arithmetic operators, Modula-2 has a set of boolean operators designated by the reserved words NOT, AND, and OR and the lexical symbols "&" and "~". The standard identifiers TRUE and FALSE, listed in Figures 2-6 and 2-10, serve as the only literals for data objects of type BOOLEAN. The word BOOLEAN is a standard identifier used to define variables of this type. Figure 2-15 lists several boolean expressions and their

Boolean Expression	Computed Result
Result1 := NOT TRUE	FALSE
Result2 := NOT FALSE	TRUE
Result3 := TRUE AND TRUE	TRUE
Result4 := TRUE AND FALSE	FALSE
Result5 := FALSE AND TRUE	FALSE
Result6 := FALSE AND FALSE	FALSE
Result7 := TRUE OR TRUE	TRUE
Result8 := TRUE OR FALSE	TRUE
Result9 := FALSE OR TRUE	TRUE
Result10 := FALSE OR FALSE	FALSE
Result11 := TRUE & Result1	FALSE

Figure 2-15   Example Boolean Expressions

computed results under the assumption that the variables used are all of type BOOLEAN.

The reserved word NOT and the lexical symbol "~" both represent negation and may be used interchangeably. OR represents logical conjunction, and AND represents logical disjunction. The lexical symbol "&" is a synonym for the symbol AND; they may be used interchangeably. In Modula-2 the operator NOT has a higher precedence than AND, which, in turn, has a higher precedence than OR. As with arithmetic expressions, parentheses alter or clarify the precedence of operations.

2:4:4 Relational Operators

Relational operators compare two expressions of the same type. The result of this operation is the boolean value TRUE if the relation holds and FALSE if it does not. Modula-2's lexical symbols for the relational operators are listed in Figure 2-16. Note that the symbol "#" is a synonym for "<>"; they may be used interchangeably.

Because relational operators compute boolean values as their result, relational expressions often serve as boolean expressions or parts of boolean expressions. Relational expressions appear in Modula-2 programs most frequently as conditions in decision and looping statements, which modify the executable flow of control in a program. Decision statements and looping statements are introduced in Chapter 4. Sometimes the expressions that control these statements involve compound relationships. In those cases we recommend that you use parentheses to clarify the

Lexical Symbol	Meaning
=	Equality
<	Less than
< =	Less than or Equal to
>	Greater than
> =	Greater than or Equal to
< >	Inequality
#	Inequality
IN	Set Membership

Figure 2-16   Relational Operators

Identifier	Current Value
Maximum	100
TOTAL	11983
Sales83	8095
Sales82	10832

Expression	Computed Result
Sales83 = Sales82	FALSE
Sales83 < Sales82	TRUE
Sales83 > Sales82	FALSE
(Maximum * 80 + 95) # Sales83	FALSE
(Sales83 < Sales82) OR (Sales83 = Sales82)	TRUE
Sales83 <= Sales82	TRUE
Total >= Sales82	TRUE
(NOT (Sales83 = Sales82)) OR (Sales83 > Sales82)	TRUE

Figure 2-17   Examples of Relational Expressions

order of the relational and boolean operators rather than rely on the precedence of the operators.

As an example of the formation of relational and boolean expressions, consider the table of data objects, current values, and expressions listed in Figure 2-17. Note that in the formation of a valid relational expression, both operands must be of the same data type.

2:4:5 Set Operators

The lexical symbols "+", "-", "*", and "/" also designate the set operations of union, difference, intersection, and symmetric difference, respectively. In addition, the reserved word IN designates the relational operation of set membership. A complete discussion of sets appears in Chapter 5. Since these lexical symbols have several meanings, the type of operands used with these symbols determines which operation is to be applied. The set operators "*" and "/" have precedence over the operators "+" and "-", just as they do when they are considered as arithmetic operators.

2:4:6 Dereferencing Operator

The lexical symbol "∧" serves as the dereferencing operator. This operation accesses dynamic data objects identified by pointer variables. A complete discussion of dynamic data objects and pointer variables appears in Chapter 9.

2:4:7 Precedence Among Operators

The dereferencing operator has the highest precedence among all of the operators because it identifies data objects in expressions. Next in the precedence hierarchy are the negation operators, NOT and "~", followed by the multiplicative operators. Next are the additive operators, then the relational operators. Lowest in precedence is the assignment operator. The multiplicative operators are "*", "/", DIV, MOD, AND, and "&". The additive operators are "+", "-", and OR.

Since expressions may become quite complex, programmers are strongly encouraged to use parentheses to clarify the order of operations. This practice serves not only to resolve any question about the order of operations in an expression but also adds considerably to the readability of the program.

Exercises

1. Using the syntax diagrams given in this chapter, follow the derivation that shows that a single *Identifier* is a valid *Expression*.

2. Determine whether or not each of the following is a valid *Expression*.

```
False - True
3.14 + 1 = 4.14
32767 - 1 * 2
3.7 + 0.1 +0.01+.001 + 0.0001
112.4 + (-7.0)
```

3. Determine the computed result for each of the valid *Expression*s given in Exercise 2, if possible.

4. According to the syntax diagrams given in this chapter, operators are grouped into the following three classifications: *Relation*, *Additive Operator*, and *Multiplicative Operator*. Can you give reasons why these groupings are used rather than those presented in the text? Note also that the boolean operator NOT does not appear in any of these three classifications; neither do the so called unary operators indicated by the lexical symbols "+" and "-". Can you explain why?

5. Using the syntax diagrams given in this chapter, work through the derivations for each of the following to determine if it is a valid *Expression*.

```
+ 19 + 21
+19+21
100+-12
```

2:5 Delimiters and Comments

Modula-2 has several lexical symbols that serve to delimit statements or clauses. Some of these symbols may be viewed as specific types of operators. However, they are treated here as delimiters primarily because of the lexical function they perform. Since delimiters appear frequently in Modula-2's syntax, this section only surveys their usefulness. A better understanding of the uses and syntax of delimiters may be obtained from the syntax diagrams appearing throughout this text and in Appendix B.

Delimiters serve two useful purposes. First, they provide a consistent structure to a programming language, thus allowing individual statements or parts of statements to be distinguished from each other. In this sense they play a role similar to that played by punctuation in a sentence. Second, they assist the language translator in its task of translating a source program into a form that the computer may directly execute.

One way of viewing a *Compilation Unit* is as a finite sequence of statements. The syntax of Modula-2 specifies that these statements be separated by the lexical symbol ";", which serves as a statement delimiter. Since the semicolon serves as a separator between statements, the last statement in a statement sequence should not be followed by this delimiter. However, the syntax of Modula-2 is flexible in this regard and, in some cases, accepts extra delimiters. Refer to Section 4:1 for more information on the semicolon as a delimiter.

Some delimiters separate clauses within statements. The lexical symbol ":", for example, is used in several statements. In particular, it serves as a delimiter in *Variable Declarations* to separate the *Identifier List* from the

Type, as discussed in Section 3:1. Chapter 5 shows the colon used in the definition of *Variant*s. The ":" also serves as a delimiter in the *Case Statement* to separate each *Case Label List* from its corresponding *Statement Sequence* (Section 4:3:2). Also discussed in this section is the role of the lexical symbol " ¦ ", which serves as a separator between *Case*s in the *Case Statement*.

The lexical symbol " , " also appears as a separator in the *Case Statement*. It serves to separate *Case Labels* in each *Case Label List*. The comma also appears in other statements as a separator. In set literals, which are discussed in Section 5:3, it serves as a separator between elements. It also appears in *Identifier List*s, *Array Type*s, *Formal Type List*s, and *Expression List*s.

The lexical symbol " .. " separates the bounds in the declaration of a *Set Element* (Section 5:3). It is also used in the declaration of a *Subrange* (Section 3:3:2). There, too, it serves to separate the bounds.

The lexical symbol " . " is the terminator for a *Compilation Unit* (Section 2:1). For a *Qualified Identifier* (Section 2:2:2) the period separates the module name from the item name. Section 5:2 discusses the use of the period in referencing components within a record structure. Of course, the " . " also serves as a decimal point in the formation of real literals.

Parentheses, the lexical symbols "(" and ")", must always be used together. These symbols have several uses. They may be used in *Expression*s (Section 2:3), in the declaration of *Enumerations* (Section 3:3:1), and with procedures to describe *Formal Parameters* and *Actual Parameters* (Chapter 6).

The remaining delimiters each have only one use and are used in pairs. For example, the single quotation mark " ' " and the double quotation mark " " " are used in the construction of *Strings* (Section 2:2:3). The lexical symbols "{" and "}" delineate the *Elements* in set notation (Section 5:3). In Section 5:1 the lexical symbols "[" and "]" are delimiters in array declarations and array references. They delineate the subscript list. Finally, the lexical symbols "(*" and "*)" delineate comments. They may be placed anywhere in a source program. Whenever the Modula-2 language translator encounters the lexical symbol "(*", it treats all that follows as a comment until a corresponding "*)" is encountered. In Modula-2 comments may be nested. That is, for every "(*" appearing in the source file, there must be a corresponding "*)" to terminate the comment.

A few comments appear in the *Program Module* `TimesTable` presented in Figure 2-4. The number of comments used in this example is insufficient to fully describe this program. Their appearance illustrates the syntax of comments in Modula-2. Usually, comments are included in a source file to serve as permanent documentation for the program. Using comments when programming has many advantages, but no attempt is made here to justify them. However, even inexperienced programmers may find the few comments given in the *Program Module* `TimesTable` helpful in understanding the relationship between Figure 2-4 and Figure 2-5.

Exercises

1. Given the following example program, identify the syntax errors.

```
(* Computes a running balance for a savings account            *)
(*                                                              *

MODULE Savings;

   FROM InOut IMPORT ReadCard, WriteCard, WriteString, WriteLn;
   FROM RealInOut IMPORT ReadReal, WriteReal;

Var
   Balance, AnnualRate, MonthlyRate, Interest : REAL;
   Months, Month : CARDINAL;

BEGIN
WriteString ('Initial Deposit?");  ReadReal (Balance);   WriteLn;
WriteString ('Interest Rate?');     ReadReal (AnnualRate);WriteLn;
WriteString ('Number of Months?'); ReadCard (Months);    WriteLn;
WriteLn;

MonthlyRate :=  (AnnualRate / 100.0) DIV 12.0;
WriteString (' Month      Balance   Interest   New Balance');
WriteLn;
WriteString (' -----    ----------   --------   -----------');
WriteLn;

FOR Month := 1 TO Months BY 1 DO
   WriteCard (Month, 6);
   WriteReal (Balance, 13);
   Interest := Balance * MonthlyRate;
   WriteReal (Interest, 10);
   Balance := Balance + Interest;
   WriteReal (Balance, 13);
   WriteLn
END;

     WriteLn
END Savings:
```

2. Using the source program given in Exercise 1, identify and classify the lexical symbols.

3 Data Fundamentals

3:1 Data Objects

In Chapter 2 a data object is defined as a programmer-declared container for values of a particular data type. This rather simple notion is consistent with the underlying memory structure of computer hardware. The type of data directly supported in a programming language is dependent upon the computer hardware. Most computer hardware allows for the representation of integer and real numbers, boolean values, and character data. Modula-2 contains elementary data types to support each of these representations.

The class of data objects consisting of constants and variables is discussed in this chapter. Each constant and variable must be declared by having an identifier associated with it and must be declared to be of some specific data type. Often the elementary data types are used, but additional data types may be declared to suit particular programming situations.

Programmers may declare either unstructured or structured data types, which may be used to declare static or dynamic data objects. An unstructured data type defines an object that stores a single value. INTEGER, CARDINAL, REAL, BOOLEAN, and CHAR are all unstructured types. Structured data types define objects that store related collections of more than one value.

Structured data types are presented in Chapter 5. Static data objects may be structured or unstructured, and they are explicitly declared in the source program. Dynamic data objects may also be either structured or unstructured, but they are not declared in the source program. Instead, they are created by a program while it executes. Dynamic data objects are presented in Chapter 9.

The purpose of this chapter is to study Modula-2's elementary data types and to introduce facilities for the declaration and use of unstructured data types and data objects.

3:1:1 Constants and the CONST Statement

Constants are static data objects that have programmer-supplied initial values when the program in which they have been declared begins execution. Furthermore, a constant may not contain any other value during the course of program execution. The CONST statement is the means by which constants are declared. Each block in a Modula-2 program may contain optional *Declaration*s in which constants, variables, and types may be declared. Figure 3-1 presents the syntax diagram illustrating the structure of a *Declaration*.

Figure 3-2 presents the syntax diagrams for *Constant Declaration*, which indicate how constants are declared. The main reason for declaring a constant is to associate a value of a specific data type to an *Identifier*. This value may be a literal or an expression. Note the similarity between

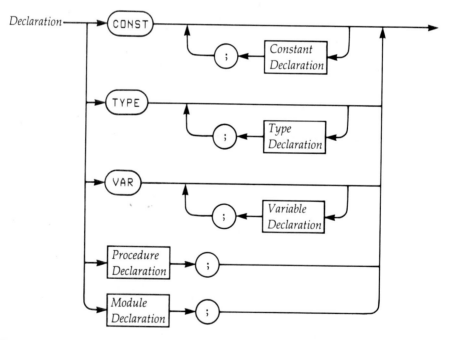

Figure 3-1   Syntax Diagram for *Declaration*

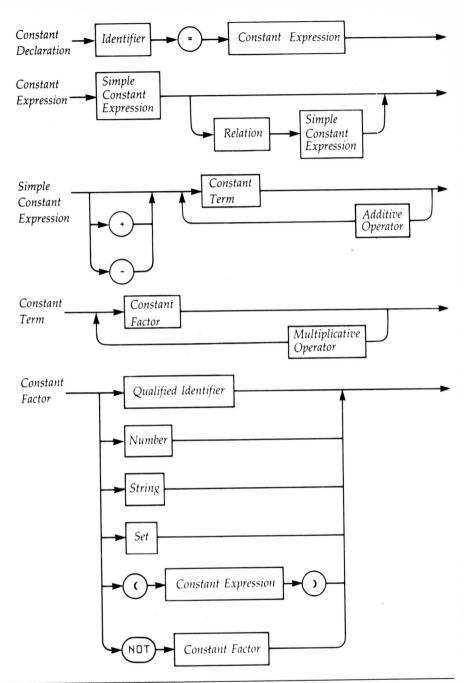

Figure 3-2   Syntax Diagram for *Constant Declaration*

these constructs and the constructs presented earlier for *Expression*; however, they are distinct syntax diagrams. After a constant is declared in a program, every reference to its *Identifier*, in effect, references the constant value.

Constants are useful in programming because they occur frequently in the models of problem solutions. Consider, for example, the *Constant Declaration*

```
CONST  DaysInWeek = 7;
```

in which an integer constant is declared. In reality, the number of days in a week is certainly not likely to change, and therefore it is appropriate to declare the constant DaysInWeek. In this particular case, we might argue that the declaration of this constant is unnecessary. The integer *Literal* 7 could be used instead. Although this argument is true, the constant improves the readability of the program. The reader of a program that uses the *Literal* 7 may be uncertain of the meaning and purpose of it, whereas the reader of a program that uses the constant DaysInWeek should have little difficulty understanding what the programmer intends. The use of a descriptive name rather than a literal value has a clearer meaning to the reader.

3:1:2 Variables and the VAR Statement

Variables are static data objects that have no values stored in them prior to the start of program execution. However, while a program executes, values are stored in variables through the assignment operation or through input. The VAR statement is the means by which variables are declared. The syntax diagram in Figure 3-1 shows, in part, the structure of the VAR statement. Figure 3-3 completes this description by presenting the syntax of a *Variable Declaration*.

Every variable is declared to be of a specific data type. The elementary data types named by the standard identifiers INTEGER, CARDINAL, REAL, BOOLEAN, and CHAR are frequently used. Additional implementation-dependent elementary data types might be used. Data types may also be declared with the TYPE statement, which is introduced in Section 3:3.

Exercises

1. Explain the essential differences between literals, constants, and variables.

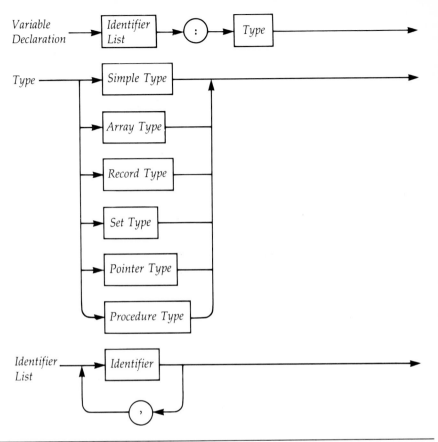

Figure 3-3   Syntax Diagram for *Variable Declaration*

2. Using the syntax diagrams given in this chapter and Chapter 2, determine if there is any syntactic difference between a *Constant Expression* and an *Expression*.

3. Consider the problem of converting standard units of measure to metric units. If you were to write a Modula-2 program to solve this problem, what constants would you foresee using? Write the corresponding CONST statements necessary to declare these data objects.

4. Consider the problem of computing and printing a payroll report for a small company. In the design of a solution to this problem, you need to consider the declaration of constants and variables. Think about this problem and write the corresponding CONST and VAR statements.

5. In programming, a constant is sometimes used to initialize a second constant. That is, the value of the second constant depends upon one

or more previously declared constants. For example, the current year determines the number of days in the year; specifically, each year divisible by 4 contains 366 days. Consider how you would go about initializing such a second constant. Also, consider the relative merits of declaring the constant as a variable and initializing it with an assignment statement.

3:2 Elementary Data Types

3:2:1 INTEGER and CARDINAL Data Types

The INTEGER data type represents whole numbers only. However, the limited size of computer memory restricts the range of integer values that may be represented. Computer memory is divided into equal-sized memory locations. Because integers are stored using a binary (base 2) representation, and each word may only store N binary digits (called bits), only the integers in the interval $-2^{(N-1)} .. +2^{(N-1)}-1$ may be represented. The number of binary digits in a computer word is determined by the computer hardware being used and is usually 16 or 32. Thus when N = 16, the range of integers is $-32768 .. +32767$, but when N = 32 the interval is $-2147483648 .. +2147483647$. The value of N is beyond the control of the programmer, since it is a built-in feature of the hardware.

The CARDINAL data type differs from the INTEGER data type in only one way. Cardinals include only nonnegative integers. Because cardinals are represented similarly to integers, using a binary representation, cardinal values in the interval $0 .. +2^N - 1$ may be represented. Thus when N = 16, the range of cardinals is 0 .. 65535. When N = 32, the interval is 0 .. 4294967295.

In practice many programming situations involve only positive whole numbers. In most of these situations, either integers or cardinals may be used. However, there are distinct advantages to using cardinals when we know that negative values do not occur. The first advantage is that the upper limit is approximately doubled. The maximum cardinal value is $2^N - 1$, whereas the maximum integer is $2^{N-1} - 1$; 65535 instead of 32767 when N = 16. The second, and probably more important, advantage is that the readability of the program is improved. Use of the CARDINAL data type conveys to the reader of the program that only nonnegative integral values are valid in the given situation. With appropriate program documentation, this information is of great help to the reader.

The operations designated by '+', '-', '*', DIV, and MOD may be applied to both cardinals and integers. We must take care to avoid expressions involving integers and cardinals together. An operation with integer operands yields an integer result, whereas an operation with cardinal operands yields a cardinal result. Expressions combining integer and cardinal operands are invalid in Modula-2. However, a number of predefined functions transfer data values from one type to another. The standard identifiers INTEGER and CARDINAL also identify the type transfer functions for these types. They act as functions to transfer between the INTEGER and CARDINAL data types. Given the *Declaration*s

```
VAR     ExampleInt : INTEGER;
        ExampleCard: CARDINAL;
```

the statement sequence

```
ExampleInt  := 37;
ExampleCard := CARDINAL (ExampleInt)
```

transfers the bit pattern representing the integer value 37 to the CARDINAL variable ExampleCard. In addition to representing the standard types CARDINAL and INTEGER, these standard identifiers, when used in arithmetic expressions, represent type transfer functions, which assist in transferring data from objects of one data type to variables of another data type. The *Expression*

```
CARDINAL (-15)
```

yields the cardinal value with the same bit pattern as the integer value −15. Similarly,

```
INTEGER (ExampleCard)
```

produces the integer value with the same bit pattern as the cardinal value in ExampleCard.

Figure 3-4 presents a Modula-2 *Program Module* that computes and prints a table of Fahrenheit and Celsius temperatures. Figure 3-5 shows the results produced by this program. More specifically, this program converts all integral Fahrenheit degree values from 0 through the value of Limit to Celsius degree values. As each conversion is performed, both degree values are printed.

The well-known Fahrenheit/Celsius conversion formula

$$C := (F - 32) * 5/9$$

is used in this program on line 15. Note that the INTEGER type transfer function also appears on this line. Because Fahrenheit degrees less than 32 have equivalent Celsius degrees that are negative, this program cannot just use cardinal data objects. For this reason the variable Celsius, de-

```
 1   MODULE IntegerTemperatures;
 2
 3   FROM InOut IMPORT WriteCard, WriteInt, WriteString, WriteLn;
 4
 5   VAR     Limit, Fahrenheit : CARDINAL;
 6           Celsius          : INTEGER;
 7
 8   BEGIN
 9   WriteString ('Fahrenheit Celsius');  WriteLn;
10   WriteString ('------------------');  WriteLn;
11     .cp 10
12   Limit := 40;
13   FOR Fahrenheit := 0 TO Limit BY 1 DO
14      WriteCard (Fahrenheit, 9);
15      Celsius := (INTEGER (Fahrenheit) - 32) * 5 DIV 9;
16      WriteInt (Celsius, 9);
17      WriteLn
18   END
19   END IntegerTemperatures.
```

Figure 3-4   Program Module with INTEGER Type Transfer

clared on line 6, is of type INTEGER. Thus since the variable Fahrenheit is of type CARDINAL and because it appears in the conversion formula, the type transfer function is necessary to avoid an invalid expression.

Note also that the *Literals* 32, 5, and 9 that appear in the *Expression* on line 15 are regarded as integer values rather than as cardinal values. Since nonnegative integral values are valid as both CARDINAL and INTEGER literals, expressions involving them are resolved based upon the types of the data objects involved. Hence in this case these literals are resolved as INTEGER literals.

Modula-2 is a strongly typed programming language, which means that programmers must explicitly avoid writing any expression that involves operands of different types. The implicit conversion of data from one type to another that occurs in some programming languages is not present in Modula-2. This feature is good because it forces better programming practices and avoids certain subtle data errors.

3:2:2 REAL Data Type

The REAL data type represents real numbers, that is, numbers that consist of an integral and a decimal part. Unlike INTEGERs and CARDINALs, which represent distinct enumerable values (that is, whole numbers in a specific interval), REALs cannot be enumerated. The number of distinct real numbers in any interval, for example, 1.0 .. 2.0, is infinite. For this reason val-

Fahrenheit	Celsius
0	-17
1	-17
2	-16
3	-16
4	-15
5	-15
6	-14
7	-13
8	-13
9	-12
10	-12
11	-11
12	-11
13	-10
14	-10
15	-9
16	-8
17	-8
18	-7
19	-7
20	-6
21	-6
22	-5
23	-5
24	-4
25	-3
26	-3
27	-2
28	-2
29	-1
30	-1
31	0
32	0
33	0
34	1
35	1
36	2
37	2
38	3
39	3
40	4

Figure 3-5   Results Printed by Program Module IntegerTemperatures

ues of this data type are represented internally using a floating point representation, which is only an approximation of a real number. In a floating point representation, a real number is approximated with a certain number of significant digits of accuracy, called the **mantissa**, and a scale factor, called the **characteristic**. Because of the limited capacity of computer memory locations, only a limited number of digits are stored. The number of significant digits stored depends upon the number of bits in the representation and how they are used. Many representations provide between 6 and 14 decimal digits of accuracy. The scale factor contains information about the placement of the decimal point. The scale factor is also system dependent, but typically allows values at least in the range of 10^{-40} to 10^{40}. Thus the range of numbers representable with the data type REAL is usually much greater than that available for INTEGER or CARDINAL.

The operations designated by the lexical symbols "+", "-", "*", and "/" may be used with the REAL data type. An operation with real operands yields a real value as its result. Because the addition, subtraction, and multiplication operators may also appear with integer and cardinal operands, programmers must be careful not to form invalid expressions involving data of different types. Addition, for example, cannot be performed combining a real operand with an integer operand. For this reason the *Expression*

        13 + 0.32

is invalid.

Just as type transfer functions exist for the CARDINAL and INTEGER data types, they also exist for the REAL data type. However, the standard identifiers FLOAT and TRUNC convert between cardinal and real values. Note that TRUNC accepts an argument of type REAL and returns a value of type CARDINAL. This cardinal value is the integral part of the real value; the fractional part is not considered, and no rounding takes place. The FLOAT function accepts an argument of type CARDINAL and returns the floating point representation of that number as a REAL.

Figure 3-6 presents a *Program Module* very similar to the one presented in Figure 3-4. This program also prints a table of Fahrenheit and Celsius temperatures but uses a variable of type REAL rather than INTEGER. The expression in line 17 uses the FLOAT function to convert a cardinal data value to its real equivalent. This function is required, since the variable Fahrenheit is of type CARDINAL and the variable Celsius is declared to be of type REAL.

Comparing this program and its results, shown in Figure 3-7, with the original program in Figure 3-4 illustrates some of the differences and similarities among the elementary data types CARDINAL, INTEGER, and REAL. The integer computation in Figure 3-4 using the Fahrenheit to Celsius conversion formula results in the truncation of the decimal part and produces the results shown in Figure 3-5. Note that 33 degrees Fahrenheit is roughly equivalent to 0.55 degrees Celsius, but in Figure 3-5 only the whole number portion of this result is retained. In the program

```
 1    MODULE RealTemperatures;
 2
 3    FROM InOut      IMPORT WriteCard, WriteString, WriteLn;
 4    FROM RealInOut IMPORT WriteReal;
 5
 6    CONST  Limit = 40;
 7
 8    VAR     Fahrenheit : CARDINAL;
 9            Celsius    : REAL;
10
11    BEGIN
12    WriteString ('Fahrenheit Celsius');  WriteLn;
13    WriteString ('-------------------');  WriteLn;
14
15    FOR Fahrenheit := 0 TO Limit BY 1 DO
16       WriteCard (Fahrenheit, 9);
17       Celsius := (FLOAT (Fahrenheit) - 32.0) * 5.0 / 9.0;
18       WriteReal (Celsius, 15);
19       WriteLn
20    END
21    END RealTemperatures.
```

Figure 3-6   Program Module RealTemperature

in Figure 3-6, a real variable is used. The result is correct, but it is printed using the exponential notation 5.5555552E-01 (5.5555552 multiplied by 10^{-1} yields 0.55555552).

3:2:3 BOOLEAN Data Type

A data object of type BOOLEAN may only be assigned either the value "true" or the value "false," designated by the standard identifiers TRUE and FALSE, respectively. Thus TRUE and FALSE are the only boolean literals, and Modula-2 programmers may declare boolean constants and variables.

Since most programs primarily manipulate numeric or character data, boolean data objects are seldom the primary data objects in a program. However, boolean data objects frequently control the flow of execution in programs. A Modula-2 program containing no boolean data objects or expressions is rare and probably performs only a limited or trivial task. The relational operators "=", "<", "<=", ">", ">=", "<>", "#", and IN compute boolean results. These boolean results frequently control the flow of execution in the various conditional and looping structures in a program. These structures are discussed in Chapter 4.

Fahrenheit	Celsius
0	-1.7777770E+01
1	-1.7222219E+01
2	-1.6666662E+01
3	-1.6111105E+01
4	-1.5555548E+01
5	-1.4999997E+01
6	-1.4444440E+01
7	-1.3888883E+01
8	-1.3333326E+01
9	-1.2777775E+01
10	-1.2222218E+01
11	-1.1666661E+01
12	-1.1111104E+01
13	-1.0555553E+01
14	-0.9999996E+01
15	-9.4444429E+00
16	-8.8888883E+00
17	-8.3333325E+00
18	-7.7777767E+00
19	-7.2222208E+00
20	-6.6666656E+00
21	-6.1111098E+00
22	-5.5555546E+00
23	-4.9999994E+00
24	-4.4444435E+00
25	-3.8888883E+00
26	-3.3333325E+00
27	-2.7777773E+00
28	-2.2222214E+00
29	-1.6666662E+00
30	-1.1111104E+00
31	-5.5555552E-01
32	0
33	5.5555552E-01
34	1.1111104E+00
35	1.6666662E+00
36	2.2222214E+00
37	2.7777773E+00
38	3.3333325E+00
39	3.8888883E+00
40	4.4444435E+00

Figure 3-7   Results Printed by the Program in Figure 3-6

As an example of the use of the BOOLEAN data type, consider the *Program Module* given in Figure 3-8. This program reads a collection of cardinal values, computes, and prints their sum. This program is straightforward, with the bulk of its work performed by the REPEAT structure on

```
 1 MODULE BooleanExample;
 2
 3 FROM InOut IMPORT ReadCard, Done, WriteCard,
 4                                    WriteString, WriteLn;
 5 CONST   MaxCard = 65535;
 6
 7 VAR     Value, Sum : CARDINAL;
 8         Overflow    : BOOLEAN;
 9
10 BEGIN
11 Sum        := 0;
12 Overflow := FALSE;
13 Value      := 0;
14
15 REPEAT
16    IF (MaxCard - Sum) < Value THEN
17        Overflow := TRUE
18      ELSE
19        Sum := Sum + Value;
20        ReadCard (Value);   WriteLn
21    END
22 UNTIL (NOT Done) OR Overflow;
23
24 WriteLn;
25 IF Overflow THEN
26     WriteString (' ---ERROR: Cardinal Overflow Attempted')
27   ELSE
28     WriteString (' The sum is ');
29     WriteCard (Sum, 5)
30 END;
31 WriteLn
32 END BooleanExample.
```

Figure 3-8   Program Module BooleanExample

lines 15 through 22. The boolean variable Overflow indicates that the values could not be summed because the sum would exceed the range of representable cardinals.

Because a collection of cardinal values may very well sum to a value too large to be represented in memory, an overflow situation is possible. This program recognizes such an overflow situation and gracefully handles it by stopping processing and printing a meaningful error message. This error checking is accomplished with the boolean variable Overflow, declared on line 8. Initially, Overflow is assigned the value FALSE. As each value is read, it is compared against the current sum to determine if its addition will cause an overflow; if so, Overflow is assigned the value TRUE. Finally, Overflow is used to determine whether the sum or the error message is printed.

The boolean operators designated by NOT, "~", AND, "&", and OR are used with boolean operands to form boolean expressions. As with the arithmetic operators, these boolean operators have a precedence hierarchy. The negation operators, NOT and "~", have the highest precedence, followed by the conjunction operators, AND and "&", followed in turn by the disjunction operator, OR. The relational operators have the lowest precedence in boolean expressions. Thus the boolean expression

```
(NOT Done) OR Overflow
```

which appears in Figure 3-8 on line 22, could have been written equivalently as

```
NOT Done OR Overflow
```

The parenthesized version is preferred, since it is straightforward, clarifies the order of evaluation, and does not require memorization of the precedence hierarchy. We must take care when relational expressions appear as operands in boolean expressions, as in the expression

```
A < 100 AND B < 100
```

Given the precedence hierarchy just presented, this expression is invalid, since the operands surrounding the AND, 100 and B, are not of type BOOLEAN and therefore are invalid operands for the AND operator. A correct way to rewrite this expression is to utilize parentheses to clarify the order of evaluation, as in the expression

```
(A < 100) AND (B < 100)
```

The exact definition of the AND and OR operators in Modula-2 specifies that the second operands are not always evaluated. Specifically, if the first operand in an AND operation is false, then the second operand is not evaluated and the operation yields the result FALSE. Likewise, if the first operand in an OR operation is true, then the second operand is not evaluated and the operation yields the result TRUE. This somewhat subtle, but extremely convenient, feature of the language is particularly important when composing conditional and looping structures and is discussed further in Sections 4:3 and 4:4.

3:2:4 CHAR Data Type

The CHAR data type represents single characters in the American Standard Code for Information Interchange (ASCII) character set. The ASCII conversion chart is shown in Figure 3-9 and Appendix C. The chart lists the

Dec	Binary	Oct	Hex	Char
000	0000000	000	00	nul
001	0000001	001	01	soh
002	0000010	002	02	stx
003	0000011	003	03	etx
004	0000100	004	04	eot
005	0000101	005	05	enq
006	0000110	006	06	ack
007	0000111	007	07	bel
008	0001000	010	08	bs
009	0001001	011	09	ht
010	0001010	012	0A	lf
011	0001011	013	0B	vt
012	0001100	014	0C	ff
013	0001101	015	0D	cr
014	0001110	016	0E	so
015	0001111	017	0F	si
016	0010000	020	10	dle
017	0010001	021	11	dc1
018	0010010	022	12	dc2
019	0010011	023	13	dc3
020	0010100	024	14	dc4
021	0010101	025	15	nak
022	0010110	026	16	syn
023	0010111	027	17	etb
024	0011000	030	18	can
025	0011001	031	19	em
026	0011010	032	1A	sub
027	0011011	033	1B	esc
028	0011100	034	1C	fs
029	0011101	035	1D	gs
030	0011110	036	1E	rs
031	0011111	037	1F	us

Dec	Binary	Oct	Hex	Char
032	0100000	040	20	
033	0100001	041	21	!
034	0100010	042	22	"
035	0100011	043	23	#
036	0100100	044	24	$
037	0100101	045	25	%
038	0100110	046	26	&
039	0100111	047	27	'
040	0101000	050	28	(
041	0101001	051	29	)
042	0101010	052	2A	*
043	0101011	053	2B	+
044	0101100	054	2C	,
045	0101101	055	2D	-
046	0101110	056	2E	.
047	0101111	057	2F	/
048	0110000	060	30	0
049	0110001	061	31	1
050	0110010	062	32	2
051	0110011	063	33	3
052	0110100	064	34	4
053	0110101	065	35	5
054	0110110	066	36	6
055	0110111	067	37	7
056	0111000	070	38	8
057	0111001	071	39	9
058	0111010	072	3A	:
059	0111011	073	3B	;
060	0111100	074	3C	<
061	0111101	075	3D	=
062	0111110	076	3E	>
063	0111111	077	3F	?

Dec	Binary	Oct	Hex	Char
064	1000000	100	40	@
065	1000001	101	41	A
066	1000010	102	42	B
067	1000011	103	43	C
068	1000100	104	44	D
069	1000101	105	45	E
070	1000110	106	46	F
071	1000111	107	47	G
072	1001000	110	48	H
073	1001001	111	49	I
074	1001010	112	4A	J
075	1001011	113	4B	K
076	1001100	114	4C	L
077	1001101	115	4D	M
078	1001110	116	4E	N
079	1001111	117	4F	O
080	1010000	120	50	P
081	1010001	121	51	Q
082	1010010	122	52	R
083	1010011	123	53	S
084	1010100	124	54	T
085	1010101	125	55	U
086	1010110	126	56	V
087	1010111	127	57	W
088	1011000	130	58	X
089	1011001	131	59	Y
090	1011010	132	5A	Z
091	1011011	133	5B	[
092	1011100	134	5C	\
093	1011101	135	5D	]
094	1011110	136	5E	^
095	1011111	137	5F	_

Dec	Binary	Oct	Hex	Char
096	1100000	140	60	`
097	1100001	141	61	a
098	1100010	142	62	b
099	1100011	143	63	c
100	1100100	144	64	d
101	1100101	145	65	e
102	1100110	146	66	f
103	1100111	147	67	g
104	1101000	150	68	h
105	1101001	151	69	i
106	1101010	152	6A	j
107	1101011	153	6B	k
108	1101100	154	6C	l
109	1101101	155	6D	m
110	1101110	156	6E	n
111	1101111	157	6F	o
112	1110000	160	70	p
113	1110001	161	71	q
114	1110010	162	72	r
115	1110011	163	73	s
116	1110100	164	74	t
117	1110101	165	75	u
118	1110110	166	76	v
119	1110111	167	77	w
120	1111000	170	78	x
121	1111001	171	79	y
122	1111010	172	7A	z
123	1111011	173	7B	{
124	1111100	174	7C		
125	1111101	175	7D	}
126	1111110	176	7E	~
127	1111111	177	7F	del

Figure 3-9　ASCII Conversion Chart

95 printable characters, consisting of 52 uppercase and lowercase letters, 10 numerals, and 33 special characters, including the blank, along with the 33 unprintable control characters designated by mnemonics. Each data object of type CHAR has, as its current value, one of these 128 distinct characters.

Computer memory stores all data in a binary format. That is, each ASCII character has a distinct binary encoding, as shown in Figure 3-9. Each ASCII code is listed with its equivalent binary, octal, decimal, and hexadecimal values. These equivalents are helpful in the formation of relational expressions involving operands of type CHAR. For example, using Figure 3-9, we can see that each of the following expressions is true:

```
"A" < "B"
"z" > "y"
("0" < "1") AND ("1" < "2") AND ("2" < "3")
("9" < "A") AND ("a" > "Z")
```

For example, "9" < "A" is true because the numeral "9" corresponds to the decimal ordinal number 57, "A" corresponds to the decimal ordinal number 65, and 57 < 65.

A number of standard procedures operate on character data. The function CHR (x) returns the value of type CHAR corresponding to the ordinal number x, where x is a constant or variable of type CARDINAL. Given the declaration

```
VAR     Example : CHAR;
```

the statement

```
Example := CHR (67)
```

stores the character value "C" in the variable Example. Likewise, the statement

```
Example := CHR (130)
```

could result in an error, since the ASCII characters correspond only to the ordinal numbers 0 through 127. Some computer systems extend the ASCII conversion chart to values up to 255. One such computer is the IBM PC. In these cases CHR (x) is valid for x < 256.

The function ORD (y) returns the value of type CARDINAL corresponding to the bit pattern of the character stored in y. Given the declaration

```
VAR     Sample : CARDINAL;
```

the statement

```
Sample := ORD("D")
```

stores the cardinal value 68 in the variable Sample.

The function CAP (z) returns the capital letter corresponding to the current value of the data object identified by the variable z of type CHAR. If z contains a lowercase letter, then the corresponding capital letter is returned; otherwise, if z already contains a capital letter, or some other character, then that character is returned.

Finally, the standard procedures INC (w,n) and DEC (w,n) return the n-th value following or preceding the value stored in w. The variable w may be of type CHAR or any other enumerable type, which makes these procedures applicable to many programming situations. The use of INC and DEC with user-defined enumerations is discussed in Section 3:3:1. Given the declarations

```
VAR   Var1, Var2 : CHAR;
```

the statements

```
Var1 := 'a';
INC (Var1, 5);
Var2 := 'N';
DEC (Var2, 1)
```

store the character value "f" in the variable Var1 and the character value "M" in the variable Var2. Note that for these two procedures the second parameter is optional and, when not present, defaults to the value 1.

The CHAR data type is extremely important because many programming problems deal with nonnumeric data. An immediate generalization of the CHAR data type is an ordered collection of characters called a string. This data type, although not directly supported by Modula-2, is very often a programmer-defined data type. Simply, a **string** is an ordered collection of character data objects, that is, a sequence of characters. In Modula-2 the string data type is most often represented as an "array of CHAR." The concepts of an array, which is a structured data type in Modula-2, and strings are both discussed thoroughly in Chapter 5.

3:2:5 BITSET Data Type

A **bit** is defined as a single binary digit whose value may be either 0 or 1. Computer memory is partitioned into equal-sized locations, where each location is N bits in length. The particular value of N is hardware dependent and, therefore, beyond the control of the programmer. The BITSET data type is predefined in Modula-2 and can provide access to low-level features in the computer system.

The BITSET data type represents an ordered collection of the integer values in the range 0 through N−1. If the bits in a memory location are considered to be addressed 0 through N−1 and a data object of type BITSET is represented by a single memory location, then the notion of a bitset may be visualized as depicted in Figure 3-10.

An exact visualization of the data type BITSET cannot be given because the order of the bits within a memory location is not defined in Modula-2. That is, whether bit 0 is the least significant or the most significant bit in a memory location is not determined. Thus different implementations of Modula-2 may specify the order of the bits that is considered most appropriate for a specific system.

A data object of type BITSET containing no elements is represented by a bit pattern containing 0's in all N positions. A data object containing the elements 1 and 6 will have 1's in the first and sixth bit positions and 0's in the remaining positions. Syntactically, the lexical symbols "{" and "}" are used to compose set literals. Given the declarations

```
VAR     X, Y : BITSET;
```

the statements

```
X := {};
Y := {1,6}
```

assign the set containing no elements, commonly referred to as the empty set, to the variable X, and the set containing 1 and 6 to the variable Y. Thus X represents a single memory location in which every bit is set to 0, and Y represents a single memory location in which only the first and sixth bits are set to 1. The ability to accomplish this apparently simple assignment operation in such a straightforward manner is a primary advantage of the BITSET data type.

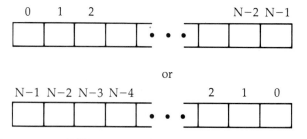

Figure 3-10   Visualization of the BITSET Data Type

Programming a computer system at a low level requires access to system features that are often not easily accessible from within high-level programming languages. The BITSET data type provides for the direct manipulation of bits, thus making it possible to set low-level switches and create bit strings.

The set operations of union, intersection, difference, and symmetric difference are represented by the lexical symbols "+", "*", "-", and "/", respectively. These set operations are binary operations and hence require two operands of the same set type. In the case of the BITSET data type, each operation requires two operands of type BITSET.

The union operator, "+", yields the bitset containing all elements that are in either of the two sets.

The difference operator, "-", forms the bitset containing all elements in the first set that are not also in the second set.

The intersection operator, "*", computes the bitset containing all elements that are in both the first set and the second set.

The symmetric difference operator, "/", produces the bitset containing those elements that are in either of the two sets but not in both sets.

The program module presented in Figure 3-11 illustrates these four set operations. In this example each of the four variables R1, R2, R3, and R4 will have the same final value, the bitset value {0,2,5}.

```
 1   MODULE BitsetExample;
 2
 3   VAR     V, W, X, Y, Z  : BITSET;
 4           R1, R2, R3, R4 : BITSET;
 5
 6   BEGIN
 7
 8   V := {1, 3, 4, 6, 7};
 9   W := {0, 1, 2, 3, 4, 5, 6, 7};
10   X := {0, 2, 5};
11   Y := {0};
12   Z := {2, 5};
13
14   R1 := Y + Z;
15   R2 := W * X;
16   R3 := W - V;
17   R4 := (X / Y ) + (Y / Z)
18
19   END BitsetExample.
```

Figure 3-11   Program Module with BITSET Operations

Operator	Meaning
=	Set equality
#	Set inequality
<>	Set inequality
<=	Subset
>=	Superset
IN	Set membership

Figure 3-12   Relational Operators for Sets

When dealing with data objects of type BITSET, the relational operators have the meanings shown in Figure 3-12. With the exception of the operator IN, each of the operators requires two operands of type BITSET. The IN operator requires that the first operand be a bitset element and the second operand be of type BITSET.

Exercises

1. For the computer system you intend to use, determine the word size (value of N) of the computer hardware used and then determine the range of integers and cardinals available on your implementation of Modula-2.

2. The type conversion function TRUNC accepts a single parameter of type REAL and returns the cardinal value representing the whole number portion of that real value. The fractional part, no matter how large, is completely ignored. Show how you could utilize this function to accomplish rounding; that is, if the fractional part is greater than or equal to 0.5, then the cardinal result is increased by 1.

3. Given the following program fragment, determine the final values stored in each of the variables used.

```
CONST   DEBUG   := TRUE;
        Online  := FALSE;
        Max     := 750;
        Print   := DEBUG OR Online;
VAR     Status, ErrorFlag : BOOLEAN;
        Count : INTEGER;

BEGIN
Count := 0;
Status := Count > Max;
ErrorFlag := NOT Print AND Status;
```

4. The standard procedure CAP converts a lowercase letter to its upper-case equivalent. Devise a scheme to convert an uppercase letter to its lowercase equivalent. **HINT:** Both the uppercase and lowercase letters occupy adjacent positions in the ASCII character set.

5. Some computer systems utilize the Extended Binary Coded Decimal Interchange Code, EBCDIC, character set rather than ASCII. Research the EBCDIC character set and devise a solution to the problem posed in Exercise 4 using EBCDIC in place of ASCII.

6. For each of the following statements, determine the resulting bitset value assigned to the variable.

```
BS1 := {14,7,8,15,1,3} + {};
BS2 := { 1, 9, 2 } + { 1, 2, 3, 4 };
BS3 := BS1 * {10,15, 12, 2};
BS4 := BS1 / {10,15,12,2};
BS5 := { 1, 2, 3, 4 } - { 1, 9, 2};
```

3:3 Unstructured Data Types

Thus far we have discussed only the elementary data types. These un-structured data types are sufficient for a surprisingly large number of pro-gramming situations and they are efficiently supported. However, many programming situations do arise that require additional data types that are specific to the particular problem being solved and are therefore not directly supported by the language. These programmer-definable, un-structured data types are divided into two categories: **subrange**s and **enumeration**s. Subranges and enumerations are declared with the TYPE statement. Figure 3-13 presents the syntax diagrams for *Type Declaration*.

3:3:1 Enumeration Types

Not all programming problems deal with numbers or individual charac-ters. Data are best quantified in problem-dependent terminology. Con-sider the classification of students at a college or university. Traditionally, undergraduate students are included in one of the following classes: freshman, sophomore, junior, or senior. It would be unnatural and possi-bly confusing if this terminology were not used in a programming situa-tion modeling this reality.

In Modula-2 a new data type may be declared by simply enumera-ting all the values that belong to this type. Syntactically, each value is an

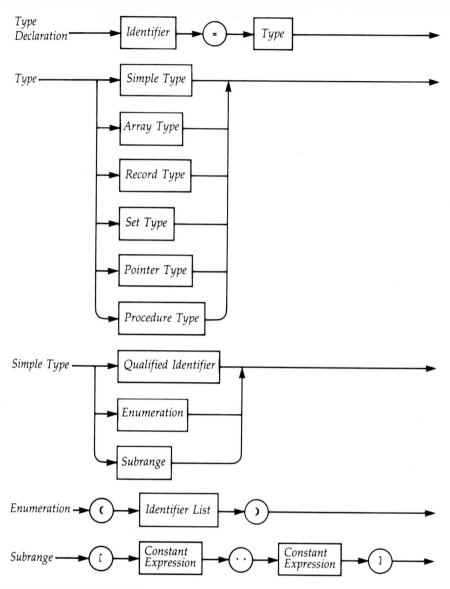

Figure 3-13   Syntax Diagram for *Type Declaration*

Identifier and must follow the rules for composing *Identifiers*. Thus the declaration

```
TYPE   Class = ( Freshman, Sophomore, Junior, Senior );
```

declares the new data type Class, consisting of the four values Freshman, Sophomore, Junior, Senior. Note that since the case of letters, upper or lower, is significant, the *Identifiers* freshmen, SOPHOMORE, junior, and SENior are not valid for the type Class.

The standard procedures INC and DEC may be used with enumerations. For example, given the enumeration of type Class, declared above, and the declaration

```
VAR   Student : Class;
```

the statement sequence

```
Student := Freshman;
INC (Student, 2);
```

places the value Junior in the variable Student. DEC functions in a similar manner. A complete discussion of INC and DEC appears in Section 7:1.

Similarly, other enumerations may be declared where appropriate, as in the following type declarations relating to the classification of students at a university.

```
TYPE   School = (ArtsAndSciences, Business, Engineering);
       Class  = (Freshman, Sophomore, Junior, Senior, Graduate);
       Status = (Parttime, Fulltime);
       Major  = (Mathematics, Chemistry, History, Accounting,
                 ComputerScience, Psychology, Communications);
```

3:3:2 Subranges

Those programming situations that require a restriction on the acceptable data values placed in a data object lend themselves to the use of *Subranges*. Every *Subrange* has a base type, which is the type from which the new type is derived. The base type must be a scalar type; this eliminates the possibility of subranges of reals. All operations available for the base type are automatically available for the *Subrange*. But remember that just as it is invalid for a data object of type INTEGER or CARDINAL to take on a value outside of its defined interval, it is invalid for a data object of a subrange type to take on a value outside of its defined range.

Consider the declarations

```
TYPE   Status   = [ -5 .. 15 ];
       MonthDay = [ 1 .. 31 ];
       Letter   = [ "A" .. "Z" ];
```

in which three subranges are declared. The type Status is declared as a subrange of the base type INTEGER, so that it includes only those integers in the specified interval. The new type MonthDay is a subrange of the base type CARDINAL, whereas the type Letter is a subrange of the base type CHAR. Now that these types have been declared, we can declare variables of these types, as in the following declarations:

```
VAR     Initial             : Letter;
        Appointment         : MonthDay;
        Score, Result,X  : Status;
```

Subranges may be formed over enumeration types. For example, with the declaration

```
TYPE    Class  = (Freshman, Sophomore, Junior,
                    Senior, Graduate);
```

a subrange may be formed as

```
TYPE    UpperClass = [Sophomore .. Senior];
```

which does not include the values Freshman and Graduate.

An advantage of using subranges is automatic range checking at execution time. That is, at execution time an error message is generated whenever an attempt is made to assign a value outside of the range.

Exercises

1. Write the statements necessary to declare the data types UHF and VHF, which accommodate the available channels for these types of television tuners.

2. Exactly how many distinct values does the following data type, AlphaNumeric, encompass?

```
TYPE    AlphaNumeric = [ '0' .. 'Z' ];
```

3. Write the statements necessary to declare the data type USCoins, which consists of the appropriate enumerated names for United States coins.

4. Given the declarations

```
VAR     Month : Months;
        Day   : Days;
        Year  : Years;
```

write the statements necessary to declare the data types Months, Days, and Years. Assume that all dates from 1900 through 2100 are to be represented.

5. The situation may arise where it is appropriate to declare two enumerations that both contain the same *Identifier*. Is this situation valid in Modula-2? Study the syntax diagrams to see if you can answer this question. In addition, write a short Modula-2 program containing such declarations and see whether your language implementation accepts or rejects it.

4 Program Structure

4:1 Overview

In Chapters 2 and 3 the emphasis was on data and for good reasons. Programming essentially involves the manipulation of data. This manipulation of data is accomplished in Modula-2 through the execution of statements. Understanding the types and representation of data is necessary before the executable statements may be studied. This chapter introduces the basic statements available in Modula-2. Many of these statements appeared in the sample programs in earlier chapters to present complete Modula-2 programs.

Consider the sample program presented in Figure 4-1. This program is the same as that presented in Figure 2-4. This program module, TimesTable, computes and prints a multiplication table. Many of the lexical components appearing in this program should be familiar to the reader, although the precise meanings of the individual statements may not be.

Lines 5 through 43 in this program correspond to the lexical component *Block*, whose syntax diagram appears in Figure 4-2. A *Block* consists of optional declarations followed by a sequence of executable statements enclosed by the reserved words BEGIN and END. A *Statement Sequence* is a collection of one or more *Statements* separated by the lexical symbol ";". The semicolons serve as separators between statements rather than as statement terminators. Thus the last statement in a sequence is not followed by a semicolon. At this point you should observe that the program module TimesTable corresponds to the syntax indicated in Figure 4-2. This program module contains two *Declaration*s and five *Statement*s.

```
 1 MODULE  TimesTable;
 2
 3 FROM InOut IMPORT ReadCard, WriteCard, WriteString, WriteLn;
 4
 5 CONST  Limit = 12;              (* Maximum allowed size of table *)
 6
 7 VAR    Size, I, Row, Column, Entry : CARDINAL;
 8
 9 BEGIN
10
11 (*  User interaction to accept desired table size  *)
12 WriteString ('Enter Size?');  ReadCard (Size);  WriteLn;
13 WriteLn;
14
15 IF Size > Limit THEN             (*  Test for valid user input  *)
16     WriteString ('---ERROR: Size exceeds the Limit of ');
17     WriteCard (Limit, 2); WriteLn
18   ELSE       (*  Write the heading across the top of the page  *)
19     WriteString ('    !');
20     FOR I := 1 TO Size BY 1 DO    (* Write the column headings *)
21        WriteCard (I, 5)
22     END;
23     WriteLn;
24     WriteString (' ---!');
25     FOR I := 1 TO Size DO
26        WriteString ('-----')
27     END;
28     WriteLn;
29                              (* Once for each row in the table *)
30     FOR Row := 1 TO Size BY 1 DO
31        WriteCard (Row, 3);
32        WriteString (' !');
33
34        FOR Column := 1 TO Size BY 1 DO (* Once for each column *)
35           Entry := Row * Column;
36           WriteCard (Entry, 5)
37        END;
38        WriteLn                  (* Terminate the output line  *)
39
40     END
41 END
42
43 END TimesTable.
```

Figure 4-1   Program Module TimesTable

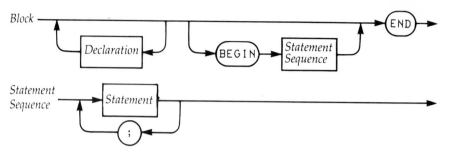

Figure 4-2   Syntax Diagrams for *Block* and *Statement Sequence*

Figure 4-3 contains the syntax diagram for the lexical component *Statement*. This diagram represents the executable statements available in Modula-2. Appearing as the first option in this syntax diagram is the *Assignment Statement*, a frequently used statement in Modula-2. The *Assignment Statement* is discussed thoroughly in Section 2:4:1, dealing with the assignment operator. Decision statements and looping statements, in their various forms, comprise the majority of executable statements available in Modula-2. These statements are important because through them programmers alter the flow of control within programs to implement decision structures and repetitive execution.

4:2 Importing and Procedure Calls

Before proceeding with this discussion of Modula-2's executable statements, we must first discuss the IMPORT statement appearing on line 3 in Figure 4-1. Such a statement may appear zero or more times in a *Program Module*, immediately preceding the *Block*. Figure 4-4 contains the syntax diagram for the *Import Statement*. The purpose of this statement is to declare, from the specified module, those identifiers that are being referenced in the current module. In the program module TimesTable, the identifiers ReadCard, WriteCard, WriteString, and WriteLn are imported from the standard module InOut. They identify procedures called to perform input and output.

A procedure is a named sequence of program instructions that performs some well-defined task. Procedures are discussed thoroughly in Chapter 6. Our interest at this point is in understanding the use of predefined procedures. The four procedures mentioned in the previous paragraph are declared in the standard module InOut, whose contents are described in Section 7:3 and whose definition appears in Appendix D. The *Import Statement*

```
FROM InOut IMPORT ReadCard, WriteCard, WriteString, WriteLn;
```

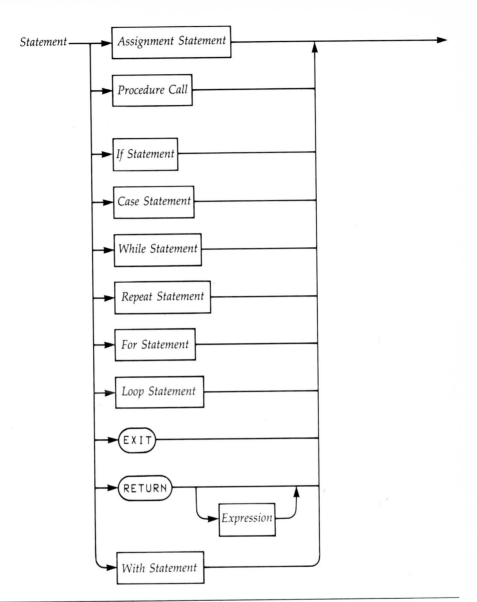

Figure 4-3   Syntax Diagram for *Statement*

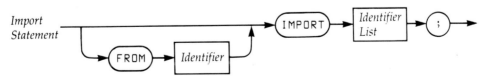

Figure 4-4   Syntax Diagram for *Import Statement*

specifies that the identifiers ReadCard, WriteCard, WriteString, and WriteLn declared in the module InOut may be referenced in the current module. This statement is necessary because in Modula-2 an identifier may not be referenced unless it has been declared. The *Import Statement* provides access in the current module to identifiers declared in another module.

The declaration

        IMPORT InOut;

illustrates the alternative form of the *Import Statement*, in which just the name of the module is specified. This form provides access to all the identifiers exported by the module. However, these identifiers may only be accessed as *Qualified Identifiers*. For example, the identifiers in InOut must be referenced as InOut.ReadCard, InOut.WriteCard, and so forth.

A procedure executes only when it is called. The syntax of a *Procedure Call* is illustrated in Figure 4-5. In most cases the *Designator* is simply an *Identifier*, whereas the *Actual Parameters* depend on the declaration of the particular procedure being called. Each procedure is declared with a fixed number of parameters, and the number of parameters in the *Procedure Call* must agree with the number of parameters in the procedure declaration. The type of each *Actual Parameter* must agree with the type of the corresponding formal parameter in the *Procedure Declaration*. To import a procedure, the name of the procedure and the name of its module must be known. In addition, the types and purposes of the formal

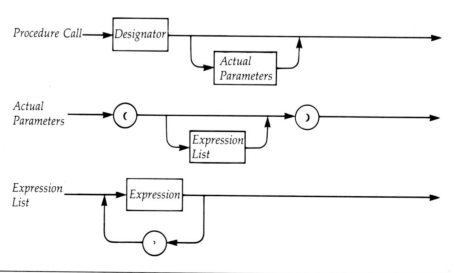

Figure 4-5   Syntax Diagram for *Procedure Call*

parameters must be known, because the actual parameters must be consistent with the formal parameters.

In the sample program the procedures ReadCard, WriteCard, WriteString, and WriteLn interact with the user, who enters the size of the multiplication table. Then the program prints the table. Specifically, the procedure ReadCard, called on line 12, takes the cardinal value entered by the user and stores it in the cardinal variable Size. WriteCard prints the current value of the specified data object of type CARDINAL using the specified number of columns. This second parameter must also be of type CARDINAL. WriteString prints a character string. The parameterless procedure WriteLn called on lines 17 and 23 terminates the current line of printed output. In some cases print operations are buffered. That is, although the various output procedures are called, nothing is actually printed until the procedure WriteLn is called.

As an example of a use of the standard module InOut, consider the program module Listing presented in Figure 4-6. This program reads and produces a listing of an ASCII data file. Each line of the listing starts with the sequence number of the line in the data file. The program reads

```
 1 MODULE Listing;
 2
 3 FROM InOut IMPORT EOL, Done, Read, Write, WriteCard, WriteLn;
 4
 5 CONST  Colon = ':';
 6         Blank = ' ';
 7
 8 VAR    Line  : CARDINAL;
 9         AChar : CHAR;
10
11 BEGIN
12 Line   := 1;
13 AChar  := EOL;
14 Done   := TRUE;
15 WHILE Done DO
16    IF AChar = EOL THEN
17        WriteLn;  WriteCard (Line, 12);   Write (Colon);
18        Write (Blank);  Line := Line + 1
19      ELSE
20        Write (AChar)
21    END;
22    Read (AChar)
23 END;
24 WriteLn
25 END Listing.
```

Figure 4-6   Program Module Listing

the input, a character at a time, and produces a sequenced listing of the input.

This program produces a numbered listing of any source program, such as those appearing as figures in this text. Source programs themselves may not contain line numbers, but line numbers provide a convenient way of referring to statements within a program. The procedures WriteCard and WriteLn, presented earlier, are used in this program. Read and Write are also procedures declared in InOut. Read reads a single character from the input device, and Write writes a single character to the output device.

The program module Listing reads and then writes a character at a time. The program determines when the end of each input line is encountered so that it can terminate each output line and place a sequence number at the beginning of the next line of output. The end of an input line is determined by comparing the variable AChar to EOL, which is a constant imported from InOut. Likewise, the program must have some way of determining when it has read all of the available input, so that it may halt. This task is accomplished with the BOOLEAN variable Done, which is also imported from InOut.

EOL, a constant of type CHAR, indicates the end of a line. EOL is an acronym for **End Of Line**. The Read procedure reads one character each time it is called; at the end of each line of input, it reads a character value equivalent to EOL. By comparing the character read with EOL, the program determines when an entire line has been read and printed.

Done, a variable of type BOOLEAN, is initialized by the procedures in InOut to indicate whether or not the specified input operation was successful. Specifically, the input procedures in InOut store the boolean value TRUE in Done whenever they were able to read a value. They store the value FALSE whenever they were not able to read a value. When all of the input values have been read and an attempt is made to read another value, the input procedure assigns the value FALSE to Done. Thus the Program Module Listing determines when to halt by observing when Done becomes FALSE. As long as Done is TRUE, all of the input has not been read. We emphasize that Done is a variable and, as such, it has no default initial value. Thus Done should not be tested until a value is assigned to it either through an assignment statement or through a call to an input procedure.

Exercises

1. Enter the Program Module TimesTable presented in Figure 4-1 into the computer system you use, translate, and execute it. You should obtain the results shown in Figure 2-5. In addition, you might investi-

gate some of the subtleties of your implementation of Modula-2. For example, add a semicolon to the end of line 36 of the program and see if your implementation forgives this extra delimiter. It should.

2. Modify the Program Module TimesTable so that it uses data objects of type INTEGER rather than CARDINAL. Not only will the declarations need to change but so will the various procedure calls.

3. Write a complete Modula-2 program module that counts the number of characters appearing in its input. The procedure Read from the standard module InOut is used to read individual characters.

4:3 Decision Statements

In programming, a decision statement is a mechanism that allows a process to perform one of several different actions, or no action, based upon the current values of specific data objects. Modula-2 contains two decision statements, the *If Statement* and the *Case Statement*, each having several valid forms.

Basically, a decision statement consists of a condition and a statement sequence. A condition is a boolean expression. Frequently, the condition is expressed as a comparison between data objects using the relational operators. If the condition holds, that is, if the boolean expression evaluates to TRUE, then the statements in the sequence are executed. This basic idea is the underlying logic behind all forms of decision statements in Modula-2.

4:3:1 The IF Statement

The most commonly used decision statement is the *If Statement*. Furthermore, the *If Statement* is sufficient for expressing all decisions necessary in any programming situation. In the next section the *Case Statement* is presented because it is a convenient notation for expressing certain types of complex decisions.

Figure 4-7 contains the syntax diagram for the *If Statement*. The simplest form of this statement consists of the reserved word IF followed by a boolean expression, followed by the reserved word THEN, followed by a *Statement Sequence*. The entire statement is terminated by the reserved word END.

The meaning of this simple form is as follows: If the boolean expression evaluates to TRUE, then and only then does the statement sequence execute. If the expression evaluates to FALSE, then execution simply by-

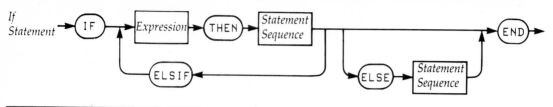

If Statement

Figure 4-7   Syntax Diagram for *If Statement*

passes the statement sequence and continues with the statement follow-ing the *If Statement*. This form is appropriate in programming situations in which an action should only be performed if a certain well-defined con-dition holds. For example, in the *Block*

```
TYPE    AgeGroup   = (Child, Adult);
        Degrees    = (MD, PhD, Other);
        Profession = (Doctor, Lawyer, IndianChief);

VAR     Age     : CARDINAL;
        Degree  : Degrees;
        Person  : AgeGroup;
        Work .  : Profession;
BEGIN
. . . (* other statements *)
Person := Child;
IF Age >= 21 THEN
      Person := Adult
END;
. . . (* other statements *)
END
```

the assignment statement

```
Person := Child
```

is unconditionally executed each time the block itself is performed. How-ever, the assignment statement

```
Person := Adult
```

executes only if the current value of the variable Age is greater than or equal to 21.

There are many programming situations in which one action is per-formed when a certain condition holds and another action is performed when the condition does not hold. A slightly more complicated form of the *If Statement* contains an optional ELSE clause to accommodate this situation. As an example of this form, consider the *If Statement*

```
IF Age >= 21 THEN
    Person := Adult
  ELSE
    Person := Child
END
```

which contains an ELSE clause. If the condition holds when this statement executes, then the statement

```
Person := Adult
```

executes; otherwise, just the assignment statement

```
Person := Child
```

is performed. One and only one of the two *Statement Sequences* executes in every case.

One advantage of using this form of the *If Statement* in this situation is that the *If Statement* encapsulates all of the logic involved. The reader of the statement sees in one statement the entire decision structure intended by the programmer. In the first example an unconditionally executed assignment statement precedes the *If Statement*. What effect does this assignment statement have on the decision structure being expressed? How likely is the reader to recognize the connection between this assignment statement and the *If Statement*? In addition, the statement

```
Person := Child
```

is executed every time, even in those cases when the value in Age is greater than or equal to 21. This unconditional execution is inefficient. The *If Statement* with an ELSE clause is usually more efficient and clearer.

Another option in the *If Statement* involves the use of additional conditions, which are evaluated sequentially. The first condition that evaluates to TRUE has its corresponding statement sequence executed. If none of the conditions hold, then none of the sequences execute and the process continues with the statement following the *If Statement*. As an example consider the *Block*

```
TYPE    AgeGroup  = ( Child, Adolescent, Adult, SeniorCitizen );
        What      = ( Working, Playing, Exploring, Retired );
VAR     Age       : CARDINAL;
        Person    : AgeGroup;
        Activity  : What;
```

```
BEGIN
   . . . (* other statements  *)
   Person   := SeniorCitizen;
   Activity := Retired;
   IF Age < 13 THEN
         Person   := Child;
         Activity := Playing
      ELSIF Age < 21 THEN
         Person   := Adolescent;
         Activity := Exploring
      ELSIF Age < 65 THEN
         Person   := Adult;
         Activity := Working
   END;
   . . . (* other statements  *)
END
```

in which the *If Statement* contains three conditions. If we assume that the variable Age currently has the value 17, then the first condition

```
   Age < 13
```

is false, but the second condition

```
   Age < 21
```

is true. Under our assumption the sequence

```
      Person   := Adolescent;
      Activity := Exploring
```

is executed. When using this form of the *If Statement*, it is possible that none of the conditions will hold. For example, if we assume that the variable AGE currently has the value 72, then none of the three specified conditions hold and none of the three statement sequences execute. The variable Person retains the value SeniorCitizen, and the variable Activity retains the value Retired. This *If Statement* may be modified to the statement

```
      IF Age < 13 THEN
            Person   := Child;
            Activity := Playing
         ELSIF Age < 21 THEN
            Activity := Exploring;
            Person   := Adolescent
         ELSIF Age < 65 THEN
            Person   := Adult;
            Activity := Working
```

```
      ELSE
         Activity := Retired;
         Person   := SeniorCitizen
      END
```

which is equivalent and illustrates another form of the *If Statement*. This form consists of a primary condition followed by one or more additional conditions, followed by an ELSE clause, which comes into play only if none of the conditions hold. In this form of the *If Statement*, one of the specified statement sequences executes in every case.

We must take care when expressing decision structures with the *If Statement*. If there is an ELSE clause, then exactly one statement sequence within an *If Statement* will perform. If no ELSE clause is present, then one of the conditions must be true for one of the statement sequences to perform.

4:3:2 The CASE Statement

The *Case Statement* in Modula-2 operates similarly to the *If Statement*. The main difference between these two decision statements is the manner in which the condition is expressed. The *If Statement* has explicit conditions expressed as boolean expressions. The *Case Statement* has implicit conditions expressed as lists of enumerated values or enumerated value ranges.

Consider the equivalent *If Statement* and *Case Statement* presented in Figure 4-8. The explicit condition

```
Age < 13
```

in the *If Statement* is equivalent to the condition implied by the range

```
0..12
```

```
IF Age < 13 THEN                CASE Age OF
   Person := Child                 0..12 : Person := Child        !
   ELSIF  Age  <  21 THEN         13..20 : Person := Adolescent   !
   Person := Adolescent           21..64 : Person := Adult
   ELSIF Age < 65 THEN            ELSE
   Person := Adult                   Person := SeniorCitizen
   ELSE                           END
   Person := SeniorCitizen
END
```

Figure 4-8   Equivalent IF and CASE Statements

in the *Case Statement*. Similarly, the condition

```
Age < 65
```

after the preceding conditions are tested, expresses the same condition as does the range

```
21..64
```

Thus the *Case Statement* consists of an expression followed by one or more specific *Cases* that the expression may satisfy, each with a corresponding *Statement Sequence*.

Figure 4-9 shows the syntax diagrams for the *Case Statement*. These syntax diagrams indicate that a *Case Statement* consists of the reserved word CASE followed by an expression that evaluates to an enumerable type, followed by the reserved word OF, followed by one or more *Cases* separated by the lexical symbol "¦". An optional ELSE clause may appear immediately before the required terminator, which is the reserved word END. Each *Case* consists of one or more literals or ranges separated by commas and followed by the lexical symbol ":", which, in turn, is followed by a *Statement Sequence*.

Although the *Case Statement* has a complex syntactic structure, there is a direct relationship between the syntax and the meaning of the state-

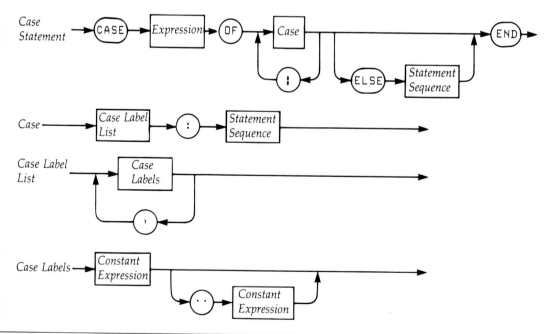

Figure 4-9   Syntax Diagram for *Case Statement*

ment. The expression in the *Case Statement* evaluates to a value that is compatible with the enumerable data type used in the *Case Labels*. INTEGER, CARDINAL, BOOLEAN, and CHAR are examples of enumerable data types, whereas REAL is not. Any programmer-declared enumeration or subrange data type is also enumerable and therefore valid. The *Case Statement* performs by evaluating the expression, determining which *Case Label List* corresponds to the value of the expression, and then executing the corresponding *Statement Sequence*.

   If the computed value of the expression in a *Case Statement* does not match one of the *Case Labels* and no ELSE clause was specified, a run time error occurs. This error is different from the similar situation with the *If Statement*, in which execution simply proceeds with the following statement.

   With regard to the syntax of the *Case Statement*, note that the lexical symbol "∎" is a separator, not a terminator, between *Cases*. This fact is illustrated in each of the examples in this section. The revised definition of Modula-2 (see Appendix A or B) allows for the inclusion of extra separators "∎".

   Enumerated data types are commonly used to compose expressions in *Case Statement*s. The following block illustrates a case structure with an enumeration type.

```
TYPE    Colonies = ( NH, MA, RI, CT, NY, NJ, PA, DE, MD,
                                            VA, NC, SC, GA);

        Areas    = ( NewEngland, MidAtlantic, Southern);

VAR     Colony   : Colonies;
        Location : Areas;

BEGIN
. . . (*  other  statements  *)
CASE Colony OF
   NH : Location := NewEngland   ∎
   MA : Location := NewEngland   ∎
   RI : Location := NewEngland   ∎
   CT : Location := NewEngland   ∎
   NY : Location := MidAtlantic  ∎
   NJ : Location := MidAtlantic  ∎
   PA : Location := MidAtlantic  ∎
   DE : Location := MidAtlantic  ∎
   MD : Location := Southern     ∎
   VA : Location := Southern     ∎
   NC : Location := Southern     ∎
   SC : Location := Southern     ∎
   GA : Location := Southern
END;
. . . (*  other  statements  *)
END
```

In this example each *Case* is a single specific value followed by a *Statement Sequence* (a single statement in this example). This form of the *Case Statement*, consisting of a separate *Case* for each possible value, is valid, but in this example it is more lengthy than necessary. Since identical statements are performed for more than one value, an alternative form of the *Case Label List* may be used. An equivalent *Case Statement*,

```
CASE Colony OF
   NH,MA,RI,CT      : Location := NewEngland  !
   NY,NJ,PA,DE      : Location := MidAtlantic !
   MD,VA,NC,SC,GA : Location := Southern
END
```

performs the same actions. In this statement only three cases are expressed, with each *Case Label List* consisting of the specific values that share the same *Statement Sequence*. This form of the *Case Statement* is shorter and clearer because we can more easily determine which values share the same action.

This example is modified to illustrate another form of the *Case Statement*. Since all enumerable data types, INTEGER and CARDINAL included, have a well-defined ordering of values, we can compose value ranges. The statement

```
CASE Colony OF
   NH..CT : Location := NewEngland  !
   NY..DE : Location := MidAtlantic !
   MD..GA : Location := Southern
END
```

is equivalent to the preceding two statements, but instead of listing each enumerated value, a convenient range notation is used. Note that this range notation may not be appropriate in all cases because it is dependent upon the ordering of the identifiers in the enumeration. For example, if, instead, the data type Colonies was declared as

```
TYPE    Colonies = ( DE, NH, MA, RI, NJ, PA, DE,
                     MD, VA, NC, CT, SC, GA )
```

then the preceding case statement would not perform correctly. It would have to be rewritten as

```
CASE Colony OF
   NH..RI,CT      : Location := NewEngland !
   MD..NC,SC..GA : Location := Southern    !
   DE,NJ..DE      : Location := MidAtlantic
END
```

to accomplish an equivalent result. The last example shows the use of specific values and value ranges within the same case. Any number of values or ranges may appear in a *Case Label List*, and, likewise, no limit exists to the number of *Cases*.

Exercises

1. Correct the syntax error(s) in the following decision statement:

```
IF Coin <# Quarter THEN
    Useful := FALSE
  ELSE;
    Useful := TRUE
END
```

2. The standard module InOut contains procedures for writing integers, cardinals, reals, characters, and strings, but how are enumerated values printed? One way of accomplishing this task is to use a *Case Statement*. Using an enumeration of your choice, write a program fragment that illustrates how this may be done.

3. Write a complete Modula-2 program module that counts the number of times a blank character appears in its input. The procedure Read from the standard module InOut is used to read individual characters.

4. Assuming that periods only terminate sentences and that one or more consecutive blanks separate words, write a complete Modula-2 program that counts the number of sentences and the number of words in its input.

4:4 Looping Statements

A looping statement is a mechanism that performs a statement sequence more than once, usually terminating the repetition when a certain condition becomes true. Modula-2 contains four looping statements. For programming purposes only one type of looping statement is sufficient. However, four statements are provided to suit the needs of certain programming situations. Learning when a certain looping statement is more appropriate than another is part of the art of programming.

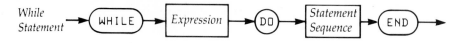

Figure 4-10   Syntax Diagram for *While Statement*

4:4:1 The WHILE Statement

A simple and general looping statement is the *While Statement*. This statement consists of a condition and a *Statement Sequence*. First the condition is tested. If it is true, then the statement sequence is executed; otherwise, execution proceeds with the statement following the *While Statement*. After the statement sequence executes, the condition is retested. If it is still true, the statement sequence executes again. This process continues as long as the condition holds, possibly forever. Thus in most programming situations it is important that the statements in the sequence cause the condition to eventually evaluate to false; otherwise, an infinite loop results. In the *While Statement* as in the *If Statement*, the condition is a boolean expression, which is frequently a comparison between data objects expressed using relational operators. Figure 4-10 shows the syntax diagram for the *While Statement*.

The example of a *While Statement* in the *Block*

```
CONST   Initial    = 1;
        Increment = 1;
        Final      = 5;

VAR   Control : INTEGER;

BEGIN
Control := Initial;
WHILE Control <= Final DO
    WriteString ('This is just a test');
    WriteLn;
    INC (Control, Increment)
END
END
```

illustrates a simple use of this statement. This example demonstrates a simple counting situation; specifically, the example prints the string "This is just a test" five times. This example shows the three necessary ingredients in a complete looping structure:

1. Proper initialization of the loop control variables. A loop control variable is a variable that appears in the loop condition.

2. The correct composition of the loop condition in terms of the loop control variables.

3. Proper adjustment of the loop control variables to cause the looping to eventually terminate.

Prior to the *While Statement*, the variable Control is assigned an initial value of 1. The condition on the *While Statement* means that the loop continues as long as the value stored in Control is less than or equal to 5. Finally, the last statement in the loop's statement sequence adjusts the value of Control so that the condition eventually becomes false.

In the *While Statement*, note that if the condition initially evaluates to false, the statement sequence of the loop does not execute. Thus in this example, if the constant Initial contained the value 7, nothing would be printed. Also, if the constant Increment contained the value -1, the loop could continue forever.

A more meaningful illustration of the *While Statement* appears in the program module Summation presented in Figure 4-11. This program reads a collection of integer values, then computes and prints their sum.

To understand this program module, we need to understand the role of the variable Done, which is imported from the standard module InOut. The statement

```
ReadInt (IntValue);
```

```
1 MODULE Summation;
2
3 FROM InOut IMPORT ReadInt, Done, WriteInt, WriteString, WriteLn;
4
5 CONST   MaxInt = 32767;
6
7 VAR     Sum, IntValue : INTEGER;
8
9 BEGIN
10 Sum := 0;
11 ReadInt (IntValue);
12
13 WHILE Done DO
14     Sum := Sum + IntValue;
15     ReadInt (IntValue)
16 END;
17
18 WriteString (' The sum is ');   WriteInt (Sum, 6);   WriteLn
19 END Summation.
```

Figure 4-11   Program Module Summation

appearing on lines 11 and 15 reads a single integer value from the current input device, initially the user's keyboard, and stores that value in the variable IntValue. The variable Done, a boolean variable, is imported from the standard module InOut. It is assigned the value TRUE by the procedure ReadInt if the read operation was completed successfully. If for some reason the read operation is unsuccessful, Done is assigned the value FALSE. In particular, Done is assigned the value FALSE when an attempt is made to read past the end of the data. The various input procedures declared in the standard module InOut initialize Done in this same way.

Thus the *While Statement* appearing on lines 13 through 16 continues processing as long as the procedure ReadInt successfully reads integer values. When all the data has been read and an attempt is made to read another value, then no value is read and Done is assigned the value FALSE. Since ReadInt is the last statement in the sequence, the loop terminates the next time the condition is evaluated.

4:4:2 The REPEAT Statement

The *Repeat Statement*, like the *While Statement*, is a looping construct, but its control logic is slightly different from that of the *While Statement*. Figure 4-12 shows the syntax of the *Repeat Statement*.

When a *Repeat Statement* executes, the *Statement Sequence* is executed and then the condition is tested. If the condition evaluates to false, then the statement sequence is executed again and the condition retested. This process continues until the condition evaluates to true, at which time execution continues with the statement following the *Repeat Statement*. To summarize: In a *While Statement* the loop continues **while** the specified condition is true; in a *Repeat Statement* the loop continues **until** the specified condition becomes true.

As with the *While Statement*, and every looping statement, we must take care to compose the *Repeat Statement* properly. Specifically, each of the following conditions must be assured:

1. Proper initialization of the loop control variables.

2. The correct composition of the looping condition in terms of the loop control variables.

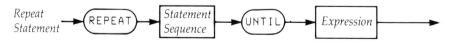

Figure 4-12   Syntax Diagram for *Repeat Statement*

3. Proper adjustment of the loop control variables to cause the looping to eventually terminate.

Every use of the *While Statement* in Modula-2 may be rewritten as a *Repeat Statement* and vice versa. Consider the two looping structures in Figure 4-13. In this example the two statements appear to be very similar, and in most situations they accomplish the same result. However, these two statements are **not** equivalent. If we assume that the value of Initial is not greater than the value of Final and that Increment has a positive value, then these statements are equivalent. However, if the value of Initial is greater than the value of Final and the value of Increment is positive, then, since the *Repeat Statement*'s sequence executes before the condition is tested, the string is printed once. Given these assumptions, the *While Statement*'s sequence does not execute even once.

Now consider the equivalent looping structures in Figure 4-14. The *Repeat Statement* is within an *If Statement*. This arrangement is necessary to avoid an initial iteration of the loop when the condition is initially false. These two structures are equivalent; they both accomplish the same result. We might argue that in this given situation the *While Statement* is more appropriate, since it appears to be less complex. How do we decide which looping statement to use? The answer depends upon the particular programming situation and, to a certain extent, on the programmer's preference.

```
BEGIN                                 BEGIN
Control := Initial;                   Control := Initial;
WHILE Control <= Final DO             REPEAT
   WriteString('Testing');              WriteString('Testing');
   Control := Control + Increment       Control := Control + Increment
END                                   UNTIL Control > Final
END                                   END
```

Figure 4-13   Comparison of WHILE and REPEAT Structures

```
Sum := 0;                             Sum := 0;
ReadInt(IntValue);                    ReadInt(IntValue);
WHILE Done DO                         IF Done THEN
   Sum := Sum + IntValue;                REPEAT
   ReadInt(IntValue)                        Sum := Sum + IntValue;
END;                                         ReadInt(IntValue)
                                          UNTIL NOT Done
                                      END;
```

Figure 4-14   Another Comparison of WHILE and REPEAT Structures

Since the *Repeat Statement* evaluates its condition after executing its statement sequence, the loop control variable can be initialized within that statement sequence rather than prior to the loop. As an example of this situation, consider the loop structure

```
Sum := 0;
REPEAT
   ReadInt (IntValue);
   IF Done THEN
      Sum := Sum + IntValue
   END
UNTIL NOT Done;
```

in which the procedure ReadInt is called just once. This loop structure is equivalent to both of those presented in Figure 4-14. Notice that an *If Statement* appears within the loop and is necessary to avoid an extra addition operation. Is it good programming practice to compose a looping structure this way? This question does not have a simple answer, since some programming situations may be more easily solved using such a structure. Generally speaking, having the loop control variable initialized prior to the looping statement is clearer to many readers.

4:4:3 The FOR Statement

The *For Statement* in Modula-2 is a looping statement used in most counting, or enumerating, situations. The syntax of the *For Statement* is somewhat more complex than that of the other looping statements, since this statement contains a *Counting Clause*, which embodies the three ingredients necessary for a successful looping structure:

1. Proper initialization of the loop control variables.

2. The correct composition of the looping condition in terms of the loop control variables.

3. Proper adjustment of the loop control variables to cause the looping to eventually terminate.

Figure 4-15 shows the syntax diagrams for the *For Statement*. The *For Statement* consists of the reserved word FOR, a *Counting Clause*; the reserved word DO followed by a *Statement Sequence*; and the reserved word END, which terminates the statement.

The *Counting Clause* consists of an *Identifier*, which represents the loop control variable; followed by the lexical symbol "`:=`"; followed by an *Expression*, which represents the initial value of the loop control variable.

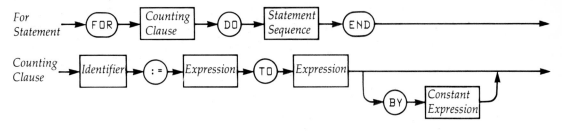

Figure 4-15 Syntax Diagram for the *For Statement*

Following this *Expression* is the reserved word TO and another *Expression*, representing the final value of the loop control variable. Each iteration of the loop results in an adjustment to the loop control variable, eventually assigning the final value to it. Execution of the loop terminates when the loop control variable is about to be assigned a value that exceeds the subrange specified by the final value. Execution continues with the statement following the *For Statement*. The *Counting Clause* also has an optional portion consisting of the reserved word BY followed by an *Expression* of type INTEGER or CARDINAL. This *Expression* defines the adjustment to be made to the loop control variable for each iteration of the loop. If this option does not appear, the adjustment is assumed to be 1. An adjustment of 1 means that the loop control variable is assigned the next value following its current value each time through the loop.

The *For Statement* is intended for counting situations, and its operation can be explained in terms of the *While Statement*. Consider the comparable looping structures in Figure 4-16. This figure illustrates a typical situation in which the *For Statement* is most appropriate, namely, counting situations. Since some programming situations require the loop control

```
Control := Initial;
WHILE Control <= Final DO
    WriteString ('Testing');
    WriteLn;
    INC (Control)
END
```

```
FOR Control := Initial TO Final DO
    WriteString ('Testing');
    WriteLn
END
```

```
Control := 5;
WHILE Control >= 1 DO
    WriteString ('Testing');
    WriteLn;
    DEC (Control)
END
```

```
FOR Control := 5 TO 1 BY -1 DO
    WriteString ('Testing');
    WriteLn
END
```

Figure 4-16 Equivalent WHILE and FOR Structures

variable to be decremented for each loop iteration, the optional adjustment clause may be specified, as shown in the second example presented in Figure 4-16.

Remember that the *For Statement* automatically assigns the initial value to the loop control variable and automatically adjusts the loop control variable after executing the statement sequence. It is important to emphasize that the loop control variable is modified only when the loop's terminating condition is not met. Thus the following program fragment causes the value 10 to be printed. This situation is also illustrated in Figure 4-17, where the first and last value in an enumeration are used in a *For Statement*.

```
VAR    I : CARDINAL;

BEGIN
FOR I := 1 TO 10 DO
    . . . (*  statements *)
END;
WriteCard ( I, 4 )
```

The *For Statement* may also iterate over a range or subrange of an enumeration, as presented in Figure 4-17. The *Counting Clause* is defined such that *Expressions* of any scalar type may appear as the initial and final values. The main point to remember is that these expressions must evaluate to a value compatible with the data type of the loop control variable. This requirement is consistent with the logic behind the *Assignment Statement*. Remember that the *For Statement* is a powerful looping structure that performs multiple assignments to the loop control variable.

The optional adjustment portion of the *Counting Clause* must, of course, contain an *Expression* of type INTEGER or CARDINAL. Figure 4-18 contains a program module similar to the one in Figure 4-17, but it illustrates a negative adjustment. The adjustment of -1 causes the loop control variable to be assigned the value preceding its current value each time through the loop.

4:4:4 The LOOP and EXIT Statements

The *Loop Statement* is unique among the four looping statements available in Modula-2 because it has no terminating condition. The syntax of the *Loop Statement* is simple. It consists of the reserved word LOOP followed by a *Statement Sequence* and terminated by the reserved word END. Figure 4-19 shows the syntax diagram for the *Loop Statement*.

The *Loop Statement* is used primarily to express cyclic processes that have no terminating condition or whose termination must be imbedded

```
 1 MODULE EnumeratedExample;
 2
 3 FROM InOut IMPORT WriteInt, WriteLn;
 4
 5 TYPE    Colonies = (NH, MA, RI, CT, NY, NJ, PA, DE, MD,
 6                                          VA, NC, SC, GA);
 7 VAR     Colony : Colonies;
 8         NECount, MACount, SCount : INTEGER;
 9
10 BEGIN
11
12 NECount := 0;  MACount := 0;  SCount := 0;
13 FOR Colony := NH TO GA DO
14    CASE Colony OF
15       NH : INC (NECount) |
16       MA : INC (NECount) |
17       RI : INC (NECount) |
18       CT : INC (NECount) |
19       NY : INC (MACount) |
20       NJ : INC (MACount) |
21       PA : INC (MACount) |
22       DE : INC (MACount) |
23       MD : INC (SCount)  |
24       VA : INC (SCount)  |
25       NC : INC (SCount)  |
26       SC : INC (SCount)  |
27       GA : INC (SCount)
28    END
29 END;
30
31 WriteInt (NECount, 10);   WriteInt (MACount, 10);
32 WriteInt (SCount, 10);   WriteLn
33 END EnumeratedExample.
```

Figure 4-17   Program Module with Enumeration FOR Statement

within the loop. Note that the *Loop Statement* is unnecessary because an infinite loop may be expressed in Modula-2 using any of the other looping statements, as in the *While Statement*

```
WHILE TRUE DO
 . . . (* statements *)
END
```

Even though the *Loop Statement* is unnecessary, it does serve two useful purposes. It is convenient for indicating a potentially infinite loop and for

```
 1 MODULE NegativeAdjustment;
 2
 3 FROM InOut IMPORT WriteInt, WriteLn;
 4
 5 TYPE    Colonies = (NH, MA, RI, CT, NY, NJ, PA, DE, MD,
 6                                                 VA, NC, SC, GA);
 7 VAR     Colony : Colonies;
 8         NECount, MACount, SCount : INTEGER;
 9
10 BEGIN
11
12 NECount := 0;   MACount := 0;   SCount := 0;
13 FOR Colony := GA TO RI BY -1 DO
14    CASE Colony OF
15       NH..RI, CT     : INC (NECount) |
16       NY, NJ..PA, DE : INC (MACount) |
17       MD..SC         : INC (SCount)  |
18       GA             : INC (SCount)
19    END
20 END;
21
22 WriteInt (NECount, 10);   WriteInt (MACount, 10);
23 WriteInt (SCount, 10);   WriteLn
24 END NegativeAdjustment.
```

Figure 4-18   Program Module Similar to Figure 4-17

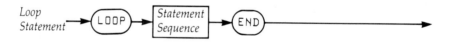

Figure 4-19   Syntax Diagram for *Loop Statement*

constructing loops whose exit does not appear at either the beginning or the end of the loop's statement sequence.

The *Loop Statement* in Modula-2 is made more powerful when used with an EXIT. The EXIT statement may only be used within the scope of a *Loop Statement*, since its execution causes the immediate termination of the enclosing *Loop Statement*. The EXIT statement is the normal means of terminating the repetition of a *Loop Statement*.

Of course, the EXIT Statement may appear in the *Statement Sequence* of any decision or looping statement within a *Loop Statement*, but remember that its execution causes the immediate termination of the enclosing *Loop Statement*. Execution continues with the statement following the END that corresponds to the *Loop Statement*.

```
FOR Control := Initial TO Final DO      Control := Initial;
    WriteString ('Testing')             LOOP
END;                                        IF Control > Final THEN
                                                EXIT
                                            END;
                                            WriteString ('Testing');
                                            Control := Control + 1
                                        END
```

Figure 4-20   Comparable FOR and LOOP-EXIT Constructs

Consider the *For Statement* and the comparable looping structure presented in Figure 4-20. This example shows the formation of a terminating *Loop Statement* in a counting situation.

Exercises

1. Modify the Program Module `TimesTable` so that it uses addition rather than multiplication to compute the entries in the multiplication table. Since computers perform addition operations much faster than multiplication operations, this change should substantially, although probably not noticeably, reduce the execution time of the program.

2. Show how every use of a *Repeat Statement* in Modula-2 may be rewritten using a While Structure. Show how every *Repeat Statement* and every *While Statement* may be rewritten using a *Loop Statement* in conjunction with an *Exit Statement*.

3. Write a complete program module that reads a Modula-2 source program as its input (using the `Read` procedure) and writes it out (using the `Write` procedure) with all comments removed. Do not worry about the possibility of nested comments in the first version of this program module. Once this first version is working, then modify it to handle all valid comments nested to any level.

5 Structured Data Types

5:1 Arrays

An **array** is a collection of related values of the same data type. Each value in an array is stored in a distinct data object and may only be identified and accessed as an element of the array. The values in an array are stored in physically sequential memory locations adjacent to each other. Each element in an array may be efficiently accessed using an index. Thus an array is a structured data type consisting of a collection of data objects that are all of the same type.

Arrays are fundamental to programming. They provide programmers with a method of storing large collections of data. Most computers have hardware features that efficiently implement arrays. Therefore most programming languages, Modula-2 included, provide programmers with an interface to these hardware features.

In Modula-2 the declaration of an array requires the specification of two pieces of information: the type of the values being stored in the array and the type of index being used to access the elements in the array. The values in an array may be of any type. Since array elements may themselves be arrays or other structured types, the declaration of complex array structures is possible. This topic is discussed in Section 5:4. An array index may be of any enumerable type, such as CARDINAL, INTEGER, BOOLEAN, CHAR, enumeration, or subrange. Typically, subrange or enumeration types are used as array indices. Arrays can occupy potentially large areas of memory, and limiting the number of elements in arrays is necessary. For example, an array declared with an index of type CARDINAL could potentially consist of tens of thousands of elements. Usually, that many elements are unnecessary, so a subrange type is used as the index, thus limiting the number of elements.

1	2	3	4	5	6	7
7.34	-654.2	0.0024	2.7182	4.4444	-84.23	0.0241

Figure 5-1   Visualization of the Array Alpha

Figure 5-1 is a visualization of an array whose elements are of type REAL and whose index is a subrange, 1..7, of type CARDINAL. Specifically, the elements in this array are indexed in the range 1 through 7, inclusive. This array, Alpha, may be declared using the Modula-2 syntax in a variety of ways. The most direct declaration is through a *Variable Declaration*, as in

        VAR   Alpha : ARRAY [1 .. 7] OF REAL;

Notice that in this declaration the type of the variable Alpha is not specified as a single *Identifier* but as an *Array Type*, with a more complex syntax (see Figure 5-2).

Several additional syntax diagrams must be referenced to fully appreciate this syntax diagram for *Array Type*. They have not been included in this figure, but may be found in Appendix B. Figure 5-2 does, however, indicate the necessary syntax and emphasize that the type of both the array element and array index is required to declare the structure of an array.

An alternative and generally preferred method of declaring an array is to first declare a type to represent the structure of the array and then use this type to declare the array. The most important reason for declaring an array in this way rather than as first illustrated has to do with using arrays as parameters to procedures, which is discussed in Chapter 6. The following declarations also result in the declaration of the array Alpha:

        TYPE   RealArray = ARRAY [1 .. 7] OF REAL;

        VAR   Alpha : RealArray;

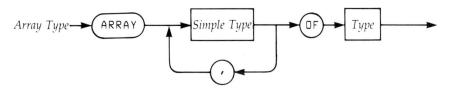

Figure 5-2   Syntax Diagram for *Array Type*

To carry this method one step further, it is often preferable to first declare the index as a type and then declare the structure of the array, as in

```
TYPE    IndexRange = [ 1 .. 7 ];
        RealArray  = ARRAY IndexRange OF REAL;

VAR     Alpha : RealArray;
```

which also results in the same declaration of the array Alpha.

Individual elements stored in an array are accessed by specifying both the name of the array and an index that identifies the specific element desired. Thus the value 2.7182 stored in the fourth position of the array Alpha may be accessed as Alpha [4], as in the statement

```
Beta := Alpha [ 4 ];
```

Likewise, values are stored in individual array elements using this same syntax. The statement

```
Alpha [ 6 ] := 3.14;
```

stores the value 3.14 in the sixth position of the array Alpha. In essence, any element in an array may be accessed, modified, or utilized in any way that a single variable of the same type may be. A review of the syntax diagrams appearing in this text will indicate that most of the executable statements make reference to the construct *Designator* rather than *Identifier*. Part of the reason for this reference is to allow for the syntax just illustrated to identify array elements. The syntax diagram for *Designator* may be found in Appendix B.

Figure 5-3 presents the program module SimpleArrayExample as an illustration of a use of arrays. This program reads a collection of real values, stores them in an array, prints each value along with its corresponding index, computes the average of the values, and determines and then prints the largest and smallest values found in the collection.

What follows is a detailed description of the program module SimpleArrayExample presented in Figure 5-3.

Lines 1 through 16

The array Number is declared on line 15. This declaration occurs as the culmination of several related declarations. On line 8 the constant MaxIndex is declared. MaxIndex specifies the upper limit of the index range for the array. The declaration of the subrange type IndexRange appears on line 10. This type is used on line 11 in the declaration of the

```
 1 MODULE SimpleArrayExample;
 2
 3 FROM InOut IMPORT  OpenInput, CloseInput, Read, ReadString,
 4                    ReadCard, WriteLn, WriteString, WriteCard;
 5
 6 FROM RealInOut IMPORT  Done, ReadReal, WriteReal;
 7
 8 CONST  MaxIndex = 100;
 9
10 TYPE    IndexRange = [ 1 .. MaxIndex ];
11         RealArray  = ARRAY IndexRange OF REAL;
12
13 VAR     Items, J, MinPosition, MaxPosition : IndexRange;
14         Sum, Average : REAL;
15         Number       : RealArray;
16
17 BEGIN
18
19 OpenInput ('DAT');
20 Items := 1;
21 ReadReal (Number [Items]);
22 WHILE (Items < MaxIndex) & Done DO
23    WriteCard (Items, 4); WriteReal (Number [Items], 15); WriteLn;
24    INC (Items);
25    ReadReal (Number [Items])
26 END;
27
28 IF Done THEN
29    WriteString ('Array too small, all data was not processed');
30    WriteLn
31   ELSE
32    DEC (Items)
33 END;
34
35 Sum := 0.0;
36 FOR J := 1 TO Items DO
37    Sum := Sum + Number [J]
38 END;
39 Average := Sum / FLOAT (Items);
40
41 WriteLn;
42 WriteString ('The Sum of the ');  WriteCard (Items, 4);
43 WriteString (' numbers is ');      WriteReal (Sum, 15);
44 WriteLn;
45 WriteString ('   The Average is ');  WriteReal (Average, 15);
46 WriteLn;
47
48 MinPosition := 1;
49 MaxPosition := 1;
```

```
50 FOR J := 2 TO Items DO
51    IF Number [J] > Number [MaxPosition] THEN
52          MaxPosition := J
53       ELSIF Number [J] < Number [MinPosition] THEN
54          MinPosition := J
55    END
56 END;
57
58 WriteString ('The smallest number is ');
59 WriteReal   (Number [MinPosition], 15);
60 WriteString (' and is in position ');
61 WriteCard   (MinPosition, 4);
62 WriteLn;
63 WriteString ('The Largest  number is ');
64 WriteReal   (Number [MaxPosition], 15);
65 WriteString (' and is in position ');
66 WriteCard   (MaxPosition, 4);
67 WriteLn
68
69 END SimpleArrayExample.
```

Figure 5-3   Program Module SimpleArrayExample

---

array type RealArray. Thus this program contains several related declarations that combine to create the array Number.

Lines 17 through 26

The variable Items, declared of type IndexRange, is an index that accesses the array elements in the loop structure of lines 22 through 26. Items is initialized to 0. Each time through the loop, Items is incremented so that as the individual real values are read, they are stored in successive array locations.

Lines 28 through 33

The loop structure terminates in one of two ways: (1) Either Done becomes false, indicating that all values have been read, or (2) the array has been filled. If the array was filled, the *If Statement* produces a message to warn that the array is not large enough to store all of the supplied data.

Lines 35 through 46

The variable Sum is initialized to 0; then the FOR statement sums the values stored in the array. The value of Sum and the computed Average are then printed.

Lines 48 through 56

This statement sequence determines the largest and smallest values stored in the array. Both MinPosition and MaxPosition are initialized to 1. As the loop executes, the *If Statement* within the loop finds the indices of the first occurrences of the largest and smallest values and stores them in the variables MaxPosition and MinPosition, respectively. After the loop terminates, Number [MinPosition] and Number [MaxPosition], the smallest and largest values, are printed.

Figure 5-3 serves as a basic demonstration of array capabilities. A closer look at the syntax diagram for *Array Type* reveals the flexibility that programmers have when declaring arrays. The elements in an array may be of any type, not just unstructured types. Arrays may also be declared with more than one index, thus defining multidimensional arrays. Examples of more complex arrays are presented in Section 5:4. This section concentrates on the study of arrays whose elements are unstructured data types using a single index.

To illustrate array use within the context of a problem, consider the problem of printing the base b representation of a cardinal number. For example, if 174 is the representation of a number in base 10, then that number may also be expressed as

10101110 in base 2

AE in base 16

where A = 10 and E = 14, or

336 in base 7

An algorithm to convert a decimal number to its representation in a base b is straightforward. The number is repeatedly divided by b, with the quotient becoming the new dividend. The remainders correspond to the digits that form the base b representation of the number. This process continues until the dividend is equal to 0.

Figure 5-4 illustrates this repeated division process. The remainder of each division is a digit in the resulting representation. In the case of bases greater than 10, the letters of the alphabet represent the numerals for the values 10 through 35.

In the division process, the remainders are ordinal values. Each ordinal value corresponds to a numeral represented by a character '0' through '9', then 'A' through 'Z'. In terms of a Modula-2 implementation of this algorithm, assume the following declarations:

```
TYPE    DigitRange       = [ 0 .. 35 ];
        NumeralArray     = ARRAY DigitRange OF CHAR;
```

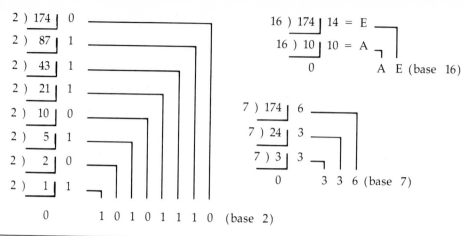

Figure 5-4   Example Conversions from Base 10

```
TYPE    RepRange            = [ 1 .. 16 ];
        RepresentationType  = ARRAY RepRange of CHAR;

VAR     Number, Quotient,
        Remainder, I, Length  : CARDINAL;
        Numeral               : NumeralArray;
        Representation        : RepresentationType;
```

The array Numeral is initialized with the statement sequence

```
FOR I := 0 TO 9 DO
    Numeral [I] := CHR (ORD ('0') + I)
END;
FOR I := 10 TO 35 DO
    Numeral [I] := CHR (ORD ('A') + I - 10)
END;
```

which stores the character values representing the numerals '0' through '9' and 'A' through 'Z' in the array Numeral so that each character is indexed by the numeral's ordinal value. Figure 5-5 illustrates this initialization.

0	1	2		9	10	11		34	35
'0'	'1'	'2'	•••	'9'	'A'	'B'	•••	'Y'	'Z'

Figure 5-5   Array Numeral After Initialization

Assume that the number to be represented is stored in the variable Number, and the base for the representation is stored in Base. The statement sequence

```
Quotient := Number;
IF Quotient = 0 THEN
    Representation [1] := '0';
    Length := 1
  ELSE
    Length := 0;
    REPEAT
        Remainder := Quotient MOD Base;
        Quotient  := Quotient DIV Base;
        INC (Length);
        Representation [Length] := Numeral [Remainder]
    UNTIL Quotient = 0;
END;
```

stores the representation of the number as a string of characters in the array Representation. The IF statement first checks to see if the number equals 0. If it does, the character '0' is stored in the first position in the array Representation; otherwise, the repetitive division process is performed. Each time through the loop, new values for Remainder and Quotient are computed and Length is incremented. Remainder is used as an index for the array Numeral to access the correct numeral and place it in Representation [Length]. Length is used as an index for the array Representation.

The representation of the number in Base may then be printed with the FOR statement,

```
FOR I := Length TO 1 BY -1 DO
    Write (Representation [I])
END;
```

Notice that the characters are printed one at a time, starting with the one stored in the array position indicated by Length and then decrementing down to 1. This process is necessary because the algorithm presented above finds the numerals in the representation starting first with the numeral furthest to the right. Thus the numerals are stored in Representation in reverse order.

A complementary algorithm takes the representation of a number in some base b and forms it into its numeric value stored as a CARDINAL. This is a repetitive multiplicative process. For example, in base 7 the string of numerals 336 represents the value of the expression

$$3 * 7^2 + 3 * 7 + 6 = (((3 * 7) + 3) * 7 + 6)$$

In general, a sequence of numerals,

$$a_1 \; a_2 \; a_3 \; \ldots \; a_n \; (\text{base } b)$$

represents the number that is the value of the expression

$$(\, (\, \ldots \, (\, (\, (v_1 * b) + v_2) * b + v_3) \, \ldots \,) * b + v_n \,)$$

for the base b, where v_i is the value that corresponds to the numeral a_i. An array is used in the solution of this problem because it simplifies the process of translating numerals, or characters, into values of type CARDI-NAL. This *Array Type* is declared with elements of type CARDINAL, and its index is of type CHAR. Consider the following declarations:

```
TYPE    CharRange           = [ '0' .. 'Z' ];
        ValueArray          = ARRAY CharRange OF CARDINAL;

TYPE    RepRange            = [ 1 .. 16 ];
        RepresentationType = ARRAY RepRange of CHAR;

VAR     Number, I, Length : RepRange;
        Value             : ValueArray;
        Representation    : RepresentationType;
```

The array Value is initialized with the statement sequence

```
FOR CH := '0' TO '9' DO
   Value [CH] := ORD (CH) - ORD ('0')
END;
FOR CH := 'A' TO 'Z' DO
   Value [CH] := ORD (CH) - ORD ('A') + 10
END;
```

This initialization requires two separate loops because the range of ASCII characters, '0' through 'Z', contains several characters (for example, ":" and ";") that do not represent numerals. This situation may be seen by referencing the ASCII conversion chart given in Appendix C.

Assume that the array Representation contains a sequence of numerals representing a number in some base and that Length contains a count of the number of positions in Representation that contain numerals. Then the statement sequence

```
Number := 0;
FOR I := 1 TO Length DO
   Number := Number * Base + Value [Representation [I] ]
END;
```

I	Length	Number	Base	Representation [I]	Value [Representation [I]]
	3	0	7		
1				'3'	3
		3			
2				'3'	3
		24			
3				'6'	6
		174			

Figure 5-6   Trace Table for Converting 336 (Base 7) to Base 10

translates this representation into a value of type CARDINAL stored in the variable Number. In this statement sequence, I serves as an index into the array Representation. The character stored at Representation [I] is used as an index into the array Value to select the numeric value that it represents. Upon completion of the loop, the variable Number contains the result.

Assume that the number 336 (base 7) is stored as the first three elements in the array Representation as the characters '3', '3', and '6'. Also assume that the variables Length, Number, and Base contain the values 3, 0, and 7, respectively. Under these assumptions the trace table in Figure 5-6 illustrates the conversion of this representation to the numeric value stored in Number.

As an illustration of the use of an enumeration type for an array index, consider the declarations

```
TYPE    Colors = (black, red, green, blue, yellow, orange,
                                            violet, white);
        RGBRange        = [ red .. blue ];
        ColorArrayType = ARRAY Colors OF INTEGER;
        RGBArrayType    = ARRAY RGBRange OF INTEGER;

VAR     Intensity    : ColorArrayType;
        RGBValue     : RGBArrayType;
        Phosphor     : Colors;
```

where Colors is an enumeration and RGBRange is a subrange of that enumeration. ColorArrayType and RGBArrayType are array types declared using this enumeration and its subrange, respectively. Intensity and RGBValue are declared as arrays of these types. The locations in the arrays Intensity and RGBValue may be accessed using either a variable of the corresponding enumeration type or a literal as an array index, as in

```
FOR Phosphor := black TO white DO
    Intensity [Phosphor] := 0
END;
```

or

```
RGBValue [blue] := 7;
```

Arrays assist in the solution of many problems, and the exercises at the end of this section suggest several uses. However, any introduction to arrays would be incomplete without a sorting example. Assume that a collection of values are to be sorted into ascending order. The declarations

```
TYPE    RealArray = ARRAY [ 1 .. 1000 ] OF REAL;
VAR     Datum : RealArray;

VAR     I, J, ActualCount : CARDINAL;
        Extra             : REAL;
```

declare the array Datum, which stores the values to be sorted. To assist in the sorting process, the variables I, J, and ActualCount are declared of type CARDINAL and Extra is declared of type REAL. The statement sequence

```
FOR I := 1 TO ActualCount - 1 DO
    J := I;
    WHILE (J > 0) & (Datum [J] > Datum [J+1]) DO
        Extra         := Datum [J];
        Datum [J]     := Datum [J+1];
        Datum [J+1]   := Extra;
        DEC (J)
    END
END;
```

implements a bubble sort that reorganizes the numbers in Datum such that Datum [1] contains the smallest number, Datum [2] contains the second smallest number, and so forth.

Assume that ActualSize contains a count of the number of positions in the array that actually contain values. That is, Datum [1] through Datum [ActualCount] contain the data to be sorted. In this algorithm, numbers in adjacent positions, indexed by J and J+1, are compared, and the smaller of the two numbers is placed in the Jth position. These comparisons are performed in a systematic fashion until the collection of values is sorted. The key to understanding this algorithm is to understand the role of the condition on the WHILE statement. This inner loop moves the value currently stored in the I+1th position in the array to its correct position relative to the values preceding it. This loop is the bubbling process. The second condition of this loop,

```
(Datum [J] > Datum [J+1])
```

continues the loop as long as the value in the Jth array position is greater than the value in the J+1th position. The first condition,

J > 0

stops the loop if a value has been moved all the way to the first position.

Exercises

---

1. Write a complete base conversion program that accepts as input the following three items: a base, the representation of a number in that base, and a new base. The program should then convert the representation to its value as a cardinal and then convert that value to a representation in the new base. Thus this program will utilize the two base conversion algorithms presented in this section.

2. For the following collection of numbers, trace through the sorting algorithm presented in this section.
   19.75, 40.0, 91.2, 17.12, 24.0, 36.0, 98.7, 7.0, 82.1, 40.0

3. Write a program to read a set of numbers, perform a bubble sort, and print the numbers in order along with their indices.

4. Research different sorting algorithms and implement either a selection sort or a Shell sort.

5. Write a program that represents vectors as arrays and computes the dot and cross product of two vectors.

6. Polynomials may be stored in a computer by storing the coefficients in an array. For example, a polynomial

   $$a_n x^n + a_{n-1} x^{n-1} + \ldots + a_2 x^2 + a_1 x + a_0$$

   may be stored in an array type declared as

   ```
   TYPE    PolyType = ARRAY [ 1 .. n ] OF REAL
   ```

   Write statement sequences to perform the following manipulations on polynomials:

   a. Compute the value of the polynomial for a given real value x. (HINT: Look at the techniques used to convert the representation of a real in a given base to the value of the expression it represents.)
   b. Given a polynomial stored in an array, place, in another array, the derivative of the given polynomial.

Remember,

$$\frac{dax^n}{dx} = anx^{n-1} \text{ when n is not 0}$$

$$= 0 \text{ when } n = 0$$

c. Form the integral of a polynomial stored in an array. (WARNING: Don't forget the constant of integration.)

5:2 Records

5:2:1 Records Without Variants

Arrays are homogeneous structures. That is, all the elements in an array contain the same type of data. Many programming situations require that related data of different types be kept together. For example, a payroll record for an employee of a company might contain components such as the employee's name, address, hourly pay rate, marital status, and number of dependents. Some of these data are strings of characters, like the employee's name and address, whereas others may be real values, like the hourly rate. Still other data may be kept as cardinal values, such as the number of dependents.

Modula-2 supports a structured type that facilitates the manipulation of related data, not necessarily of the same type. Such a structure is a record. Records may be declared directly with a *Variable Declaration*, such as

```
VAR     AnEmployee,
        AnotherOne  : RECORD
                      Name,
                      AddressLine1,
                      AddressLine2    : ARRAY [ 1 .. 20 ] OF CHAR;
                      HourlyRate,
                      Hours,
                      GrossPay,
                      Taxes,
                      NetPay          : REAL;
                      NoOfDependents  : CARDINAL;
                    END;
```

which declares the variables AnEmployee and AnotherOne as records. The *Identifiers*, Name, AddressLine1, and so forth, specified in this declaration are called the **components**, or **fields**, of the record. Each compo-

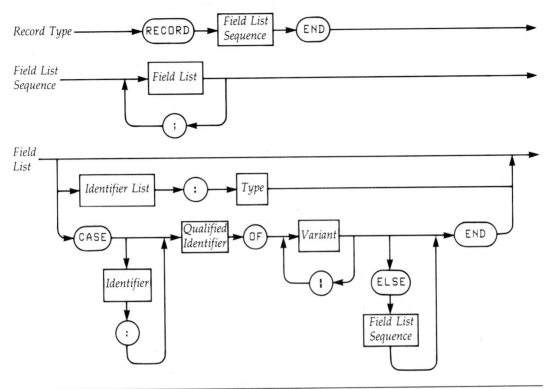

Figure 5-7   Syntax Diagram for *Record Type*

nent has a name and stores data of a specified type. These components may be of any type.

Figure 5-7 shows the syntax diagram for *Record Type*, which describes the structure of a record. Although the syntax of *Field List* appears quite complex, in most situations the complex syntax is not used. Usually, as in the example just presented, only the first alternative of *Field List* is used. The second alternative, using the reserved words CASE, OF, ELSE, and END, is used in the declaration of variant records. Variant records are discussed later in this section.

Although records may be declared directly with a *Variable Declaration*, as presented in the preceding declaration, the preferred approach declares the record structure in a *Type Declaration*, then declares variables of that type. For example, the record and variables declared in the first example could also be declared with the following declarations:

```
TYPE   EmployeeRecord = RECORD
                  Name,
                  AddressLine1,
                  AddressLine2    : ARRAY [ 1 .. 20 ] OF CHAR;
```

```
                              HourlyRate,
                              Hours,
                              GrossPay,
                              Taxes,
                              NetPay           : REAL;
                              NoOfDependents : INTEGER;
                          END;

      VAR     AnEmployee, AnotherOne  : EmployeeRecord;
```

The components in a record are accessed individually by specifying the name of the variable and the component and separating them by a period, as in

```
      AnEmployee.HourlyRate
```

which accesses the component of type REAL, identified as HourlyRate in the record variable AnEmployee. Such a reference may appear anywhere in a program where any reference to a real value may appear, such as

```
      WriteReal ( AnEmployee.HourlyRate, 10 )
```

or

```
AnEmployee.GrossPay := AnEmployee.Hours * AnEmployee.HourlyRate
```

or

```
IF AnEmployee.HourlyRate > AnotherOne.HourlyRate THEN
       . . . (* statements *)
```

Many times when records are manipulated in a program, one record at a time is accessed. In these cases every reference to a component must include the identification of the record, which tends to make the program wordy and less clear. Access to components of a record may be simplified in these situations by using the *With Statement*. The *With Statement* allows programmers to specify a record variable once and then just identify its components within the scope of the *With Statement*. Within this scope all components are assumed to be in the specified record. Use of this statement greatly improves program readability by eliminating the repetitive reference to the record variable. For example, a statement like

```
AnEmployee.GrossPay := AnEmployee.Hours * AnEmployee.HourlyRate
```

when written within the scope of a *With Statement* becomes

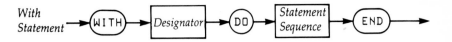

Figure 5-8   Syntax Diagram for *With Statement*

```
WITH AnEmployee DO
    . . . (*   other statements   *)
    GrossPay := Hours * HourlyRate;
    . . . (*   other statements   *)
END;
```

which improves the readability of the statement. Figure 5-8 shows the syntax diagram for the *With Statement*.

Usually, memory allocation for records is physically sequential; that is, components in a record are stored in the memory in sequence, one after the other. However, there might be some implementation dependent variations of this arrangement because of byte addressing on some computer systems. To illustrate, assume no byte addressing and the following memory requirements:

1. CHAR: 1 location

2. INTEGER: 2 locations

3. REAL: 4 locations

Given these assumptions, the memory allocation for the record type EmployeeRecord is visualized in Figure 5-9. It requires 82 locations of memory.

Records are useful because they allow related data objects to be grouped together in one place. This grouping not only stores these objects in adjacent memory locations but, more importantly, allows the entire collection to be manipulated as a unit. Records support two important aspects of computing: dynamic storage allocation and file processing. These topics are discussed in more detail in Chapters 9 and 10.

As an illustration of the use of records, consider the problem of performing complex arithmetic. The declarations

```
TYPE    ComplexRecord = RECORD
                        Re,        (* Real Part *)
                        Im          (* Imaginary Part *)
                            : REAL;
                        END;

VAR     U, V, W, Z : ComplexRecord;
```

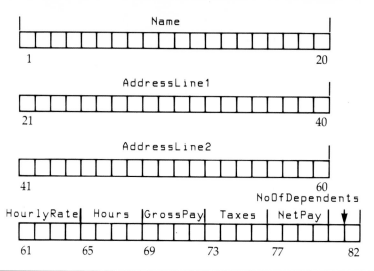

Figure 5-9   Visualization of EmployeeRecord

declare a record type, which may be thought of as a representation of complex numbers, and several variables of this type. A complex number is a number z, such that

$$z = z_{Re} + iz_{Im}$$

where z_{Re} and z_{Im} are real numbers and i is the square root of -1. This variable declaration declares four variables, U, V, W, and Z, as variables of type ComplexRecord. With these declarations each complex arithmetic operation is performed as a sequence of two real arithmetic operations, one to compute the real part of the complex number and one to compute the imaginary part. For example, multiplication of the complex numbers stored in the records W and Z is accomplished by the two assignment statements

```
U.Re := W.Re * Z.Re - W.Im * Z.Im;
U.Im := W.Re * Z.Im + W.Im * Z.Re;
```

which store the resulting product in appropriate components within the record U. The first statement computes the real part of the complex product, and the second statement computes the imaginary part. Similarly, the statements

```
V.Re := W.Re + Z.Re;
V.Im := W.Im + Z.Im;
```

compute the complex sum of W and Z and place the result in V. If we assume that the variable Mag is declared as a real, then the *With Statement*

```
WITH Z DO
    Mag := sqrt ( Re*Re + Im*Im )
END;
```

computes the magnitude of the complex number. sqrt is the square root function, which is imported from the standard module MathLib0. MathLib0 is described in Section 7:5.

5:2:2 Variant Record Structures

Although most programming situations, like those just presented, involving records manipulate fixed record structure, certain situations require the declaration of a record type with alternative internal structures. This capability is referred to as **variant records**. Variant records are declared using a caselike syntax to describe the alternative structures within the record type. Figure 5-7 contains the syntax diagram for *Field List*, which indicates the syntax of a variant record declaration. Figure 5-10 shows the syntax diagram for *Variant* necessary to complete this description.

To illustrate this concept, consider the type EmployeeRecord declared in Figure 5-9. Many companies have employees whose pay is computed according to different formulas, but EmployeeRecord supports

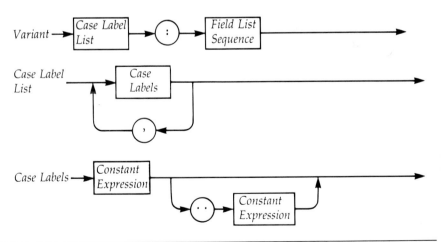

Figure 5-10   Syntax Diagram for *Variant*

```
TYPE   PayType = (Salaried, Hourly, PieceRate);
       VariantEmployeeRecord = RECORD
                     Name,
                     AddressLine1,
                     AddressLine2     : ARRAY [ 1 .. 20 ] OF CHAR;
                     CASE PayMethod : PayType OF
                          Salaried   : Salary : REAL;
                       !     Hourly   : HourlyRate, Hours  : REAL
                       ! PieceRate    : Pieces : INTEGER;
                                        PerPiece : REAL;
                     END;
                     GrossPay,
                     Taxes,
                     NetPay           : REAL;
                     NoOfDependents   : INTEGER;
                     END;

VAR    Employee, OtherOne   : VariantEmployeeRecord;
```

Figure 5-11   Example Variant Record with Tag Component

only hourly employees. Suppose a company has three methods of paying its employees: salaried, hourly, and piece rate. In this situation the record structure for an employee varies depending upon the employee's pay method. An hourly employee's record must have components for the hourly rate and the number of hours. A salaried employee needs components only for the salary, and a piece rate employee needs components for the piece rate and the number of pieces.

Figure 5-11 presents the declaration of a variant record structure that handles all three payment methods. The enumeration PayType identifies the three pay methods. The case syntax in a variant record declaration specifies the alternative structures in the record. For each case the corresponding components appear in the record. Thus for the type VariantEmployeeRecord declared in Figure 5-11, the component PayMethod of type Paytype distinguishes between the possible variants. Such a component in a variant record is often referred to as the **tag field** or **tag component**. One and only one of the possible variants within a variant record exists at any point in time.

The programmer is responsible for properly initializing and using the appropriate components within a record. Typically, the tag component is initialized, and then a CASE statement or IF statement processes the record depending upon the value stored in the tag component. To illustrate this process, assume that Employee.PayMethod has been initialized with one of the payment values, Salaried, Hourly, or PieceRate.

The variant structure within the Employee record may then be initialized from input with the statement sequence

```
WITH Employee DO
    CASE PayMethod OF
        Salaried : ReadReal ( Salary )                                        :
        Hourly   : ReadReal ( HourlyRate ); ReadReal ( Hours ) :
        PieceRate: ReadReal ( PerPiece );   ReadInt ( Pieces )
    END
END;
```

where the appropriate values are read into one of the record variants.

There is no limit on the number of variants declared in a record. What's important to remember is that variables of a variant record type occupy an area of memory whose size is determined by the components declared in the record. For records with variants the area allocated must be large enough to store the case or cases requiring the most space. Memory allocation for variant records declared with variable declarations are handled in this way. Variant records allocated dynamically are discussed in detail in Section 9:7. For the variant record variables described in this section, space for the record is allocated so that any one of the variants may be stored in the available space. Figure 5-12 illustrates a possible representation for VariantEmployeeRecord using the same set of assumptions about space requirements presented earlier. Assume that the type PayType requires one location of memory.

Since the variant that needs the most space determines the amount of space allocated for the record, we can easily determine that the variant occurring when PayMethod contains Hourly requires eight locations, and this value is the largest. Thus when PayMethod contains either the value Salaried or PieceRate, some locations are not used. Figure 5-12 shows the space allocation for the variant record VariantEmployeeRecord.

Tag components are unnecessary in variant records. However, there must be some method of determining which variant is present in a particular record. Figure 5-13 shows a declaration of a variant record without a tag component. In this example the type PayType is the identifier in the case structure, but no component of this type actually exists in the record.

The choice whether to use a tag component in variant records is discussed in more detail in Chapter 9, on dynamic storage allocation, because of the role tag components play in efficient memory allocation of dynamically allocated records.

The revised definition of Modula-2 specifies two changes to the syntax that affect the declaration of variant records. Appendices A and B both identify these changes. The first change is in *Field List* and requires that the type must be preceded by a semicolon when tag components are

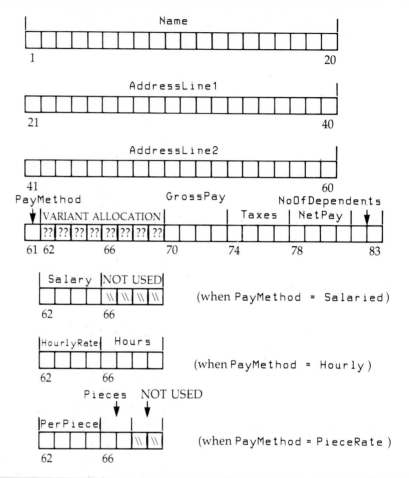

Figure 5-12   Visualization of VariantEmployeeRecord

not used. Thus the case structure presented in Figure 5-13 must be rewritten as

```
CASE : PayType OF
      Salared   : Salary : REAL
   !    Hourly : HourlyRate, Hours : REAL
   ! PieceRate : Pieces    : INTEGER;
                 PerPiece : REAL
END;
```

The second change is in *Variant*. It allows *Variant*s to be empty, thus permitting extra vertical bars. With this change the case structure presented

```
TYPE    PayType = (Salaried, Hourly, PieceRate);
        NoTagEmployeeRecord = RECORD
                        Name,
                        AddressLine1,
                        AddressLine2    : ARRAY [ 1 .. 20 ] OF CHAR;
                        CASE PayType OF
                           Salaried   : Salary : REAL
                        !    Hourly : HourlyRate, Hours : REAL
                        ! PieceRate : Pieces    : INTEGER;
                                       PerPiece : REAL
                        END;
                        GrossPay,
                        Taxes,
                        NetPay           : REAL;
                        NoOfDependents : INTEGER
                        END;

VAR     Employee, OtherOne  : VariantEmployeeRecord;
```

Figure 5-13   Example of a Variant Record Without a Tag Component

in Figure 5-13 may be rewritten as

```
CASE : PayType OF
   !   Salared   : Salary : REAL
   !     Hourly : HourlyRate, Hours : REAL
   ! PieceRate : Pieces    : INTEGER;
                  PerPiece : REAL
   END;
```

Exercises

1. Write the declarations of a record type that may be used to store mailing list data consisting of components for name, house number, street, and so forth.

2. Write the declarations of a record type containing components for the statistical measures mean, median, mode, minimum, and maximum. Write a program that reads in a collection of real values and computes these measures using this record type.

3. Write the declarations for an "inventory record" containing components for part number, cost, quantity, order point, and so forth.

5:3 Sets

The type BITSET is introduced in Section 3:2:5. Recall that BITSET is defined as a set of cardinal values in the range 0 through N − 1. Thus a bitset contains a maximum of N elements, one corresponding to each bit in a memory location. Each element is represented by a cardinal value in the subrange 0..N − 1. N represents some cardinal value, the actual value of which is machine dependent and, in many implementations, is 16 or 32. This section presents the generalization of the bitset concept, which allows for the declarations of sets whose elements may be of types other than CARDINAL. However, a set may contain only a limited number of elements, as specified by N. This restriction is important to remember when programming with sets in Modula-2.

As an illustration of set declarations, consider the following type declarations and variable declarations:

```
TYPE   Colors  = (red, green, blue, yellow, orange, violet,
                                          white, black);
       ColorSet = SET OF Colors;

VAR    Rainbow, RGBMonitor, RasterScan      : ColorSet;
       Phosphor, Brush                      : Colors;
```

The enumeration Colors is used in the declaration of the set type ColorSet. Figure 5-14 shows the syntax diagram for *Set Type*.

Figure 5-15 shows the syntax diagram for *Set*, which indicates the construction of set literals. Modula-2 requires that all set literals, except those of type BITSET, be qualified using the type identifier for the set, as in the statement

```
       RGBMonitor := ColorSet {red, green, blue};
```

which initializes the variable RGBMonitor with the set elements red, green, and blue. In this statement the reference to the identifier ColorSet is required and identifies the type of set involved.

The set operations of union, intersection, difference, and symmetric difference may be performed on sets. Figure 5-16 summarizes the set op-

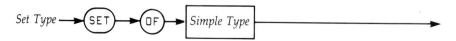

Figure 5-14   Syntax Diagram for *Set Type*

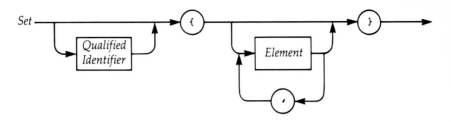

Figure 5-15   Syntax Diagram for *Set*

Operation	Example	Description
Union	A + B	Set of all elements in A **or** B
Intersection	A * B	Set of all elements in A **and** B
Difference	A − B	Set of all elements in A but **not** in B
Symmetric difference	A / B	Set of all elements in A **or** B **but not in both** A and B
Set inclusion	x IN A	TRUE if element x is in A
Set equality	A = B	TRUE if sets A and B are identical
Subset	A <= B	TRUE if A is a subset of B
Superset	A >= B	TRUE if the set A contains the set B
Set inequality	A <> B or A # B	TRUE if the sets are not identical

Figure 5-16   Set Operations

erations. The set qualifier is not specified in references to variables of set types, as in the statement

```
Rainbow := RGBMonitor + RasterScan,
```

which stores the union of the sets RGBMonitor and RasterScan in the variable Rainbow.

Given the meanings of the set operators presented in Figure 5-16, we construct expressions involving sets with the same syntax used for data objects of other types. As an example, consider the expression

```
(RGBMonitor - RasterScan) + (RasterScan - RGBMonitor)
```

Likewise, sets may be compared. Two sets may be compared for equality, as in

```
IF Rainbow = RasterScan THEN
    . . . (* statements *)
END
```

or for the subset relationship, using the lexical symbol "<="; or for the subset relationship, using the lexical symbol ">=", as in

```
IF Rainbow <= RasterScan THEN
   . . . (* statements *)
 ELSIF Rainbow >= RasterScan THEN
       . . . (* statements *)
END
```

The set inclusion operator, represented by the reserved word IN, tests for a relationship between a set and an element that could be in the set. This relationship is tested by expressions such as

```
Phosphor IN ColorSet {red, green blue}

blue IN Rainbow
```

and

```
Brush IN Rainbow
```

To demonstrate a use of sets in the context of a real programming situation, consider the problems of implementing error detection and error correction. Before data is transmitted, additional information is added in such a way that the receiver can manipulate the bit pattern and determine if an error occurred during the transmission of the pattern. In certain circumstances the error can be corrected. One method of forming error correction codes uses set relationships. This method is the Hamming error-correcting coding scheme.

A bit pattern is said to have **even parity** if the number of 1's in the pattern is even; otherwise, the pattern is said to have **odd parity**. The string of bits 10010011 has even parity, and the string 10110110 has odd parity.

Figure 5-17 illustrates the use of a Venn diagram in creating an error-correcting code. The circles subdivide the Venn diagram into eight areas, labeled A through H. A Hamming error-correcting code is constructed by adding four error-correcting bits to four data bits by associating the bits to areas of the Venn diagram as follows:

1. Associate the four data bits to the areas labeled E, F, G, and H.

2. Assign a 0 or 1 to areas B, C, and D so that the parity of the bits in each circle is odd.

3. Assign a 0 or 1 to area A so that the parity of bits in the entire Venn diagram is odd.

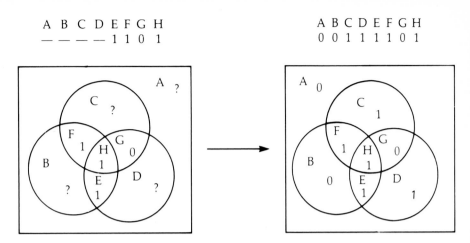

A B C D E F G H
— — — — 1 1 0 1

A B C D E F G H
0 0 1 1 1 1 0 1

Figure 5-17   Example of a Venn Diagram and the Creation of an Error-Correcting Code

The result of applying the preceding rules is an eight-bit error-correcting code. Assume that the four bits 1101 (see Figure 5-17) are to be transmitted. First, these four bits are corresponded to areas E through H. Next, values are assigned to areas B through D to produce odd parity in each circle. Area B is assigned 0, area C is assigned 1, and area D is assigned 1. These assignments produce the bit pattern

A B C D E F G H
— 0 1 1 1 1 0 1

Finally, A is assigned the value 0 to produce odd parity in the entire bit pattern, and the result is the bit pattern

A B C D E F G H
0 0 1 1 1 1 0 1

An error-correcting code algorithm can be implemented with sets and arrays in Modula-2. The declarations

```
TYPE AreaElements = (A, B, C, D, E, F, G, H);
     AreaGroups   = [A .. D];
     AreaSet      = SET OF AreaElements;
     AreaType     = ARRAY AreaGroups   OF AreaSet;
     ParityArray  = ARRAY AreaGroups   OF BOOLEAN;
     BitArray     = ARRAY AreaElements OF BOOLEAN;
```

```
VAR   Bit        :  BitArray;
      Parity     :  ParityArray;
      Area       :  AreaType;
      MapGroup   :  AreaGroups;
      Element    :  AreaElements;
      Item       :  AreaElements;
      Index      :  AreaGroups;
      TheSet     :  AreaSet;
```

declare the types and variables sufficient to support an error-correcting code. The relationships between areas in the Venn diagram are described by the variable Area of type AreaType. Area is initialized with the statement sequence

```
Area [A]  :=  AreaSet {A .. H};
Area [B]  :=  AreaSet {B, E, F, H};
Area [C]  :=  AreaSet {C, E, G, H};
Area [D]  :=  AreaSet {D, F, G, H};
```

This statement sequence defines four area groupings: the whole diagram (Area [A]) and the three circles (Area [B], Area [C], and Area [D]). These four area groupings are associated to four Modula-2 sets. The array Area is an array of four sets: The first set, indexed by A, represents the entire Venn diagram. Each of the remaining sets, indexed by B, C, and D, represents one of the circles.

The array Bit contains the bit pattern represented by BOOLEAN values, with FALSE corresponding to 0 and TRUE corresponding to 1. After four values are placed in Bit [E], Bit [F], Bit [G], and Bit [H], the other four bits are initialized to 0 (FALSE) with the FOR statement

```
FOR Index := A TO D DO
   Bit [Index] := FALSE;
END;
```

Then the parity of the three circles is determined with the statement sequence

```
FOR Index := B TO D DO
   Parity [Index] := FALSE;
END;
FOR Item := A TO H DO
   IF Bit [Item] THEN
        FOR Index := B TO D DO
           IF Item IN Area [Index] THEN
               Parity [Index] := NOT Parity [Index];
           END;
        END;
   END;
END
```

Each position in the Parity array is set to TRUE to indicate odd parity. The nested FOR statements determine if the number of 1's in each circle is odd by setting the corresponding position in the Parity array to TRUE. The Parity array is used to reset Bit [B], Bit [C], and Bit [D] to produce the correct parity in each circle. This parity is accomplished with the statement sequence

```
FOR Index := B TO D DO
    IF NOT Parity [Index] THEN
        Bit [Index] := NOT Bit [Index];
    END;
END;
```

Now Bit [A] may be set to produce odd parity in the entire bit pattern. This odd parity is accomplished with the statement sequence

```
Parity [A] := FALSE;
FOR Item := A TO H DO
    IF Bit [Item] THEN
        Parity [A] := NOT Parity [A];
    END;
END;
IF NOT Parity [A] THEN
    Bit [A] := NOT Bit [A];
END;
```

If a single bit is changed during the transmission of any eight bit pattern, the error can be corrected. If two bits are changed, the error can be detected but not corrected. To see this concept, assume the bit pattern

```
A B C D E F G H
0 0 1 1 1 1 0 1
```

is modified during transmission to the pattern

```
A B C D E F G H
0 0 1 1 1 0 0 1
```

The receiver associates this bit pattern to a Venn diagram and determines which circles no longer have odd parity. In this case the circles without odd parity are the circles B and C. The intersection of these two circles is the region in the diagram associated to F; hence the bit associated to area F must be corrected, and the pattern is returned to its correct form,

```
A B C D E F G H
0 0 1 1 1 1 0 1
```

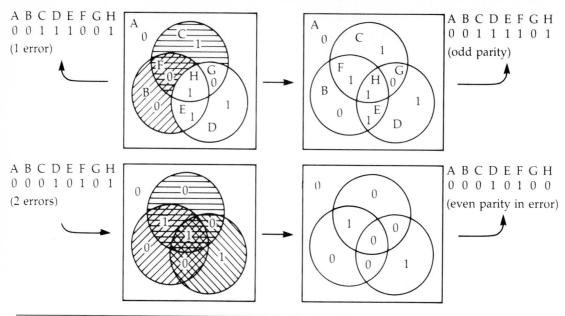

ABCDEFGH
0 0 1 1 1 0 0 1
(1 error)

ABCDEFGH
0 0 1 1 1 1 0 1
(odd parity)

ABCDEFGH
0 0 0 1 0 1 0 1
(2 errors)

ABCDEFGH
0 0 0 1 0 1 0 0
(even parity in error)

Figure 5-18   Error Correcting Using a Venn Diagram

Once the circles are error corrected, the parity of the entire bit pattern can be checked to determine if two bits might have been changed during transmission. For example, suppose that the original pattern

A B C D E F G H
0 0 1 1 1 1 0 1

has two bits changed during transmission and the pattern becomes

A B C D E F G H
0 0 0 1 0 1 0 1

When this bit pattern is associated to a Venn diagram (see Figure 5-18) and the parity of the circles is checked, the parity in each of the circles is even; hence the error is in the intersection of the circles, which is area H. The result of this error correcting produces the bit pattern

A B C D E F G H
0 0 0 1 0 1 0 0

Note that the parity of the corrected bit pattern is even. Since odd parity is desired, an even bit pattern indicates that two bits were changed during transmission. Although this error has been detected, the algorithm cannot correct it.

The error detection and correction can be performed by the receiver with an algorithm that uses some of the same statement sequences that were used to create the bit pattern. When a bit pattern is received in the array Bit, the statement sequence

```
FOR Index := B TO D DO
    Parity [Index] := FALSE;
END;
FOR Item := A TO H DO
    IF Bit [Item] THEN
        FOR Index := B TO D DO
            IF Item IN Area [Index] THEN
                Parity [Index] := NOT Parity [Index];
            END;
        END;
    END;
END
```

determines the parity of the circles. We assume that an error is some-where in that part of the bit pattern corresponding to the three circles. This assumption is expressed with the statement

```
TheSet := AreaSet {B .. G};
```

If the parity of a circle is odd (TRUE), the elements that correspond to that circle are removed from TheSet. If the parity is even (FALSE), TheSet is intersected with the Area of the corresponding circle with the statement sequence

```
FOR Index := B TO D DO
    IF Parity [Index] THEN
        TheSet := TheSet - Area [Index]
    ELSE
        TheSet := TheSet * Area [Index];
    END;
END;
```

If TheSet is empty, then no error was detected in the bits corresponding to the circles. If an error is detected, then the appropriate bit is corrected with the statement sequence

```
IF TheSet # AreaSet {} THEN
    FOR Index := B TO H DO
        IF Index IN TheSet THEN
            Bit [Index] := NOT Bit [Index];
        END;
    END;
END;
```

If two bits had been changed during the transmission of the bit pattern, then the statement sequence

```
Parity [A] := FALSE;
FOR Item := A TO H DO
    IF Bit [Item] THEN
            Parity [A] := NOT Parity [A];
    END;
END;
```

sets Parity [A] to TRUE if the pattern is correct.

Exercises

1. Write a complete program to test the error-correcting process described in this section.

2. That the error detection is performed using odd parity is not important. Error-correcting bit patterns can be created with even parity. Modify the program developed for Exercise 1 to use even parity.

3. The error-correcting process described in this section used three sets, represented by three circles, and eight elements. Other error-correcting codes can be developed using n subsets and 2^n elements. For example, with four sets, eleven data bits can be transmitted with only five error-correcting bits if we assume that at most two bits will be changed during transmission. Research Hamming error-correcting codes (see **Scientific American**, January 1985); then develop and test algorithms for a Hamming error-correcting code for patterns that are 16 bits long.

5:4 Multidimensional Arrays and Other Combinations of Structured Types

Modula-2, like Pascal and several other programming languages, supports strong data typing. Strong data typing means that rather than contriving the representation of information into the limited number of predefined data types, the programmer may declare data types that appropriately and logically represent the information that is manipulated. The variety of combinations of structured data types that programmers create by combining arrays, records, and sets is limited only by the programmer's imagination and the syntax structure of Modula-2. Fortunately, the syntax is not very limiting.

The most basic extension of arrays are multidimensional arrays. Multidimensional arrays are declared with multiple index ranges. For example, an **m by n matrix** structure, a two-dimensional array type, is declared with the *Type Declaration*

```
TYPE   MatrixType = ARRAY [ 1 .. m ] [ 1 .. n ] OF REAL;
```

assuming that m and n are declared constants. Matrices may then be declared, as in the declaration

```
VAR     A, B, C : MatrixType;
```

Elements in such an array are identified using two indices, one for each of the index ranges specified in the array declaration, as in

```
A [I, J]
```

Assuming that the constants m and n store the cardinal values 3 and 4, respectively, we can visualize each of the variables A, B, and C as a 3-by-4 arrangement of 12 real numbers, as shown in Figure 5-19. The value -1 stored in the fourth column of the second row is accessed as A [2, 4].

The result of the addition of two matrices B and C is a matrix A, satisfying

```
A [I,J] = B [I,J] + C [I,J]
```

for all I and J, where $1 <= I <= 3$ and $1 <= J <= 4$. If three matrices are identified by the variables A, B, and C declared above, then matrix addition is performed by the statement sequence

```
FOR I := 1 TO m DO
    FOR J := 1 TO n DO
        A [I, J] := B [I, J] + C [I, J]
    END
END;
```

	1	2	3	4
1	45	-3	55	40
2	84	29	-7	-1
3	15	41	88	99

Figure 5-19   A Visualization of MatrixType

As another example of complex array structures, consider the structure of a volume of an encyclopedia. Each page could be composed of columns of text. Each column is 40 lines long, and each line of text might contain 35 characters. In addition, suppose each volume contains 400 pages and there are 30 volumes in the encyclopedia. This structure could be declared with the following declarations:

```
TYPE   Line         = ARRAY [ 1 .. 35 ] OF CHAR;
       Column       = ARRAY [ 1 .. 40 ] OF Line;
       Page         = ARRAY [ 1 ..  2 ] OF Column;
       Volume       = ARRAY [ 1 .. 400 ] OF Page;
       Encyclopedia = ARRAY [ 1 .. 30 ] OF Volume;
```

If these types are used to declare a variable, as in the declaration

```
VAR  Britanica : Encyclopedia;
```

then the individual characters on each page are accessed or modified with a reference that may appear in one of two ways:

```
Britanica [3] [126] [1] [15] [3] := 'T';
```

or

```
Britanica [3, 126, 1, 15, 3] := 'T';
```

These statements are equivalent. In either case the letter 'T' is stored as the third letter on the fifteenth line of column 1 on page 126 of volume 3. An entire line may be printed with the statements

```
WriteString ( Britanica [3, 126, 1, 15] );  WriteLn;
```

As another example of multidimensional array declarations, consider

```
TYPE   Saying      = ARRAY [ 1 .. 128 ] OF CHAR;
       Verse       = ARRAY [ 1 .. 99 ] OF Saying;
       Chapter     = ARRAY [ 1 .. 199 ] OF Verse;
       Evangelists = (Matthew, Mark, Luke, John);
       GospelType  = ARRAY Evangelists OF Chapter;

VAR  Gospel : GospelType;
```

which declares the variable Gospel as an array whose most basic element is of type CHAR and requires five indices to reference. Furthermore, if we assume that the array is properly initialized, the first verse in the first chapter of Luke is printed with the statement sequence

```
WriteString ( Gospel [ Luke, 1, 1 ] );   WriteLn;
```

Although these two examples seem quite natural, several disadvantages of this approach should be mentioned. The first disadvantage is observed in both the Encyclopedia and the Gospel examples. In the Encyclopedia example not all books are the same length; in the Gospel example not all volumes contain the same number of pages. Hence array ranges that are the maximum for each particular application would have to be selected. As a result memory would be wasted. A second limitation is the actual size of many computer memories. Most computer systems would not have sufficient memory to store a structure of type Encyclopedia. If an attempt is made to declare a data structure too large for the computer system, an error message is generated by the language translator to convey this fact.

New structured data types can be declared by combining arrays, records, and sets in any syntactically valid combination. Section 5:2 discusses an example of a record that contains an array. Arrays of records may also be formed. For example, expanding on the EmployeeRecord type presented in Section 5:2 leads to the declarations presented in Figure 5-20, which declare an array of employee records.

```
CONST   NoOfEmployees = 1000;

TYPE    EmployeeRecord = RECORD
                        Name,
                        AddressLine1,
                        AddressLine2    : ARRAY [ 1 .. 20 ] OF CHAR;
                        HourlyRate,
                        Hours,
                        GrossPay,
                        Taxes,
                        NetPay          : REAL;
                        NoOfDependents  : INTEGER
                      END;

        EmployeeArray = ARRAY [ 1 .. NoOfEmployees ] OF EmployeeRecord;

VAR     Employee    : EmployeeArray;
        ExtraRecord : EmployeeRecord;
        ActualCount,
          I, J      : INTEGER;
```

Figure 5-20   Example Declarations for an Array of Records

The variable `Employee` is an array of `EmployeeRecords`. To access an employee's record, we must know the index to that record. For example, the name of the Jth employee is printed with the statement

```
WriteString ( Employee [J].Name );
```

As a further example, the following statement sequence sorts this array of employee records into ascending order based upon the component GrossPay.

```
FOR I := 1 TO ActualCount-1 DO
   J := I;
   WHILE ( J > 0 ) &
         ( Employee [J].GrossPay > Employee [J+1].GrossPay ) DO
      ExtraRecord     := Employee [J];
      Employee [J]    := Employee [J+1];
      Employee [J+1] := ExtraRecord;
      DEC (J)
   END
END;
```

Note that in the comparison made between the gross salaries in the expression

```
Employee [J].GrossPay > Employee [J+1].GrossPay
```

the indices J and J+1 identify the records to be compared and

```
.GrossPay
```

identifies the component in the record.

Exercises

1. Write and test a program containing algorithms to perform multiplication and addition of matrices stored in two-dimensional arrays.

2. Write and test a program that reads a set of numbers into a two-dimensional array and locates a minmax if it exists. A minmax is a matrix element that is simultaneously the mimimum number in its row and the maximum number in its column.

3. Write and test a program to solve sets of simultaneous linear equations by storing the coefficients in a two-dimensional array and performing the Gaussian Elimination Algorithm.

6 Procedures

6:1 Overview

Modularization is an important system design capability, and good programming languages are expected to support it. Excellent support of modularization is one of the main features of Modula-2. In Modula-2 this support is provided through both procedures, which are described in this chapter, and modules, which are described in Chapters 7 and 8. Procedures provide direct support of good programming practices such as top-down design and the logical partitioning of a system. In addition to this support for modularization, procedures also support the control of the flow of information through a program. This additional support is another strength of Modula-2.

From a modularization point of view, procedures may directly represent the logical design of a system. For example, if a program must read, sort, and print a set of numbers, the program module to perform these tasks might appear as

```
BEGIN
Initialize;
ReadTheData;
SortTheData;
PrintTheData
END
```

where Initialize, ReadTheData, SortTheData, and PrintTheData are the names of four procedures that perform the tasks indicated by their names. This representation directly assists programmers throughout the life cycle of a system, because the names of the procedures meaningfully

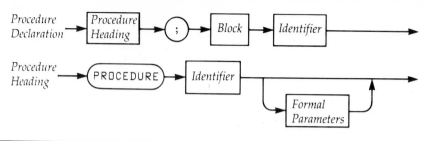

Figure 6-1   Syntax Diagram for *Procedure Declaration*

identify the procedures and provide an overview of how the system is logically partitioned. To gain a deeper understanding of how each particular procedure carries out its task, programmers may consult the implementation, or body, of the procedure.

Figure 6-1 shows the syntax diagram for *Procedure Declaration*. The example,

```
PROCEDURE NameOfTheProcedure;

BEGIN
   . . . (*  statements  *)
END NameOfTheProcedure;
```

follows the syntax indicated by *Procedure Declaration*. A *Procedure Heading* consists of the reserved word PROCEDURE followed by an *Identifier*, which serves as the name of the procedure. This *Identifier* appears twice in each *Procedure Declaration*: once after the reserved word PROCEDURE and again after the corresponding reserved word END.

Figure 6-2 illustrates the use of procedures in a program that reads, sorts, and prints collections of real numbers. Lines 72 through 77 comprise the executable part of the program module. Each of these lines contains a call, or reference, to a procedure. Each procedure carries out the task implied by its name.

Program execution always begins with a program module's statement sequence. In Figure 6-2, execution begins with line 72. As the sequence of statements executes, calls to procedures transfer control from the point where the procedure is called to the procedure's statement sequence. When a procedure terminates, control is transferred back to the statement following the procedure call. In Figure 6-2 the procedure Initialize is performed first. This procedure is followed by the execution of procedure ReadTheData, then SortTheData, and, finally, PrintTheData. Coincidentally, the order of appearance of the procedure declarations happens to be the same order in which they execute. Some relationships exist between the location of a procedure in a program module and how a procedure is called. This relationship is discussed next.

```
 1 MODULE SimpleProcedureExample;
 2
 3 FROM InOut IMPORT  OpenInput, CloseInput,
 4                    WriteLn, WriteString, WriteCard;
 5
 6 FROM RealInOut IMPORT  Done, ReadReal, WriteReal;
 7
 8 CONST  ArraySize  = 1000;
 9        NumberPerLine = 4;
10
11 TYPE   ArrayRange  = [ 1 .. ArraySize ];
12        RealArray   = ARRAY ArrayRange OF REAL;
13
14 VAR    ActualCount,
15        I, J, Dist   : INTEGER;
16        Number       : RealArray;
17        ExtraReal    : REAL;
18
19 PROCEDURE Initialize;
20    BEGIN
21    CloseInput;
22    OpenInput ('DAT')
23    END Initialize;
24
25 PROCEDURE ReadTheData;
26    BEGIN
27    ActualCount := 1;
28    ReadReal (Number [ActualCount]);
29    WHILE (ActualCount < ArraySize) & Done DO
30       INC (ActualCount);
31       ReadReal (Number [ActualCount])
32    END;
33    IF Done THEN
34       WriteString ('Array too small, all data not processed');
35       WriteLn
36     ELSE
37       DEC (ActualCount)
38    END;
39    END ReadTheData;
40
41 PROCEDURE SortTheData;
42    BEGIN
43    Dist := ActualCount DIV 2;
44    REPEAT
45       FOR I := 1 TO ActualCount-Dist DO
46          J := I;
47          WHILE (J > 0) & (Number [J] > Number [J+Dist]) DO
48             ExtraReal := Number [J];
49             Number [J] := Number [J+Dist];
50             Number [J+Dist] := ExtraReal;
```

```
51                J := J - Dist
52            END
53         END;
54         Dist := Dist DIV 2
55      UNTIL Dist = 0
56      END SortTheData;
57
58
59  PROCEDURE PrintTheData;
60      BEGIN
61      WriteString ('Data Printed in ascending order');
62      WriteLn;
63      FOR I := 1 TO ActualCount DO
64          WriteCard (I, 4);   WriteReal (Number [I], 15);
65          IF (I MOD NumberPerLine) = 0 THEN
66              WriteLn
67          END
68      END;
69      WriteLn
70      END PrintTheData;
71
72  BEGIN
73  Initialize;
74  ReadTheData;
75  SortTheData;
76  PrintTheData
77  END SimpleProcedureExample.
```

Figure 6-2   Program Module SimpleProcedureExample

Procedures may be nested; that is, the declaration of one procedure may occur within another procedure. Figure 6-3 presents an alternative declaration for the procedure SortTheData. The procedure Interchange is contained within the new version of SortTheData. In this version the procedure Interchange is called each time through the inner loop. Interchange performs the operation of exchanging the values in the Jth and J+1st positions in the array Number. Because it is nested within SortTheData, Interchange cannot be called by the other procedures or by the program module itself.

The rules for calls of one procedure by another are straightforward:

1. Two procedures B and C directly nested within procedure A may access each other and procedure A. Also, both procedures B and C may be accessed by A. The term **directly nested** means that there is not a procedure D such that A contains D and D contains B or C.

```
 1 PROCEDURE SortTheData;
 2
 3    PROCEDURE Interchange;
 4
 5       BEGIN
 6       ExtraReal        := Number [J];
 7       Number [J]       := Number [J+Dist];
 8       Number [J+Dist] := ExtraReal
 9       END Interchange;
10
11    BEGIN  (* of Sort The Data *)
12    Dist := ActualCount DIV 2;
13    REPEAT
14       FOR I := 1 TO ActualCount-Dist DO
15          J := I;
16          WHILE (J > 0) & (Number [J] > Number [J+Dist]) DO
17             Interchange;
18             J := J - Dist
19          END
20       END;
21       Dist := Dist DIV 2
22    UNTIL Dist = 0
23 END SortTheData;
```

Figure 6-3   Example of Nested Procedures

2. If procedure A contains procedure B, no procedure outside of A may call B.

3. If procedure A contains procedure B, procedure B may call any procedure that A may call.

The program module is considered a phantom procedure in the statement of the rules.

Figure 6-4 presents a collection of procedures and attempts to call one procedure by another. The errors in the program, marked with error number 73, are instances where one procedure could not call another procedure.

As an illustration of rule 1, Alpha and Gamma are two procedures nested within the program module AlphaBetaTheta, which, for the sake of the rules, is considered a procedure. Alpha and Gamma may be called by the program module and by each other (see lines 14, 19, and 61).

Figure 6-4 contains many examples of the first part of rule 2, for example, the calls in Alpha of Beta, on line 19, and in Beta of Alpha, on line 14. All of the error messages in Figure 6-4 resulted from the attempts

```
 1     MODULE AlphaBetaZeta;
 2
 3     PROCEDURE Alpha;
 4
 5        PROCEDURE Beta;
 6
 7           PROCEDURE Delta;
 8              BEGIN (* Delta *)
 9              Alpha;   Beta;   Delta;
10              Gamma;   Mu;      Epsilon
*****                    ^ 73          ^ 73
11              END Delta;
12
13           BEGIN (* Beta *)
14           Alpha;   Beta;   Delta;
15           Gamma;   Mu;      Epsilon
*****                    ^ 73          ^ 73
16           END Beta;
17
18        BEGIN (* Alpha *)
19        Alpha;   Beta;   Delta;
*****                         ^ 73
20        Gamma;   Mu;      Epsilon
*****                 ^ 73          ^ 73
21        END Alpha;
22
23     PROCEDURE Gamma;
24
25        PROCEDURE Mu;
26
27           PROCEDURE Epsilon;
28              BEGIN (* Epsilon *)
29              Alpha;   Beta;   Delta;
*****                             ^ 73     ^ 73
30              Gamma;   Mu;      Epsilon;
31              Theta;   Zeta
*****                             ^ 73
32              END Epsilon;
33
34           BEGIN (* Mu *)
35           Alpha;   Beta;   Delta;
*****                          ^ 73     ^ 73
36           Gamma;   Mu;      Epsilon;
37           Theta;   Zeta
*****                          ^ 73
38           END Mu;
39
40        PROCEDURE Theta;
41
```

```
  42          PROCEDURE Zeta;
  43             BEGIN (* Zeta *)
  44             Alpha;  Beta;  Delta;
 *****                        ^ 73    ^ 73
  45             Gamma;  Mu;     Epsilon;
 *****                                  ^ 73
  46             Theta;  Zeta
  47             END Zeta;
  48
  49          BEGIN (* Theta *)
  50          Alpha;  Beta;  Delta;
 *****                     ^ 73     ^ 73
  51          Gamma;  Mu;     Epsilon;
 *****                              ^ 73
  52          Theta;  Zeta
  53          END Theta;
  54
  55       BEGIN (* Gamma *)
  56       Alpha;  Beta;  Delta;
 *****                  ^ 73    ^ 73
  57       Gamma;  Mu;     Epsilon
 *****                          ^ 73
  58       END Gamma;
  59
  60    BEGIN
  61    Alpha; Beta; Delta;
 *****               ^ 73   ^ 73
  62    Gamma; Mu; Epsilon
 *****             ^ 73        ^ 73
  63    END AlphaBetaZeta.
```

Figure 6-4   Example of Procedure Declarations and Calls

---

to violate the second part of rule 2. For example, on line 19 Delta cannot be called by Alpha because Delta is declared within Beta, which, in a sense, hides Delta from Alpha. Similarly, on line 62 Mu and Epsilon cannot be called by the program module because they are contained within other procedures, Gamma and Mu, respectively.

Access following rule 3 is illustrated in several cases in Figure 6-4. For example, since Beta is in Alpha and Alpha may access Gamma, Beta may access Gamma on line 15. Also, since Epsilon is nested inside Mu, it may access any procedure that Mu may access. By recursive application of rule 3, Epsilon may also access all of the procedures that Gamma may access, since Epsilon is nested in Mu and Mu is nested in Gamma.

To clarify the access rules, consider the block diagram in Figure 6-5, which illustrates the nesting structure of the procedures in the program

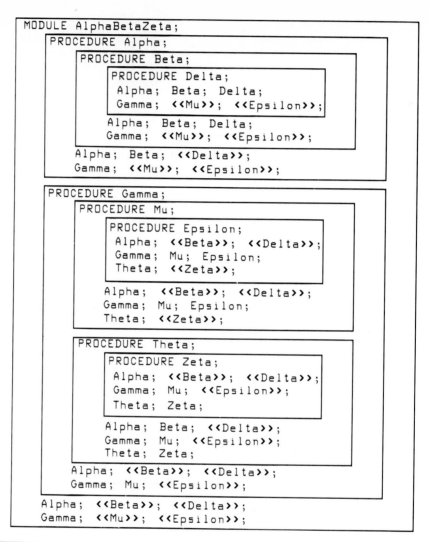

Figure 6-5   Block Diagram of Figure 6-4

skeleton presented in Figure 6-4. Informally, in the block diagram the
rules for procedure access are visually presented. A procedure hides the
procedures within it. For example, Beta may access Delta, but it hides
access to Delta from all the other procedures. Procedures can see out of
the procedure that contains them; hence Delta may access Alpha, Beta,
and Gamma. However, Delta cannot access Mu and Epsilon because they
are hidden within other procedures.

6:2 Variables and Parameters

Procedures are the fundamental tools for modularization. An important part of modularization is the control of the flow of data between modules. The procedures in the sorting example discussed in Section 6:1 do not control the flow of data between procedures. This situation is undesirable in large programming systems. What is desirable are methods of restricting access to data. Two methods control access to information: the scope of identifiers and the use of parameters with procedures.

The program module presented in Figure 6-6 is a modification of the program module in Figure 6-2, which reads, sorts, and prints collections of real numbers. This program module contains examples of both methods of controlling access to information. First we must explore the scope of identifiers and the concept of locality. The scope, or locality, of an identifier is where it may be accessed. To illustrate, in Figure 6-6 the procedures SortTheData and PrintTheData both contain variables named I. The variable I in SortTheData exists only in SortTheData while that procedure is executing. It is not the same variable as the variable I in PrintTheData, although it has the same name. The variable I in SortTheData may only be accessed within the procedure SortTheData and any procedure, such as Interchange, declared within it. This concept of locality, or scope, also applies to any identifier, constant, type, variable, or procedure declared within a given procedure. Also, if any other procedure outside of SortTheData or the program module contained a reference to any identifier declared in SortTheData, such as ExtraReal, that reference would be flagged with an error message by the language translator because the identifier is not visible at that point in the program.

The rules for the scope of identifiers are normally stated as follows (from **Programming in Modula-2** by Nicklaus Wirth):

1. The scope of an identifier is the procedure in which it is declared and all other procedures enclosed within that procedure, except for the restriction stated in rule 2.

2. If procedure Q is declared within procedure P and both procedures contain identifiers with the same name, I, then Q and all procedures declared within Q are excluded from the scope of the identifier I in P.

3. The standard identifiers in Modula-2 (INTEGER, REAL, and so forth) are considered as declared in an imaginary procedure enclosing the program module.

The program module itself should be thought of as a procedure when determining the scope of its identifiers.

```
 1  MODULE ProceduresWithParameters;
 2
 3  FROM InOut IMPORT  OpenInput, CloseInput,
 4                     WriteLn, WriteString, WriteCard;
 5
 6  FROM RealInOut IMPORT  Done, ReadReal, WriteReal;
 7
 8  CONST   ArraySize  = 1000;
 9          NumberPerLine = 4;
10
11  TYPE    ArrayRange  = [ 1 .. ArraySize ];
12          RealArray   = ARRAY ArrayRange OF REAL;
13
14  VAR     Number      : RealArray;
15          ActualCount : INTEGER;
16
17  PROCEDURE Initialize;
18      BEGIN
19      CloseInput;
20      OpenInput ('DAT')
21      END Initialize;
22
23  PROCEDURE ReadTheData (VAR   RealValue      : RealArray;
24                         VAR   NumberOfItems : INTEGER);
25      BEGIN
26      NumberOfItems := 1;
27      ReadReal (RealValue [NumberOfItems]);
28      WHILE (NumberOfItems < ArraySize) & (Done) DO
29         INC (NumberOfItems);
30         ReadReal (RealValue [NumberOfItems])
31      END;
32      IF Done THEN
33         WriteString('Array too small, all data not processed');
34         WriteLn
35        ELSE
36         DEC (NumberOfItems)
37      END
38      END ReadTheData;
39
40  PROCEDURE SortTheData (  VAR   Value   : RealArray;
41                           MaxNumber : INTEGER);
42
43      VAR   I, J, Dist : INTEGER;
44
45      PROCEDURE Interchange;
46
```

```
47        VAR     ExtraReal  : REAL;
48
49        BEGIN
50        ExtraReal := Value [J];
51        Value [J] := Value [J+1];
52        Value [J+1] := ExtraReal
53        END Interchange;
54
55    BEGIN  (* of Sort The Data *)
56    Dist := MaxNumber DIV 2;
57    REPEAT
58      FOR I := 1 TO MaxNumber-Dist DO
59        J := I;
60        WHILE (J > 0) & (Value [J] > Value [J+Dist]) DO
61            Interchange;
62            J := J - Dist
63        END
64      END;
65      Dist := Dist DIV 2
66    UNTIL Dist = 0
67    END SortTheData;
68
69 PROCEDURE PrintTheData (       Number : RealArray;
70                         ActualCount, NumberPerLine : INTEGER);
71
72    VAR    I: INTEGER;
73
74    BEGIN
75    WriteString ('Data Printed in ascending order');  WriteLn;
76    FOR I := 1 TO ActualCount DO
77      WriteCard (I, 4);  WriteReal (Number [I], 15);
78      IF (I MOD NumberPerLine) = 0 THEN
79          WriteLn
80      END
81    END;
82    WriteLn
83    END PrintTheData;
84
85 BEGIN
86 Initialize;
87 ReadTheData   (Number, ActualCount);
88 SortTheData   (Number, ActualCount);
89 PrintTheData (Number, ActualCount, NumberPerLine)
90 END ProceduresWithParameters.
```

Figure 6-6   Example of Procedures with Parameters

Rule 2, although straightforward and logical, may appear confusing to some programmers. When using good approaches to programming, rule 2 should seldom come into play because programmers should use meaningful and unique identifiers. In selecting names, programmers should select different names for different variables.

A by-product of the scope of identifiers is that variables declared within a procedure exist only during the execution of that procedure. This fact implies that a value cannot be left in a variable with the assumption that the value will be in the variable the next time the procedure is called. When a procedure is called, its variables are allocated; when a procedure terminates, its variables are deallocated. Variables that are local to a procedure but whose allocation remains even after the procedure terminates (thereby allowing information to be maintained from one call of a procedure to the next) are termed **own variables**. Own variables are discussed in Section 8:3.

Conceptually, parameters are a way of passing information to a procedure when it begins execution; hence, they control the flow of information. In Figure 6-2 all the procedures access what are referred to as global variables. An identifier is **global to a procedure** if the scope of the identifier properly contains the procedure. Good programming practices discourage the direct access and modification of global variables by procedures.

The preferred method for procedures to access information is through parameters. Again, consider the procedure SortTheData. In its declaration,

```
PROCEDURE SortTheData (  VAR  Value    : RealArray;
                              MaxNumber : INTEGER   );
```

Value and MaxNumber are referred to as **formal parameters**. In any call to SortTheData, for example, in

```
    SortTheData (Number, ActualCount);
```

Number and ActualCount are called the **actual parameters**. When a procedure is called, the current value of each actual parameter is used in place of its corresponding formal parameter. The actual parameters associate to the formal parameters by position: first actual parameter to first formal parameter, second actual parameter to second formal parameter, and so forth. Figure 6-7 contains the relevant syntax diagrams for creating procedure declarations.

The two parameters, Value and MaxNumber, in SortTheData illustrate the two methods of specifying the transfer of data through parameters. The distinction between the two methods is indicated with the reserved word VAR, which may precede a formal parameter. When

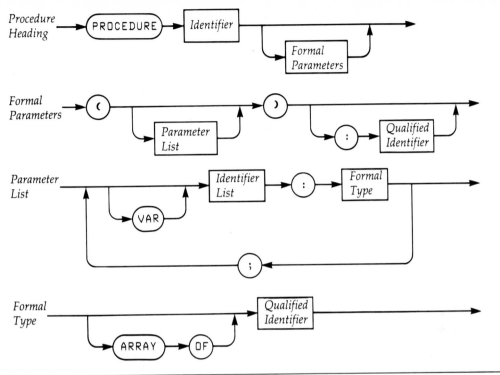

Figure 6-7   Syntax Diagrams for *Procedure Heading*

the reserved word VAR is used, the actual parameter is said to be associated to the formal parameter **by address**. When a formal parameter is not VARed, the parameter is said to be associated **by value**.

A VARed formal parameter is capable of a two-way flow of information between a procedure and its call. That is, when a formal parameter is VARed, the actual location of the variable, its address, is passed to the procedure; hence the procedure may change the value of the actual parameter.

On the other hand, when a formal parameter is not VARed, only the value of the actual parameter is passed to the formal parameter and copied into another area of memory. The value may be used, but if modified, the copy of the value is modified; hence the actual parameter does not change. For example, consider the following procedure declaration:

```
PROCEDURE Sample ( Able : INTEGER );

    BEGIN
    . . . (* statements  *)
    Able := 26;
    . . . (* statements  *)
    END Sample;
```

If this procedure is called within the statement sequence

```
Sam := 2;
Sample (Sam);
WriteInt (Sam, 5);
```

the value 2 would be printed. The value 2 is printed because the value in Sam, not the address of Sam, was passed to the procedure Sample. The formal parameter, Able, is initialized with that value of Sam; and although the value in Able is changed to 26, that change does not affect Sam because Able was not VARed.

Since formal parameters are declared within procedures, the rules for scope of identifiers also apply to formal parameters. Proper use of the scope of identifiers helps to control the flow of information in a program. For example, the preferred programming practice for a procedure is to modify only those variables declared within itself. In this way the only values that may be passed back from a procedure to its call are VARed parameters.

By following this approach to programming, programmers avoid what are termed **procedure side effects**. Essentially, this term means modifying a global variable from within a procedure. A variable is said to be global to a procedure if the procedure is properly contained in the scope of the variable. Note that the variable is declared outside of the procedure. Side effects are the access to global variables, especially the modification of global variables. These accesses tend to create problems in large programming systems because they are usually programming shortcuts and, frequently, are not properly documented.

An important feature of formal parameters in Modula-2 procedures is the **open array parameter**. This feature allows a formal parameter to be specified as an array without declaring its index range. In this way, calls to the procedure may associate similar arrays to this formal parameter. The procedure call must specify an actual parameter that is an array whose elements are the same type as the corresponding formal parameter. To illustrate, suppose a program contains several arrays that must be sorted:

```
TYPE   SmallArray = ARRAY [ -5 .. 50 ] OF REAL;
       BigArray   = ARRAY [ 1 .. 2000 ] OF REAL;

VAR    Able  : SmallArray;
       Baker : BigArray;
```

One solution would be to write separate procedures to sort each array type, but this is both inefficient and potentially confusing. Modula-2, through the use of open array parameters, provides a way to build one procedure that sorts numbers stored in any array composed of the same

```
 1   PROCEDURE SortTheData2 ( VAR Value   : ARRAY OF REAL;
 2                                MaxNumber : INTEGER);
 3
 4      VAR    I, J, Dist : INTEGER;
 5
 6      PROCEDURE Interchange;
 7
 8         VAR    ExtraReal : REAL;
 9
10         BEGIN  (* of Interchange *)
11         ExtraReal       := Value [J];
12         Value [J]       := Value [J+Dist];
13         Value [J+Dist] := ExtraReal
14         END Interchange;
15
16      BEGIN  (* Sort Procedure *)
17      DEC (MaxNumber); (* open array indices begin at 0, not 1 *)
18      IF MaxNumber > INTEGER (HIGH (Value) ) THEN
19          MaxNumber := INTEGER (HIGH (Value) )
20      END;
21      Dist := MaxNumber DIV 2;
22      REPEAT
23         FOR I := 0 TO MaxNumber - Dist DO
24            J := I;
25            WHILE (J >= 0) & (Value [J] > Value [J+Dist]) DO
26               Interchange;
27               J := J - Dist
28            END
29         END;
30         Dist := Dist DIV 2
31      UNTIL Dist = 0
32      END SortTheData2;
```

Figure 6-8   Procedure with an Open Array Parameter

type of elements. Figure 6-8 illustrates a procedure that sorts real numbers stored in any array whose elements are of type REAL.

The use of open array parameters requires some additional effort in the development of the procedure. Consider the procedure Sort-TheData2 presented in Figure 6-8. This procedure has a parameter with an open array declaration. When open array parameters are used, the size of the array is determined by calling the standard procedure HIGH. HIGH is a function procedure of one parameter that returns a count of the number of items in the array minus 1. For example, with the declarations

```
TYPE    SmallArray = ARRAY [ -5 .. 50 ] OR REAL;
        BigArray   = ARRAY [ 1 .. 2000 ] OF REAL;
```

```
VAR     Able: SmallArray;
        Baker: BigArray;
```

and the procedure call

```
SortTheData2 (Able, N);
```

HIGH (Number) from lines 18 and 19 of the procedure returns the value 55 ($50 - (-5)$). When the procedure is called as

```
SortTheData2 (Baker, N);
```

then HIGH (Number) is 1999.

Regardless of the index range of the array, a formal parameter, p, with an open array declaration is considered to be an array over the index range

```
0 .. HIGH (p)
```

The only limitation of open array parameters is that the actual parameter and corresponding formal parameter must both be declared as arrays whose elements are the same type. There is no limit on the index ranges of the arrays passed as formal parameters nor is there any limitation on the type of elements in the array.

Exercises

1. Write a procedure that reads data into a record structure declared to store "inventory data" consisting of components for part number, cost, quantity, order point, and so forth.

2. Rewrite your procedure for Exercise 1 so that it accepts a parameter that indicates whether or not a prompt should be displayed prior to reading each component value. This procedure may then be used both to read data from a file and to read data interactively.

3. Write a program module that reads in a collection of real values, stores them in an array, and then calls procedures to determine the minimum and maximum values in the collection. Add procedures to compute other statistical measures as well.

4. Write a collection of procedures, each of which performs a separate matrix operation such as addition and multiplication.

6:3 Functions

Modula-2 has several predefined functions, such as HIGH described in Section 6:2. A collection of mathematical functions is available in the standard module MathLib0. Many other functions exist in other modules. There are many advantages to functions; in particular, functions may appear in expressions, most notably in conditions and in assignment statements.

A function procedure in Modula-2 is best understood by comparing it with the mathematical concept of a function. Intuitively, a function is an operation that takes a set of data and produces a single answer. A simple example of a function is given by the equation

$$z(x,y) = x^2 + y^2$$

where x and y are the independent variables and z is the dependent variable. For a given set of x and y values, there is only one corresponding z value. For example, if x = 5 and y = 7, then z = 72. Every time x = 5 and y = 7, z will be 72.

There are many programming situations in which a procedure takes a set of actual parameter values and produces a single result. For example, the procedure

```
PROCEDURE SumSquares (  VAR Z : REAL;   X, Y : REAL );

    BEGIN
    Z := X * X + Y * Y
    END  SumSquares;
```

performs the functional calculation just described. However, the procedure cannot be called as a mathematical function in arithmetic expressions. For example, if the function's value is to appear in a statement, such as

```
IF   z[u,v]   > 100.0 THEN ...
```

or

```
ZETA := (2.5 + z[4.1, W] ) / z[13, 5];
```

it would require either that the function not formally appear in the expressions at all, which could be misleading, or that it appear as several program statements, such as

```
SumSquares (Z, X, Y);
IF  Z  > 100.0 THEN ...
```

or

```
SumSquares (Z1, 4.1, W);
SumSquares (Z2, 13, 5);
ZETA := (2.5 + Z1) / Z2;
```

A function procedure may be declared as

```
PROCEDURE Z ( X, Y : REAL ) : REAL;

    BEGIN
    RETURN (X * X) + (Y * Y)
    END Z;
```

This function may appear as part of any real expression, for example,

```
IF Z (U, V) > 100.0 THEN . . .
```

or

```
ZETA := (2.5 + Z (4.1, W) ) / Z (13, 5);
```

and directly demonstrates the role of the function in these expressions.

Functions of any unstructured data type may be declared. That is, functions return CHAR, INTEGER, REAL, BOOLEAN, enumeration, subrange, or pointer values, but cannot return arrays or records as values. The reserved word RETURN serves two purposes:

1. Associates the value of the following expression to the name of the function.

2. Terminates the function and returns control to the origin of the procedure call.

The reserved word RETURN may appear more than once in the function because it might be required by an algorithm. When a RETURN statement executes, it associates the value of the expression following the reserved word RETURN to the name of the function, terminates the function, and returns control to the statement containing the function call.

To illustrate, consider the function Colinear presented in Figure 6-9. Given three points in a plane, (x_1, y_1), (x_2, y_2), and (x_3, y_3), if the coor-

```
1    PROCEDURE Colinear (x1, y1, x2, y2, x3, y3 : REAL) : BOOLEAN;
2
3       BEGIN
4       RETURN ((x3 - x1) * (y2 - y1)) = ((x2 - x1) * (y3 - y1))
5       END Colinear;
```

Figure 6-9   Example of a Boolean Procedure

dinates of these three points are passed as the indicated six formal parameters, the function `Colinear` is TRUE when the points share the same straight line; otherwise, `Colinear` is FALSE.

Since function procedures are a special type of procedure, any operation performed by a procedure may also be performed by a function. As another illustration, consider the function `Middle` presented in Figure 6-10. If the three formal parameters were placed in ascending order of their values, the function `Middle` would pick the value that appears between the other two. This function contains a procedure, which in turn contains another procedure. Note the use of VARed and non-VARed parameters between `Middle` and `Order`. Since `Middle`'s parameters are not VARed, the actual parameters are passed to `Middle` by value. But `Middle` passes these values on to `Order`, whose parameters are VARed. Hence within `Middle`, the values in p, q, and r, which are `Middle`'s formal parameters, are placed in order by the procedure `Order`.

Whenever possible, function procedures should closely follow the mathematical concept of a function. Specifically, none of the parameters should be VARed nor should there be any side effects. Simply stated, a function should compute only one value, namely, the value associated to the function's name.

As one final example, consider the generation of the sequence of numbers

1, 1, 2, 3, 5, 8, 13, ...,

which is called the Fibonacci sequence. The first two numbers in this sequence are 1, and each subsequent value is the sum of the two preceding values. Figure 6-11 is an example of a function procedure that computes Fibonacci numbers. For example, the statement

```
WriteInt (Fibonacci (7), 5);
```

prints the value 13, the seventh Fibonacci number. The procedure has been written to first verify the parameter value passed to it. If Nth is less than 1, the function returns with a value of 0. If Nth is less than 3 (actually just 1 or 2, since the test for Nth < 1 appears in line 6), a 1 is re-

```
1     PROCEDURE Middle (p, q, r: REAL) : REAL;
2
3        PROCEDURE Order (  VAR x, y, z : REAL);
4
5           PROCEDURE Switch ( VAR a, b : REAL);
6
7              VAR    ExtraReal : REAL;
8
9              BEGIN
10             ExtraReal := a;
11             a := b;
12             b := ExtraReal
13             END Switch;
14
15          BEGIN  (* Order *)
16          IF y < x THEN Switch (x, y) END;
17          IF z < y THEN
18               Switch (z, y);
19               IF y < x THEN
20                    Switch (x, y)
21               END
22          END
23          END Order;
24
25       BEGIN  (* Middle *)
26       Order (p, q, r);
27       RETURN q
28       END Middle;
```

Figure 6-10   Example of a Real Procedure

turned. On line 11 the third value in the sequence is formed in Sum. If Nth is 3, the loop in lines 12 through 16 is bypassed and the value in Sum is returned. Otherwise, the loop iterates until the desired Fibonacci number is computed. When the loop terminates, the computed value is in Sum and is the value returned when the function terminates.

A useful recommendation for the naming of procedures and function procedures appears in **Programming in Modula-2** by Nicklaus Wirth. Simply stated, functions, as well as variables and other identifiers, should be named so that the name facilitates the reading of the program's statements. The naming recommendations are:

1. BOOLEAN procedures normally appear in expressions that are testing conditions (qualifications). Qualifications are normally indicated by adjectives or adverbs. It is recommended that adjectives be used to name BOOLEAN function procedures. Also, boolean variables should be named with verbs.

```
1    PROCEDURE Fibonacci (Nth : CARDINAL) : CARDINAL;
2
3      VAR    First, Second, Sum, Count : CARDINAL;
4
5      BEGIN
6      IF Nth < 1 THEN
7          RETURN 0
8        ELSIF Nth < 3 THEN
9          RETURN 1
10       ELSE
11         First := 1;  Second := 1;  Sum := 2;
12         FOR Count := 4 TO Nth DO
13            First   := Second;
14            Second  := Sum;
15            Sum     := First + Second
16         END;
17         RETURN Sum
18       END
19     END Fibonacci;
```

Figure 6-11   Example of a Cardinal Procedure

2. All other functions produce unstructured data objects. Objects are normally represented by nouns; hence, it is recommended that all non-BOOLEAN functions be named using nouns. Similarly, all non-BOOLEAN variables should be named with nouns.

3. All non-function procedures are actions. Actions are described with verbs. Verbs should be used to describe all regular procedures.

6:4 Recursion

Recursion is the notion of self-reference. It appears frequently in mathematics in various definitions. A classical example is the definition of the factorial function. For a positive integer n, the factorial of n, written n!, is the product of the integers between and including 1 and n. For example,

$$6! = 6 * 5 * 4 * 3 * 2 * 1 = 720$$

Mathematically, the factorial function is defined recursively as

$$n! = 1, \text{ if } n = 0 \text{ or } 1$$
$$= n * (n - 1)!, \text{ for } n > 1$$

That is, $6! = 6 * (6 - 1)! = 6 * 5!$. Then the factorial function is recursively applied to 5!, $5! = 5 * 4!$, and so forth until the value of 6! expands to

$$6! = 6 * 4 * 4 * 3 * 2 * 1!$$
$$= 720$$

and since $1! = 1$, the expression is completed.

An important aspect of recursive definitions is that a procedure must have a way for the recursion to terminate. This aspect is an integral component of the preceding factorial definition and all recursive definitions implemented on a computer.

Not only may procedures be called from a program module and from other procedures but they may also be called from within themselves. A procedure calling itself is an example of **recursion**. Although the details of how recursion is carried out are not that important at this point, many programmers find recursion confusing because they do not understand how it is implemented. It is sufficient, from a programmer's point of view, to consider recursion to be implemented as follows: When a procedure calls itself, assume that this recursion is implemented in a computer by creating another copy of the procedure, including the procedure's variables and parameters. That is, each recursive call does not use the same allocation for the procedure's local variables and parameters that were used before the call.

Figure 6-12 contains a recursive implementation of the procedure Factorial. It is a direct representation of the recursive definition of factorial. To see how it performs the calculation, assume that the Factorial function was called from the following arithmetic assignment statement:

```
X := Factorial ( 4 );
```

A key to understanding recursion is to understand how the execution of the statement

```
RETURN FLOAT (I) * Factorial (I-1);
```

is performed.

Recursion is implemented through the allocation of memory locations for local variables and formal parameters with each recursion. For example, with the call to the procedure

```
X := Factorial ( 4 );
```

the decision structure leads to line 7. In line 7 the value associated to Factorial (4) is

```
4.0 * Factorial ( 4-1 )
```

```
1    PROCEDURE Factorial (I: CARDINAL) : REAL;
2
3       BEGIN
4       IF I <= 1 THEN
5           RETURN 1.0
6         ELSE
7           RETURN FLOAT (I) * Factorial (I-1)
8       END
9       END Factorial;
```

Figure 6-12   Example of a Recursive Real Procedure

This value causes a recursive call to Factorial with the result of passing the expression in the actual parameter, $4 - 1 = 3$, to the formal parameter, I. There is a new allocation of I for this execution of the procedure Factorial. This recursive call, in turn, forces another recursion, which returns the value

```
3.0 * Factorial ( 3-1 )
```

Another recursion occurs with the value 2 passed to I. This recursion produces still another recursion when it returns the value

```
2.0 * Factorial ( 2-1 )
```

Finally, with I associated to 1, the value of 1 is returned in line 5. This association terminates the last call to Factorial and returns a value of 1 for Factorial (2-1) to the previous call. Now the value is computed for

```
2.0 * Factorial ( 2-1) = 2.0 * 1.0 = 2.0
```

which, in turn, is passed as the value to the previous recursive call,

```
3.0 * Factorial ( 3-1 ) = 3.0 * 2.0 = 6.0
```

This value is passed back to the previous recursive call, which computes the value

```
4.0 * Factorial ( 4-1 ) = 4.0 * 6.0 = 24.0
```

which is finally returned to the first call as the result.

As another example of recursion, consider the generation of the Fibonacci sequence,

1, 1, 2, 3, 5, 8, 13, ...,

presented in Section 6:3. A nonrecursive function for generating this sequence appears in Figure 6-11. Figure 6-13 is a recursive procedure that

```
1    PROCEDURE RecursiveFibonacci (Nth : CARDINAL) : CARDINAL;
2
3       BEGIN
4       IF Nth < 1 THEN
5          RETURN 0
6        ELSIF Nth < 3 THEN
7          RETURN 1
8        ELSE
9          RETURN RecursiveFibonacci(Nth-1) +
10                 RecursiveFibonacci(Nth-2)
11      END
12      END RecursiveFibonacci;
```

Figure 6-13   Example of a Recursive Cardinal Procedure

generates Fibonacci numbers. The procedure is a direct implementation of the recursive definition of Fibonacci numbers given by

$$F(i) = 1, \text{ if } i = 1 \text{ or } 2$$
$$= F(i - 1) + F(i - 2), \text{ otherwise}$$

In this example the RETURN statement contains two recursive calls. It is an interesting exercise to work through the memory allocation and determine the number of recursive calls required to compute this function. This implementation should also be compared with the nonrecursive Fibonacci function presented in Figure 6-11. This example is a good illustration of a procedure that should **not** be implemented recursively. Specifically, the nonrecursive version is more efficient than the recursive one. This comparison is suggested as an exercise.

As an example of a problem solution that uses a recursive procedure, consider the ancient problem known as the Tower-of-Hanoi problem. The problem may be described as follows:

The Tower-of-Hanoi Problem: Three pegs, identified as A, B and C, are each capable of storing disks. Each disk is unique in that it has a diameter different from all of the other disks. The two constraints are:

1. Only one disk at a time may be moved.

2. At no time may a larger disk be placed on top of a smaller disk.

The initial configuration has all of the disks stored on peg A. As required, the largest disk is the bottommost disk. The objective is to move all of the disks from peg A to peg B. Figure 6-14 illustrates this initial configuration.

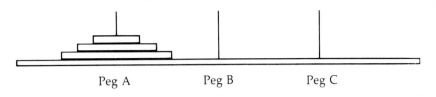

Figure 6-14   Illustration of the Tower-of-Hanoi Problem

```
 1 MODULE TestTowerOfHanoi;
 2
 3 FROM InOut IMPORT Done, ReadCard, WriteCard, WriteString,
 4                                         Write, WriteLn;
 5
 6 VAR    N : CARDINAL;
 7
 8 PROCEDURE TowerOfHanoi (NumberOfDisks : CARDINAL;
 9                                        From, To, Temp : CHAR);
10
11     BEGIN
12     IF NumberOfDisks > 0 THEN
13         IF NumberOfDisks > 1 THEN
14             TowerOfHanoi ((NumberOfDisks - 1), From, Temp, To   );
15             TowerOfHanoi (1,                   From, To,  Temp );
16             TowerOfHanoi ((NumberOfDisks - 1), Temp, To,  From )
17           ELSE
18             WriteString (' Move a disk from peg ');  Write (From);
19             WriteString (' to peg ');  Write (To);  WriteLn
20         END
21       ELSE
22         WriteString (' ... Null problem');  WriteLn
23     END
24     END TowerOfHanoi;
25
26 BEGIN
27 REPEAT
28     WriteLn;
29     WriteString ('Enter number of disks:');
30     ReadCard (N); WriteLn;
31     IF Done THEN TowerOfHanoi (N, 'A', 'B', 'C') END
32 UNTIL NOT Done
33
34 END TestTowerOfHanoi.
```

Figure 6-15   Program Module Containing the Procedure TowerOfHanoi

```
Enter number of disks:0
... Null problem

Enter number of disks:1
Move a disk from peg A to peg B

Enter number of disks:2
Move a disk from peg A to peg C
Move a disk from peg A to peg B
Move a disk from peg C to peg B

Enter number of disks:3
Move a disk from peg A to peg B
Move a disk from peg A to peg C
Move a disk from peg B to peg C
Move a disk from peg A to peg B
Move a disk from peg C to peg A
Move a disk from peg C to peg B
Move a disk from peg A to peg B
```

Figure 6-16   Example of a Dialog with the Program Module TestTowerOfHanoi

Figure 6-15 presents a program module that contains the recursive procedure TowerOfHanoi that solves this problem. Figure 6-16 shows a dialog obtained from the execution of this program.

The key to the solution of this problem is to observe how the third peg, C, is used for the temporary storage of disks. Specifically, since the bottom disk on peg A is the first disk that must be permanently moved to peg B, the only solution is:

1. Temporarily move the topmost $N - 1$ disks from peg A to peg C.

2. Permanently move the bottom disk from peg A to peg B.

3. Move the $N - 1$ disks currently stored on peg C to peg B.

These three steps correspond to the procedure calls appearing on lines 14 through 16 in Figure 6-15.

Step 2 is elementary because it always involves the movement of just one disk. Furthermore, the disk moved in step 2 is the largest disk, which means that any disk may later be placed on top of it. This fact allows for the later use of that peg for temporary storage.

Steps 1 and 3 usually involve the movement of more than one disk. Fortunately, the problem presented by these steps is exactly the same as the original Tower-of-Hanoi problem, but with one fewer disk. That is, move a collection of $N - 1$ disks from one peg to another. The solution to this problem then is exactly the same as the solution to the original problem. The procedure TowerOfHanoi is thus recursive. Each call to this procedure produces one line of output and gets one step closer to the final solution of the problem.

Exercises

1. Compare the number of loop iterations and recursive calls in the recursive and nonrecursive versions of the Fibonacci functions.

2. Write a test program to interactively test the functions and procedures presented in this section. Determine how much clock time it takes for the recursive and nonrecursive versions of the Fibonacci functions to compute their results? How do these figures compare with your answer for Exercise 1?

3. Write recursive and nonrecursive functions to generate the following series summations:

    a. $S(n) = 1 + 3 + 5 + ... + 2n - 1$

    b. $T(n) = 1 + 2 + 3 + ... + n$

    c. $U(n) = 1/1 + 1/2 + 1/3 + ... + 1/n$

    d. $V(n) = 1 + 1/2 + 1/4 + ... + 2^{-(n-1)}$

6:5 Using Procedures

Procedures support the logical modularization of programs and provide programmers with a method of declaring one copy of a procedure for processes that are used many times. To illustrate the use of procedures, consider the problem of manipulating strings, declared as arrays of characters. These processes could be valuable for a variety of systems that perform a substantial amount of character manipulation, ranging from text processing to forming strings of control codes to be transmitted to graphics terminals and other special purpose devices. Rather than justifying the importance of this collection of string-processing procedures, we have created several exercise problems to suggest their value.

We can implement strings in a variety of ways. The most obvious method is with an array of character elements, as illustrated in Figure 6-17. The procedures in Figures 6-19 through 6-23, inclusive, manipulate strings of characters stored in arrays as illustrated in Figure 6-17. One restriction on the following processes is that the maximum length of a string has a limit. The reason for this limit is that the method uses the

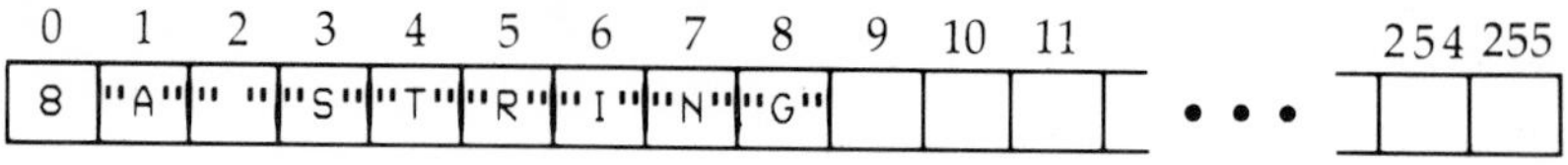

Figure 6-17   Visualization of STR255

first position in an array to store the size of the string. Since a cardinal value between 0 and 255 is stored in a byte, and 0 indicates an empty string, 255 is the maximum number of characters that may be stored in the string.

The approach just discussed is preferred to other alternatives for several reasons. First, storing the length of the string in the first position of the array provides immediate access to the length of the string. A typical alternative allows arrays of arbitrary length, but requires the use of a special character as a terminator of the string. This requirement leads to a problem in determining what character should be used and, hence, cannot appear in the string. This option is explored in more detail as an exercise.

Most of the procedures presented in the remainder of this section perform exception handling. For example, if a string of characters is larger than the array in which the characters are stored, the characters that fit are placed in the array and a boolean variable, STRXception, is set to TRUE to indicate an error. STRXception is a variable that is set as a procedure side effect. That is, it is not passed as a parameter. STRXception is always set as a side effect so that after calls to the procedures, this variable may be tested to learn if an exception has occurred. In some instances an exception is expected. These situations are discussed as each procedure is explained.

Any program module containing the procedures developed in this section requires the declarations presented in Figure 6-18. Read and Write are imported from InOut and are used by STRRead and STRWrite to support string I/O. EOL is also imported from InOut and used in STRRead. The TYPE, STR255, defines the structure of a string. The variable, STRXception, is declared along with a comment about its use.

Three procedures initialize strings and one procedure writes strings. They are:

1. STRNull: Create a null (empty) string.

2. STRRead: Read a string from the input device.

3. STRFromCHARs: Take a normal array of characters and store them in an array using the format expected by these string-handling procedures.

4. STRWrite: Write a string of characters to the output device.

```
 1   MODULE StringProcessing;
 2
 3   FROM InOut IMPORT EOL, Read, Write;
 4
 5   CONST  MaxSTRSize = 255;
 6
 7   TYPE   STR255 = ARRAY [ 0 .. MaxSTRSize ] OF CHAR;
 8     (*
 9      *  These procedures process any ARRAY OF CHAR regardless of
10      *  size up to 256 bytes long
11      *  The first byte, byte 0, is used to contain the length
12      *)
13
14   VAR    STRXception : BOOLEAN;
15     (*
16      *  STRXception is set as a side effect of all of the string
17      *  procedures
18      *     = FALSE, means the last procedure performed correctly
19      *                without any exception handling
20      *     = TRUE, means an exception was handled
21      *)
```

Figure 6-18   Declarations for STR255 Processing

Figure 6-19 presents the procedure STRNull, which creates a null string. Because of the method used here to store strings, a null string is placed in a character array simply by storing 0, CHR (0), in the first position of the array to indicate an empty string, that is, a string of size 0.

Two other typical ways of initializing a string of characters are to either read characters from the input device or to copy an array of characters into an array using the string format. Procedures for these actions appear in Figure 6-20. STRRead reads character input directly into a string. The input is read until one of two conditions is satisfied. The first condition determines if the array, into which the string is being placed, is filled. If the array is filled, additional characters may not have been read from the input device; hence the boolean variable, STRXception, is set to TRUE. The other test in the loop process looks for the normal line terminator, EOL.

```
1   PROCEDURE STRNull ( VAR A : ARRAY OF CHAR );
2
3      BEGIN
4      A [0] := CHR (0)
5      END  STRNull;
```

Figure 6-19   Procedure STRNull

```
1    PROCEDURE STRRead ( VAR A : ARRAY OF CHAR );
2    (* Exception:  Attempt to read more than 255 characters *)
3
4        VAR     I, Size : CARDINAL;
5                Ch      : CHAR;
6
7        BEGIN
8        I := 0;
9        Size := HIGH (A);
10       Read (Ch);
11       WHILE ( I < Size ) & (Ch # EOL ) DO
12          INC (I);   A [I] := Ch;   Read (Ch)
13       END;
14       IF (Ch = EOL) THEN
15          STRXception := FALSE;
16          A [0] := CHR (I)
17        ELSE
18          STRXception := TRUE;
19          A [0] := CHR (Size)
20       END
21       END STRRead;
22
23   PROCEDURE STRFromCHARs ( VAR A : ARRAY OF CHAR;
24                             B : ARRAY OF CHAR; Number : CARDINAL );
25   (* Exception:  Too many characters to put in A or A too large *)
26
27       VAR    I : CARDINAL;
28
29       BEGIN
30       IF (Number > HIGH (A)) OR (HIGH (A) > MaxSTRSize) THEN
31          STRXception := TRUE;
32           IF (Number > HIGH (A)) & (HIGH (A) > MaxSTRSize) THEN
33              Number := MaxSTRSize;
34            ELSIF Number > HIGH (A) THEN
35              Number := HIGH (A);
36          END;
37        ELSE
38          STRXception := FALSE
39       END;
40       A [0] := CHR (Number);
41       FOR I := 1 TO Number DO
42          A [I] := B [I-1]
43       END
44       END  STRFromCHARs;
```

Figure 6-20   Procedures STRRead and STRFromCHARs

The procedure STRFromCHARs initializes a string from an array of characters. This procedure processes the array into the correct form for the string-processing procedures. Note that since the second parameter is not VARed, this procedure may be called with the first two actual parameters referencing the same array, for example,

STRFromCHARs (Able, Able, 50)

STRFromCHARs handles two possible exceptions. One exception is an attempt to move more characters from the second parameter than there are positions available in the first parameter. The other exception is the possibility that the first parameter is an array of more than 256 bytes (one for holding the size and 255 for holding characters).

The procedure STRWrite is presented in Figure 6-21. It is a straight-forward looping process and needs no detailed explanation. The same is true for the function procedure STRLength, which returns the size of the specified string.

Four basic string-manipulating procedures appear in Figure 6-22. STRCopy (string copy) transfers a copy of a string to a second array. STR-ConCat (string concatenation) joins two strings together into one: the second string is placed into the first string so that the first array contains the combined contents, the first string followed by the second. STRInsert and STRDelete insert and delete, respectively, characters from strings.

```
 1   PROCEDURE STRWrite ( VAR A : ARRAY OF CHAR );
 2
 3      VAR    I : CARDINAL;
 4
 5      BEGIN
 6      STRXception := FALSE;  (* No exceptions occur *)
 7      FOR I := 1 TO ORD (A[0]) DO
 8         Write ( A[I] )
 9      END
10      END  STRWrite;
11
12   PROCEDURE STRLength ( VAR A : ARRAY OF CHAR ): CARDINAL;
13
14      BEGIN
15      STRXception := FALSE;  (* No exceptions occur *)
16      RETURN ORD ( A[0] )
17      END  STRLength;
```

Figure 6-21   Procedures STRWrite and STRLength

```
1    PROCEDURE STRCopy ( VAR A, B : ARRAY OF CHAR );
2       (* Exception:  A not big enough *)
3
4       VAR    I, Transfer : CARDINAL;
5
6       BEGIN
7       IF ORD ( B[0] ) > HIGH (A) THEN
8          Transfer := HIGH (A);
9          STRXception := TRUE
10        ELSE
11          Transfer := ORD ( B[0] );
12          STRXception := FALSE
13      END;
14      A [0] := CHR (Transfer);
15      FOR I := 1 TO Transfer DO
16        A [I] := B[I]
17      END
18      END  STRCopy;
19
20   PROCEDURE STRConCat ( VAR A, B : ARRAY OF CHAR );
21      (*  Exception:  A not large enough to hold the result *)
22
23      VAR    I, AIndex, Transfer : CARDINAL;
24
25      BEGIN
26      IF ( ORD (A[0]) + ORD (B[0]) ) > HIGH (A) THEN
27          STRXception := TRUE;
28          Transfer    := HIGH (A) - ORD (A[0]);
29        ELSE
30          STRXception := FALSE;
31          Transfer    := ORD (B[0]);
32      END;
33      AIndex := ORD (A[0]) + 1;
34      A[0]   := CHR ( ORD (A[0]) + Transfer );
35      FOR I := 1 TO Transfer DO
36        A [AIndex] := B [I];
37        INC (AIndex)
38      END
39      END  STRConCat;
40
41   PROCEDURE STRInsert ( VAR A, B : ARRAY OF CHAR;
42                                     Position : CARDINAL );
43      (*  Exception:  A not big enough to hold the result *)
44      VAR    I, Size, SizeOfA : CARDINAL;
45
46      BEGIN
47      IF ( ORD (A[0]) + ORD (B[0]) ) > HIGH (A) THEN
48          STRXception := TRUE
49        ELSE
```

```
50              STRXception := FALSE
51          END;
52          Size      := ORD(B[0]);
53          SizeOfA := HIGH (A);
54          FOR I := ORD(A[0]) TO Position BY -1 DO
55              IF (I+Size) <= SizeOfA THEN
56                  A [I+Size] := A [I]
57              END
58          END;
59          FOR I := 1 TO Size DO
60              IF (Position + I - 1) <= SizeOfA THEN
61                  A [Position + I - 1] := B [I]
62              END
63          END
64      END  STRInsert;
65
66  PROCEDURE STRDelete ( VAR A : ARRAY OF CHAR;
67                                  Location, Size : CARDINAL );
68      VAR    I : CARDINAL;
69
70      BEGIN
71      IF (Location + Size - 1) > ORD(A[0]) THEN
72          STRXception := TRUE;
73          A [0] := CHR (Location-1);
74        ELSE
75          STRXception := FALSE;
76          A [0] := CHR (ORD(A[0])-Size);
77          FOR I := Location+Size TO ORD(A[0]) DO
78              A [Location+I-1] := A [I]
79          END;
80      END
81      END  STRDelete;
```

Figure 6-22   Fundamental String-Processing Procedures

The copy process of STRCopy is straightforward, but it is preceded by possible exception handling, specifically, when the array for the first parameter is not large enough to hold the string. String concatenation, as performed by STRConCat, is a typical string process. For example, if

```
Able := "The big "
```

and

```
Baker := "bad wolf"
```

then

        STRConCat (Able, Baker)

forms

        "The big bad wolf"

in Able. This process must also handle the possible exception that the resulting combined string is too large for the array passed in the first parameter.

STRDelete (string delete) deletes a substring from a string. The second and third parameters indicate the position and the length of the substring. When a substring is deleted, that part following the deleted substring is moved forward in the array and the string size is reset. For example, if

        Able := "The big bad wolf"

then

        STRDelete (Able, 9, 4)

would change the contents of Able to

        "The big wolf"

A variety of possible exceptions must be handled by this procedure, including attempts to delete more from the array than is actually in the string.

STRInsert (string insert) inserts one string into another. For example, if

        Able := "The big wolf"

and

        Baker := "bad "

then

        STRInsert (Able, Baker, 9)

changes Able to

```
"The big bad wolf"
```

String-processing support is completed by the three function procedures presented in Figure 6-23. The first procedure locates substrings in a string, and the other two are boolean procedures used for comparisons between strings. For example, if

```
Able := "The big bad wolf"
```

and

```
Baker := "big"
```

then

```
WriteCard (STRFindSub (Able, Baker) )
```

prints 5, the position of the first character of `Baker` in `Able`. If the second parameter is not contained in the first parameter, the function returns a value of 0 to indicate this condition. This situation is also considered to be an exception, and the global variable `STRXception` is set accordingly.

`STRLess` and `STREqual` perform comparisons between strings. The string equality test is straightforward. `STRLess` performs a series of comparisons between `A [I]` and `B [I]`. The result is established and returned depending upon the first nonequal pair of characters. If all pairwise comparisons are the same up to the length of the smaller of the two strings, then the procedure is set using the string length. For example, if

```
Able := "The big bad wolf"
```

and

```
Baker := "The big"
```

then

```
STRLess (Able, Baker)
```

returns a value of FALSE, whereas

```
STRLess (Baker, Able)
```

returns TRUE.

```
1    PROCEDURE STRFindSub ( VAR A, B : ARRAY OF CHAR ) : CARDINAL;
2
3       VAR    I, Max, SizeOfB, J : CARDINAL;
4
5       BEGIN
6       Max := ORD (A[0]) - ORD (B[0]) + 1;
7       FOR I := 1 TO Max DO
8          J := 0;
9          SizeOfB := ORD (B[0]);
10         WHILE ( J < SizeOfB ) & ( A [I+J] = B [J+1] ) DO
11            INC (J)
12         END;
13         IF J = SizeOfB THEN
14            STRXception := FALSE;
15            RETURN I
16         END
17      END;
18      STRXception := TRUE;
19      RETURN 0
20      END STRFindSub;
21
22   PROCEDURE STREqual ( VAR A, B : ARRAY OF CHAR ): BOOLEAN;
23
24      VAR    I : CARDINAL;
25
26      BEGIN
27      STRXception := FALSE;  (* No exceptions occur *)
28      IF ORD (A[0]) # ORD (B[0]) THEN
29         RETURN FALSE
30       ELSE
31         FOR I := 1 TO ORD (A[0]) DO
32            IF A[I] # B[I] THEN
33               RETURN FALSE
34            END;
35         END;
36         RETURN TRUE
37      END
38      END  STREqual;
39
40   PROCEDURE STRLess ( VAR A, B : ARRAY OF CHAR ): BOOLEAN;
41
42      VAR    I, Size : CARDINAL;
43
44      BEGIN
45      STRXception := FALSE;  (* No exceptions occur *)
46      IF ORD (A[0]) < ORD (B[0]) THEN
47         Size := ORD (A[0])
48       ELSE
49         Size := ORD (B[0])
```

```
50        END;
51        FOR I := 1 TO Size DO
52           IF A[I] < B[I] THEN
53                RETURN TRUE
54              ELSIF B[I] < A[I] THEN
55                RETURN FALSE
56           END
57        END;
58        IF A[0] < B[0] THEN
59             RETURN TRUE
60           ELSE
61             RETURN FALSE
62        END
63        END   STRLess;
```

Figure 6-23   Additional String-Processing Procedures

Exercises

1. Write a simple line editor using the string-processing procedures presented in this section.

2. Use the string procedures to develop device I/O drivers for a graphics device or to manipulate all of the features of some dot matrix printer.

3. Create a set of procedures to support polynomials stored in an array.

4. An alternative to storing strings of characters in arrays is to store them using CHR (0), CHR (255), or some other user-specified string terminator. That is, this terminator is placed at the end of the string; hence there is no predefined limit to allowable string sizes. Rewrite the string-processing procedures in this chapter using this approach.

5. Critically analyze the relative advantages and disadvantages of the two approaches presented for string processing. Carefully evaluate the limitations, space, and time requirements for each approach.

6. Another approach to representing strings is with records, as in the declarations

```
CONST MaxLength = ???;   (*   Fill in   *)

TYPE StrRec = RECORD
                LogicLength:  CARDINAL;
                Char : ARRAY [ 1 .. MaxLength ] OF CHAR
              END;
```

Analyze the advantages and disadvantages of using this approach.

6:6 Procedure Types

In Modula-2, procedures can be passed as parameters to other procedures. Actually, the procedure itself is not passed, but rather the identification, that is, the address, of the procedure. This powerful feature of Modula-2 makes programming general cases much more convenient because one procedure can perform different operations depending upon the procedure passed to it as a parameter. Figure 6-24 shows the syntax diagrams relevant to the declaration of procedure types.

As an example of the declaration and use of a *Procedure Type*, consider the declarations

```
TYPE   Ordering = PROCEDURE (REAL, REAL) : BOOLEAN;

PROCEDURE Ascending (Item1, Item2 : REAL ) : BOOLEAN;
   BEGIN
   IF Item1 < Item2 THEN
      RETURN TRUE
    ELSE
      RETURN FALSE
   END
   END Ascending;

PROCEDURE Descending (Item1, Item2 : REAL ) : BOOLEAN;
   BEGIN
   IF Item1 > Item2 THEN
      RETURN TRUE
    ELSE
      RETURN FALSE
   END
   END Descending;
```

in which the type Ordering and the procedures Ascending and Descending are declared. Ordering is a procedure type; specifically, it is a function procedure that returns a BOOLEAN result and is passed two parameters of type REAL. Notice that the procedures Ascending and Descending are declared in a manner compatible with the type Ordering. Because of this compatibility, either of these procedures may become the value of any object of type Ordering. Thus given the declaration

```
   VAR   AVariable : Ordering;
```

the statement

```
   AVariable := Ascending
```

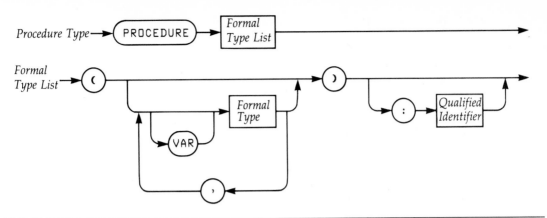

Figure 6-24   Syntax Diagrams for *Procedure Type*

is perfectly valid. We can now rewrite the procedure SortTheData presented in Figure 6-6 so that it sorts real values in either ascending or descending order. This procedure, SortRealData, appears in Figure 6-25.

In Figure 6-25 notice that the formal parameter OutOfOrder is of type Ordering. In this way the call to the procedure SortRealData specifies a third actual parameter that is a procedure compatible with type Ordering. In other words, a BOOLEAN function with two REAL parameters must be passed as an actual parameter. Ascending and Descending are two possible choices. They specify two possible conditions for interchanging in the sorting process. Thus given the declaration

```
VAR   ARealArray : ARRAY [ 1 .. 100 ] OF REAL;
```

and the statement

```
SortRealData ( ARealArray, 52, Descending );
```

the expression

```
( J > 0) & (OutOfOrder (Number [J-Dist], Number [J]))
```

appearing on line 22 essentially becomes the expression

```
( J > 0) & (Descending (Number [J-Dist], Number [J]))
```

The standard type PROC is predefined, in the same way that INTEGER, CARDINAL, CHAR, BOOLEAN, and BITSET are predefined. PROC

```
1    PROCEDURE SortRealData ( VAR   Value   : RealArray;
2                                   MaxNumber   : INTEGER;
3                                   OutOfOrder  : Ordering);
4
5       VAR    I, J, Dist : INTEGER;
6
7       PROCEDURE Interchange;
8
9          VAR     ExtraReal   : REAL;
10
11         BEGIN
12         ExtraReal := Value [J];
13         Value [J] := Value [J+1];
14         Value [J+1] := ExtraReal
15         END Interchange;
16
17      BEGIN  (* of SortRealData *)
18      Dist := MaxNumber DIV 2;
19      REPEAT
20         FOR I := 1 TO MaxNumber-Dist DO
21            J := I;
22            WHILE (J > 0) &
23                  (OutOfOrder (Value [J], Value [J+Dist])) DO
24               Interchange;J := J - Dist
25            END
26         END;
27         Dist := Dist DIV 2
28      UNTIL Dist = 0
29      END SortRealData;
```

Figure 6-25   Example of a Procedure with a Procedure Type Parameter

specifies a parameterless procedure and is considered to be defined as

```
TYPE  PROC = PROCEDURE;
```

PROC is important in the context of the definition of coroutines and processes and is discussed further in Chapter 10.

Exercises

1. Write a function

```
PROCEDURE Area (F : Function; a, b : REAL; N : CARDINAL ) : REAL
```

that estimates the area under a curve represented by the function F between the x coordinate values a and b using N rectangles. Declare

```
TYPE Function = PROCEDURE (REAL) : REAL;
```

to be passed to the function Area.

2. As in Exercise 1, write a function

```
PROCEDURE Area (F : Function; a, b : REAL) : REAL
```

that estimates the area under the curve using Simpson's method.

3. Write a function

```
PROCEDURE PartialSum ( S : Sequence; N : CARDINAL ) : REAL
```

that forms the partial sum of the first N terms in the Sequence passed to it, where

```
TYPE Sequence = PROCEDURE ( CARDINAL ) : REAL;
```

7 Standard Procedures and Modules

7:1 Standard Procedures

In addition to having several predefined data types, such as INTEGER and CHAR, Modula-2 also contains several predefined procedures, some of which have been informally introduced earlier in this text. This section describes all of the predefined procedures that are part of Modula-2. These standard procedures perform useful operations and are frequently used when programming in Modula-2. These identifiers are not imported, but are immediately available for use. Programmers should resist the temptation to write their own versions of these procedures, since the procedures provided here are efficient implementations. These procedures are presented for reference in alphabetical order in Figure 7-1.

Some of these procedures have been used or mentioned earlier in this text; others are detailed in later chapters. The standard procedures may be categorized into three groups: basic operations, type transfer and conversion, and arithmetic manipulation. Procedures in these groups are discussed in each of the following three subsections.

7:1:1 Basic Operations

Sometimes it might not be desirable in a program to distinguish between lowercase and uppercase alphabetic characters. The CAP (ch) function accepts a single parameter of type CHAR, ch. If the value of ch is a lowercase alphabetic character, this function procedure returns the corresponding uppercase character. That is, an "A" for an "a", "B" for a "b", and so forth; otherwise, the value of ch is returned as the result.

Example	Description
ABS (x)	The absolute value function. For x of type INTEGER or REAL, this function returns a value of the same type.
CAP (ch)	A function procedure whose argument must be of type CHAR and that returns a character value as follows: If ch is a lowercase alphabet character, CAP (ch) returns the corresponding capital letter; otherwise, CAP (ch) returns ch.
CHR (x)	For an ordinal number x of type INTEGER or CARDINAL, this function procedure returns the character value whose internal representation is equivalent to x. Equivalently, $$CHR\ (x)\ =\ VAL\ (CHAR,\ x)$$
DEC (x)	The decrement procedure. For x of type T, DEC (x) assigns to x the value that precedes x in T. Equivalently, $$DEC\ (x)\ =\ VAL\ (T,\ ORD\ (x)\ -\ 1)$$
DEC (x, n)	This variation assigns to x the nth preceding value in T. Equivalently, $$DEC\ (x,\ n)\ =\ VAL\ (T,\ ORD\ (x)\ -\ n)$$
DISPOSE (p)	This procedure is used in dynamic storage allocation and is described in detail in Chapter 9. The parameter, p, must be of some pointer type because it passes to DISPOSE the address of a memory area to be deallocated. Equivalently, $$DISPOSE\ (p)\ =\ DEALLOCATE\ (p,\ TSIZE\ (T))$$ where p is declared as $$VAR\ p\ :\ POINTER\ TO\ T$$ and T is some data type. DEALLOCATE is a procedure in the module Storage, which is described in Section 7:7 and discussed in Chapter 9.
DISPOSE (p, t1, t2, ...)	This variation is for disposing of variant records, where t1, t2, and so forth are specific values of the tag components . This variation is described in more detail in Section 9:7.
EXCL (s, i)	For a set s and element i, this procedure excludes the element i from s.
FLOAT (x)	For x of type CARDINAL, this function procedure returns a value of type REAL representing the same value as x.
HALT	This parameterless procedure immediately terminates program execution.

Example	Description
HIGH (a)	For a, an array type, this function procedure returns the high bound of the index range, where the index range is assumed to start with 0. That is, consider a declared as VAR a : ARRAY [0 .. HIGH (a)] OF ...
INC (x)	The increment procedure. For x of type T, INC (x) assigns to x the value that follows x in T. Equivalently, INC (x) = VAL (T, ORD (x) + 1)
INC (x, n)	This variation assigns to x the nth following value in T. Equivalently, INC (x, n) = VAL (T, ORD (x) + n)
INCL (s, i)	For a set s and element i, this procedure includes the element i in the set s.
MAX (t)	For an unstructured type t, this function returns the maximum value for this type.
MIN (t)	For an unstructured type t, this function returns the minimum value for this type.
NEW (p)	This procedure is used in dynamic storage allocation and is described in detail in Chapter 9. The parameter p must be of some pointer type, because NEW assigns to p the address of a memory area allocated to satisfy this request for memory. The size of the area allocated is dependent upon T; equivalently, NEW (p) = ALLOCATE (p, TSIZE (T)) where p is declared as VAR p : POINTER TO T and T is some data type. ALLOCATE is a procedure in the module Storage, which is described in Section 7:7 and discussed in Chapter 9.
NEW (p, t1, t2, ...)	This variation is for allocating instances of variant records, where t1, t2, and so forth are specific values of the tag components . This variation is described in more detail in Section 9:7.
ODD (x)	For x of type INTEGER or CARDINAL, this function procedure returns a value of type BOOLEAN as follows: If (x MOD 2) # 0, then TRUE; otherwise, ODD is FALSE.

Example	Description
ORD (x)	For x of type T, where T is any enumeration type, CHAR, INTEGER, or CARDINAL, this function procedure returns the CARDINAL value of the position of x in T.
TSIZE (p)	For any type T, this function procedure returns a CARDINAL value that represents the size of the memory area needed to store objects of that type.
TRUNC (x)	For x of type REAL, this function procedure returns the integral part of x as a value of type CARDINAL. That is, it truncates x to its integral part.
VAL (T, x)	For any type T and number x, which must be an ordinal number of type INTEGER or CARDINAL, this function procedure returns the value in T whose position in T is indicated by x. T must be an enumeration, CHAR, INTEGER, or CARDINAL.

Figure 7-1   Standard Modula-2 Procedures

HALT is a standard procedure that terminates the execution of a program. It is useful for terminating a program because of an error, exception handling, and debugging. HIGH determines the number of elements in an array. Descriptions and examples of the use of this function appear in Sections 6:2 and 10:2.

DEC and INC are standard procedures that efficiently decrement and increment, respectively, variables of any enumerable type, CHAR, INTEGER, CARDINAL, and so forth. DEC (x) accepts a variable x and assigns to x the value that precedes x in that type. For INTEGER and CARDINAL variables, this procedure is equivalent to subtracting 1 from the actual parameter. For variables of type CHAR, DEC (x) assigns the character value that precedes x in collating order. For example, for computers using ASCII, if x contains "C", then DEC (x) reassigns to x the character value "B". If x is an enumeration, DEC (x) assigns to x the value that precedes x in the enumeration. DEC (x, n) functions similarly to DEC (x), except that it decrements x by n instead of 1.

The procedure INC directly complements DEC. INC (x) also accepts any enumerable parameter. It assigns to x the next value in sequence following the current value in x. INC (x, n) increments by n instead of 1.

Both procedures INC and DEC correspond to the type transfer functions ORD and VAL, described as follows: If x is a variable of type T, then

DEC (x)   = VAL (T, ORD (x) - 1)

DEC (x, n) = VAL (T, ORD (x) - n)

and

$$INC \ (x) \qquad = \ VAL \ (T, \ ORD \ (x) \ + \ 1)$$

$$INC \ (x, \ n) \ = \ VAL \ (T, \ ORD \ (x) \ + \ n)$$

In all cases DEC and INC manipulate bit patterns that represent values, regardless of the variable's type. At the bit level, all DEC and INC operations are equivalent to performing addition or subtraction, by 1 or n, on the binary value represented by the bit pattern in x. For example, in declaring an enumeration such as

WeekDay = (Monday, Tuesday, Wednesday, Thursday, Friday)

the internal representations of these five values in the enumeration are, in fact, equivalent to the ordinal values 0, 1, 2, 3, 4, respectively. Therefore if a variable x of type WeekDay contains the value Wednesday, then

INC (x)

reassigns the value Thursday to x. The value Thursday is produced because the internal representation of Wednesday is 2, and 2 + 1 is 3, which represents Thursday.

One question concerning INC and DEC might be, What occurs at the bounds? That is, if x is of type CARDINAL and x contains 0, what happens when DEC (x) executes? What should occur is equivalent to an arithmetic overflow or a range check error. However, do not depend on a range check error because the error checking might be different from one Modula-2 implementation to another. On one implementation we tested, when x is INTEGER or CARDINAL, an arithmetic overflow error occurs; but for CHAR and enumerations, no error occurs. Therefore programmers should not assume that the implementation performs bounds checking.

The revised definition of Modula-2 includes the additional standard functions MIN and MAX. These functions are useful in helping to determine the range of admissible values for any enumerable type. Frequently, it is useful to know the smallest and largest allowable values for a given type.

The procedures INCL and EXCL manipulate sets. For a set s of type T, where i is an element in the set type T,

INCL (s, i) is equivalent to s := s + T {i}

and

EXCL (s, i) is equivalent to s := s - T {i}

INCL is equivalent to the set union of the set s with the set containing the single element i. EXCL removes an element from a set. Once again, the reason for these procedures is efficiency. Consider the method used to represent sets. For the enumeration WeekDay described previously, consider the declaration

```
TYPE  WorkSet = SET OF WeekDay;
```

If WorkDay is declared

```
VAR WorkDay : WorkSet;
```

then the internal representation of WorkDay may be thought of as an array of bits,

```
WorkDayRep : ARRAY WeekDay OF BOOLEAN;
```

Including an element in a set is equivalent to setting its corresponding bit, or boolean value, in the array to TRUE. Excluding an element from a set is equivalent to setting its corresponding bit to FALSE. For example, the statement

```
WorkDay := WorkSet {Monday, Wednesday, Friday};
```

would be equivalent to the following statement sequence if WorkDayRep was declared as a boolean array:

```
FOR Day := Monday TO Friday DO
   WorkDayRep [Day] := FALSE;
END;
WorkDayRep [Monday]    := TRUE;
WorkDayRep [Wednesday] := TRUE;
WorkDayRep [Friday]    := TRUE;
```

7:1:2 Type Transfer and Type Conversion

INTEGER, CARDINAL, CHAR, and enumerations are all countable collections of values, whereas REAL is not countable. A collection of values is countable if it can be placed into a one-to-one correspondence with any subset of the natural numbers (the positive integers and 0). VAL and ORD are type transfer functions that move bit patterns between variables of type CARDINAL and the other countable types. For a variable x of any enumerable type, ORD (x) returns the ordinal value (position) of x in its type. Another way of viewing this function is that ORD (x) returns the CARDINAL value represented by the bit pattern in the variable x. VAL performs the complementary operation.

ORD transfers a bit pattern from a variable of an enumerable type to CARDINAL. VAL takes a bit pattern in a CARDINAL variable and transfers it to an enumerable variable. If T is one of these types and x a CARDINAL, then

    VAL (T, x)

is the value y of type T satisfying

    x = ORD (y)

CHR is a special form of VAL for converting ordinal values to values of type CHAR:

    CHR (x) = VAL (CHAR, x)

The identifiers for types, either the standard identifiers, like INTEGER and CARDINAL, or identifiers for user-declared enumerations, also serve as type transfer functions. For example, if J is an INTEGER variable,

    J := INTEGER ("A")

transfers the ASCII bit pattern for the letter "A" to the variable J.

Type transfer functions **move** bit patterns from variables of one type to variables of another. Type conversion functions **convert** values from variables of one type to bit patterns that represent the same value in another type. For example, in most computer systems the bit pattern for the INTEGER representation of 1 is different from the bit pattern for the REAL representation of 1.0. Two type conversion procedures, TRUNC and FLOAT, are discussed in the following section.

7:1:3 Arithmetic Manipulation

Determining the absolute value of an INTEGER or REAL number is a mathematical operation supported through the ABS function. ABS accepts arguments of both types and returns the same type of value as was passed to it as a parameter.

ODD is a BOOLEAN function that accepts an INTEGER or CARDINAL parameter and returns the value TRUE if the argument is odd; otherwise,

ODD returns the value FALSE. Given the variable x, ODD is equivalent to the BOOLEAN expression

```
( x MOD 2 ) # 0
```

The function ODD provides a good illustration of why these procedures are predefined in Modula-2. Although ODD may be defined in terms of a boolean expression, this operation is faster at the machine level. Specifically, since integer and cardinal values are stored in a computer using binary representations, determining if such a number is odd is equivalent to selecting the bit that represents the least significant digit. For many computers this selection can be accomplished with a very fast low-level operation.

FLOAT and TRUNC are type conversion functions for values of type CARDINAL and REAL. In most computer systems the method for representing cardinals and reals is not directly compatible. That is, the representation for the real value 10.0 is not the same as the representation of the cardinal value 10. The real and cardinal representations of the same numeric value are typically two completely different bit patterns. As a result, when values are converted between REAL and CARDINAL variables, the representation must be modified.

TRUNC (x) is a function that obtains the integral part of its parameter, x of type REAL, and returns it as a CARDINAL value. Half-rounding may be performed with TRUNC, as in the function call

```
TRUNC (x + 0.5)
```

The function TRUNC may be efficiently implemented by taking advantage of specific information about the format used by the computer system to represent real numbers. With this information TRUNC can typically be performed at the machine level with a few fast bit-manipulating operations.

One possible limitation of TRUNC should always be considered. Because of the wide range of real values and the limited range of cardinal values, it is possible for TRUNC (x) to fail because of a range error. For example, consider the case in many computer systems where cardinal values are represented with 16 bits. The range of cardinal values is

```
0 .. 65536
```

If the real number is not within that range, a run time error occurs. For example, if x contains 1.0E+6 (one million), then

```
TRUNC (x)
```

produces a range error.

FLOAT does the type conversion from CARDINAL to REAL. However, although

TRUNC (FLOAT (i)) = i

for all i, it is **not** true that

FLOAT (TRUNC (y)) = y

for all y. This fact is easily verified by considering the case where y contains 2.5. This condition is also true for any other real number that is not a cardinal, or any real that would produce a range error during the conversion.

7:2 The MODULE Concept

In Modula-2, procedures are just the first step in program modularization. The second step is the module capability, which, among other things, supports the independent development of logically related components. Throughout the remainder of this chapter, the modules that are typically available on most implementations of Modula-2 are discussed. Chapter 8 describes how modules may be constructed.

Modules support several important programming features:

1. The ability to separately compile and maintain parts of a program or system.

2. The ability to effectively hide implementational details. That is, a user of a module is only aware of those identifiers in the module to which access has been allowed.

3. The ability to provide for the declaration of own variables. As you may recall, an own variable is a variable declared within a module in such a way that it is global to the procedures in that module, but inaccessible outside of that module.

Modules have been alluded to throughout the earlier chapters in this text. This capability is one of the major strengths of this programming language. Modules are collections of identifiers (types, variables, constants, procedures) that perform a well-defined collection of tasks.

A large part of any discussion on modules centers around the roles of four items:

1. **Definition Module**: Specifies the necessary information that a user must know about the identifiers exported by a library module.

2. **Implementation Module**: Contains the details of the declarations and procedures in a library module.

3. **Export**: Lists the identifiers available to users of a module. The revised definition of Modula-2 has made the *Export Statement* obsolete in library modules. Newer implementations of Modula-2 implicitly export all identifiers declared in a definition module.

4. **Import**: Informs the Modula-2 language translator of those identifiers being referenced from another module.

To illustrate, consider a module that has been used throughout the early chapters in this text, InOut. Access to the identifiers declared in InOut is obtained through the statement

```
FROM InOut IMPORT ... (* identifiers *)
```

For example,

```
FROM InOut IMPORT EOL, Done, termCH,
          OpenInput, OpenOutput, CloseInput, CloseOutput,
          Read, ReadString, ReadInt, ReadCard,
          Write, WriteLn, WriteString, WriteInt,
          WriteCard, WriteOct, WriteHex;
```

provides access to all of the identifiers declared in InOut.

A description of the role of each identifier appears in the Definition Module InOut, presented in Figure 7-2. Descriptions of the contents of typical Modula-2 modules appear in Appendix D. A definition module contains the information that the author of the module wishes to convey to users of that module.

A definition module defines the features available to users of that module. The specifics of writing definition modules and their corresponding implementation modules are discussed in Chapter 8. Figure 7-2 presents the Definition Module InOut for the Lilith and MRI IBM PC implementations of Modula-2. It is a good example of the primary components of a definition module. However, note the use of comments to inform users of the module about the results of procedures and possible side effects.

```
DEFINITION MODULE InOut;    (* NW 11.10.81 *)

  FROM SYSTEM IMPORT WORD;
  FROM FileSystem IMPORT File;

  EXPORT QUALIFIED
            EOL, Done, termCH, OpenInput, OpenOutput, CloseInput,
            CloseOutput, Read, ReadString, ReadInt, ReadCard,
            Write, WriteLn, WriteString, WriteInt, WriteCard,
            WriteOct, WriteHex;

  CONST EOL = 36C;
  VAR Done:  BOOLEAN;
    termCH:  CHAR;  (*  Terminating character in
                     *  ReadInt and ReadCard
                     *)
  PROCEDURE OpenInput ( defext: ARRAY OF CHAR );
    (*  Request a file name and open input file.
     *  Done := "file was successfully opened".
     *  If open, subsequent input is read from this file.
     *  If name ends with ".", append extension defext
     *)
  PROCEDURE OpenOutput ( defext: ARRAY OF CHAR );
    (*  Request a file name and open output file.
     *  Done := "file was successfully opened.
     *  If open, subsequent output is written on this file
     *)
  PROCEDURE CloseInput;
    (*  Closes input file; returns input to terminal
     *)
  PROCEDURE CloseOutput;
    (*  Closes output file; returns output to terminal
     *)
  PROCEDURE Read ( VAR ch: CHAR );
    (*  Done := TRUE when End-of-file encountered
     *)
  PROCEDURE ReadString ( VAR s: ARRAY OF CHAR );
    (*    Read a sequence of characters not containing blanks nor

     *    control characters; leading blanks are ignored. Input
     *    is terminated by any blank or any control character,
     *    that is, CHR (I), I <= 32. This character is assigned
     *    to termCH. DEL is used for backspacing when input from
     *    terminal
     *)
  PROCEDURE ReadInt ( VAR x: INTEGER );
    (*  Read a string of characters and convert to integer.
     *  Leading blanks are ignored.
```

```
     *   Done := TRUE means that an integer was read
     *)
PROCEDURE ReadCard ( VAR x: CARDINAL );
   (*   Read a string of characters and convert to cardinal.
    *   Leading blanks are ignored.
    *   Done := TRUE if a CARDINAL was read
    *)
PROCEDURE Write ( ch: CHAR );
   (*   Write the character, ch, to the output file
    *)
PROCEDURE WriteLn;
   (*   Write the line termination character, EOL
    *)
PROCEDURE WriteString ( s: ARRAY OF CHAR );

PROCEDURE WriteInt ( x: INTEGER; n: CARDINAL );
   (*   Write integer x with (at least) n characters to the
    *   output file. If n is greater than the number
    *   of digits needed, blanks are added preceding the number
    *)
PROCEDURE WriteCard ( x,n: CARDINAL );

PROCEDURE WriteOct ( x,n: CARDINAL );

PROCEDURE WriteHex ( x,n: CARDINAL );

END InOut.
```

Figure 7-2   Definition Module InOut

The *Export Statement*,

```
EXPORT QUALIFIED
      EOL, Done, termCH, OpenInput, OpenOutput,
      CloseInput, CloseOutput, Read, ReadString,
      ReadInt, ReadCard, Write, WriteLn, WriteString,
      WriteInt, WriteCard, WriteOct, WriteHex;
```

appearing in Figure 7-2, lists the identifiers in InOut that can be accessed by users of the module. The role of the reserved word QUALIFIED is explained in Chapter 8. The identifiers in the export list are precisely the identifiers that may be imported by other modules.

The *Import Statement* provides access to a module. Following the reserved word FROM is the name of the library module, which in turn is followed by the reserved word IMPORT. The list of *Identifiers* being imported from the module follows the reserved word IMPORT. For example,

```
FROM InOut IMPORT
        EOL, Done, termCH, OpenInput, OpenOutput,
        CloseInput, CloseOutput, Read, ReadString,
        ReadInt, ReadCard, Write, WriteLn, WriteString,
        WriteInt, WriteCard, WriteOct, WriteHex;
```

provides access to all of the identifiers exported by InOut. The *Import Statement* in a module lists the *Identifiers* that are accessible by that module. No error occurs if valid *Identifiers* appear in an *Import Statement* and are not used. However, this practice is not good, since it could slow down the compilation process and confuse those who might read the program.

Identifiers imported as just shown can be referenced without being qualified. An alternative form of the *Import Statement*, for example,

```
IMPORT InOut;
```

imports all of the identifiers in a library module, but the identifiers may be accessed only as *Qualified Identifiers*. If InOut is imported using this alternative form, then the identifiers exported from InOut, like ReadInt, are accessed with qualification, for example, InOut.ReadInt.

An implementation module contains the details of a module's identifiers, procedures, processes, and so forth that are **hidden** from users of the library module. In most programming situations, when a programmer plans to use a module, only the definition module is referenced to see what is available. Programmers rarely need to look at the implementational details. The development of implementation modules is described in Chapter 8.

7:3 The Module InOut

This section describes the typical contents of the module InOut. Modula-2 does not directly support input or output operations. All I/O is supported through modules. To some extent this support could make the I/O characteristics of each Modula-2 implementation unique. However, we expect elementary characteristics to be exhibited by certain fundamental I/O devices, such as keyboards, CRT screens, and printers. This section discusses the identifiers exported from a typical implementation of the module InOut.

The definition module InOut in Figure 7-2 is typical of most versions of this module. Precisely which identifiers are made available through this standard module varies slightly from system to system. However, a large group of identifiers is common to all implementations of Modula-2.

A significant portion of this definition module is self-explanatory, but a review of the module is helpful. This module exports several data objects and procedures. Note, however, that InOut imports identifiers from two other modules, SYSTEM and Terminal. A VAX/VMS version of InOut imports several identifiers from the modules SYSTEM and FileSystem. Although these details are different, reflecting possible hardware differences as well as philosophical differences in implementation, the results are quite similar from the point of view of users, who generally are not interested in low-level implementational details.

The one constant exported by InOut is EOL. The value of EOL is equivalent to a code used to indicate the end of a line. That is, it corresponds to the code inserted in files to separate one line or record of data from the next.

The variable Done of type BOOLEAN is set to TRUE when an I/O procedure has successfully performed its task. In many situations Done, having the value FALSE, indicates that the end of the input has been reached. The variable termCH is initialized by several of the input procedures. After a call to any of these procedures, termCH contains the character value following the data that was last read and translated. This variable could be useful to a programmer in case that character value is important.

The four procedures OpenInput, OpenOutput, CloseInput, and CloseOutput make and break linkages between files and the other I/O procedures. Typically, OpenInput and OpenOutput prompt the user at run time to enter the name of the file to be opened. The parameter passed to them is the default file name extension, which is used only if no extension is specified. For example, if the file NUMBER.DAT is to be opened for input with the statement

```
OpenInput ('DAT');
```

when prompted for the name of the file, the user responds with

```
NUMBER
```

The default extension is added, and the file NUMBER.DAT is accessed. However, if the user wishes to access the file ABC.XYZ, or just the file ABC, the procedure call

```
OpenInput ('DAT');
```

allows for this too. When a period is included in the file name, the default extension is not used. Hence the user simply enters the complete name, ABC.XYZ, or, in the case when a file name does not include a default extension, the name followed by a period, ABC., to access the file ABC.

CloseInput and CloseOutput return their respective I/O processes to the default device, typically the keyboard and CRT screen. A program tests to see if the last procedure call was successful by testing the variable Done, which is set to TRUE when an I/O operation succeeds and to FALSE when an I/O operation fails.

Inputting values to variables of the predefined types CHAR, INTEGER, and CARDINAL is supported by the procedures Read, ReadInt, and Read-Card, respectively. The procedure Read reads one character and stores its value in the specified parameter. The procedures ReadInt and ReadCard perform translations from strings of numerals, which may be preceded by blanks, to their equivalent internal representations as integer or cardinal numbers. The ReadString procedure reads a string of characters and stores them in the specified parameter, which must be declared as an array of characters. ReadString ignores leading blanks and control codes and then reads characters until it encounters a blank character or a control character. A control character is any character y satisfying

$y = $ CHR (x) for all x less than 32

The output procedures Write, WriteInt, and WriteCard comple-ment the corresponding input procedures. Write transfers a single char-acter to the output device. The procedures WriteInt and WriteCard translate the internal representations of integer and cardinal values to a string of numerals that forms the decimal representation of the number. Both WriteInt and WriteCard have a second parameter that specifies the minimum length of the string that is written. Numbers are printed right justified and are padded on the left with blanks.

WriteLn terminates a line of output, and WriteString writes the characters in the specified string. WriteString requires a single parameter that must be an array of characters. It writes the characters in the array up to but not including the first blank or control character.

The procedures WriteOct and WriteHex write cardinal values as strings of numerals in base 8 and base 16, respectively. As with the proce-dures WriteInt and WriteCard, the second parameter indicates the length of the output string. For example, if the identifier Num contained the cardinal value 59, then

WriteHex (Num, 6)

writes

_ _ _ _3B

where the underscores indicate blanks. The procedures ReadWrd and WriteWrd are system dependent and are discussed in Section 10:3, deal-ing with nontext I/O.

Various other modules might be available to support I/O processing. `Terminal`, `FileSystem`, and others are available on various Modula-2 implementations. These modules provide file and device support for I/O. For example, the module `Terminal` typically contains procedures that provide direct access to device controllers. This access helps programs establish efficient implementations of I/O processes. In these cases and all others, users should locate the definition module for the particular module in question. The definition module contains the information a user of the module needs in order to use the facilities provided by the module. The implementational details are hidden. How library modules are created is explained in Chapter 8.

7:4 Additional Standard Modules for I/O

The standard module `InOut` described in Section 7:3 supplies support for only one input device and one output device at a time. Typically, I/O defaults to the keyboard and CRT. The standard module `Terminal` is a lower-level module that provides hardware dependent support. Several standard modules may be supplied to support I/O. This section provides a brief overview of the functionality of some typical standard modules.

To some extent it is unfortunate that Wirth did not directly include I/O support within Modula-2. Because of this omission, different implementations of Modula-2 can have different variables and procedures exported from their standard modules. For example, the Hamburg/Logitech implementation of Modula-2 for VAX/VMS provides support for real I/O within the standard module `InOut`, whereas most other implementations provide this support through another module, `RealInOut`.

Although this situation opens the door for unnecessary criticisms of Modula-2, this problem is not as serious as it sounds. Because I/O is very system dependent, implementors of Modula-2 are not shackled to any predetermined I/O conventions within the language. Hence they can provide the most efficient and practical implementation of I/O on the specific computer system they are using. Interestingly, the I/O modules available on different implementations of Modula-2 are not a major obstacle to transportability, because most implementors of Modula-2 compilers seem to be concerned with maintaining compatibility.

An exhaustive treatment of I/O file support in Modula-2 is not appropriate for this text. Most programmers know what type of file structures they need (sequential, random, keyed, and so forth) and can determine, by reading descriptions in the relevant definition modules, which standard module provides them with the appropriate support. Which standard modules to consider can only be determined by reading the appropriate documentation.

To illustrate, the standard module InOut typically supports only one input and one output device at a time. However, certain programming situations require that several input and/or several output devices or files be open at one time. The Hamburg/Logitech implementation of Modula-2 supplies the standard module TextIO, which is useful in this situation. TextIO, which is presented in Appendix D, exports several procedures with similar names and similar functionality as the procedures declared in InOut. These procedures each have an additional parameter, which identifies the file being accessed. For example, InOut exports the procedure

```
ReadInt (v : INTEGER)
```

whereas TextIO exports the procedure

```
ReadInt (f : File; v : INTEGER)
```

TextIo provides multiple file support by declaring and exporting a hidden type, File, along with the procedures

```
OpenInput  (VAR f : File; defnam : ARRAY OF CHAR);

OpenOutput (VAR f : File; defnam : ARRAY OF CHAR);

CloseInput (VAR f : File; defnam : ARRAY OF CHAR);
```

and

```
CloseOutput (VAR f : File; defnam : ARRAY OF CHAR);
```

which are similar to the procedures with the same names in InOut. As a result multiple files may be opened and used at any moment during a program's execution. In addition, TextIO declares and exports the procedures

```
OpenIn (VAR f : File; filnam : ARRAY OF CHAR);
```

and

```
OpenOut (VAR f : File; filnam : ARRAY OF CHAR);
```

which associate disk files to file variables under program control without the need for terminal interaction.

InOut and TextIO support what are frequently referred to as **text files**. A text file is a data file that essentially stores printable character values representing data. The procedures in these modules support the reading and writing of data values of types INTEGER, CARDINAL, and sometimes REAL. Reading is accomplished by translating a string of character values, representing a value, into the internal representation of that value. Writing is accomplished by translating the internal representation of a value into a string of character values. Thus text files provide a readable external representation of data. For keyboard input and printed output, this translation is necessary, but in other situations it might not be desirable. Consider the case where data is kept on a storage device, such as a disk, and the data is not intended to be read by people. In this case, performing the translation is unnecessary and inefficient. Performing the translation consumes time, and the resultant string representation usually requires more storage space than the internal representation.

The standard modules Files and FileSystem typically support direct sequential I/O without translation. Such a file is referred to as a **stream**. Both of these modules declare procedures, with names such as Create and Close, that associate variables of type File with disk files. The standard module Files declares the procedures ReadBlock and WriteBlock, which transfer large collections of data between memory and a storage device. The standard module FileSystem declares the procedures ReadChar and WriteChar, which transfer values of type CHAR, and ReadWord and WriteWord, which transfer values whose internal representation is stored in one location of memory. The notion of a word and the declaration of the standard type WORD are discussed in Section 10:1.

The typical contents of the standard modules Terminal, TextIO, Files, and FileSystem appear in Appendix D. Programmers are encouraged to review the definition modules for the I/O modules available on their particular implementation of Modula-2 rather than just assume the descriptions in the appendix. The names and functionality of the identifiers supplied by a particular implementation of Modula-2 may have implementation dependent characteristics that make this research necessary.

7:5 The Module MathLib0

The module MathLib0 contains a collection of standard mathematical functions. The functions typically found in MathLib0 appear in Figure 7-3. They include several trigonometric and other transcendental functions as well as the square root and functions for the conversion between integers and reals.

The function procedures arctan, cos, exp, ln, sin, and sqrt are self-explanatory to anyone familiar with their typical roles in mathematics. We will not attempt to explain them here. The functions real and entier are type conversion functions for converting between values of

Example	Parameter Type	Description
arctan (x)	REAL	Returns the angle y in radians, satisfying x = tan (y); y satisfies the relation -PI / 2 <= y <= PI / 2, where PI = 3.1415927...
cos (x)	REAL	Given x in radians, this function procedure returns the trigonometric cos (x).
entier (x)	REAL	Returns a value of type INTEGER, which is the integer representation of the integral part of x.
exp (x)	REAL	Returns e^x where e = 2.71828...
ln (x)	REAL	The natural logarithm of x. The inverse of the e function.
real (x)	INTEGER	Returns a value of type REAL, which is the real representation of the integer value x.
sin (x)	REAL	Given x in radians, this function procedure returns the trigonometric sin (x).
sqrt (x)	REAL	Returns the square root of the parameter x.

Figure 7-3   Procedures Normally Found in MathLib0

types REAL and INTEGER. The function procedure

    real (x)

accepts a parameter x of type INTEGER and returns the equivalent real arithmetic representation. For example, the statement

    A := real (3)

converts the integer representation of 3 into the real arithmetic representation of 3 and places the result in the variable A, which must be declared to be of type REAL.

The function

    entier (x)

accepts a parameter x of type REAL and returns the integer representation of the integral part of x. For example, if x contains 2.175, then entier (x) returns the integer value 2 as its result.

7:6 The Module SYSTEM

The module SYSTEM provides access to low-level, system dependent features. This module is not explicitly imported; it is automatically imported by the compiler. Because it is system dependent, the contents of SYSTEM might vary from one computer to another or between Modula-2 implementations on the same computer. In any case it contains the identifiers that give programmers access to the low-level systems programming facilities.

The module SYSTEM is presented here to complete the discussion on typical standard modules. Applications of this module to access low-level features of a computer system are presented in Chapter 10. Two basic types declared in SYSTEM are WORD and ADDRESS. WORD refers to an individually addressable location of memory. Most data objects are represented by one or more contiguous WORDs. The specific capacity of a WORD is very implementation dependent and is thus not assumed in Modula-2. Objects of type WORD cannot appear in expressions because the only operation allowed for this type is assignment.

A data object of type ADDRESS stores the address of a memory location and is compatible with any pointer type. Pointer types are described in detail in Chapter 9. Formally, the type ADDRESS may be thought of as a POINTER TO WORD. Values of this type are manipulated as if they were cardinal values; but we must take great care when performing calculations with address variables because of the different addressing schemes used on various computers. However, expressions involving both of the types CARDINAL and ADDRESS are not allowed. Values of type CARDINAL may be converted to type ADDRESS with the type transfer

```
ADDRESS (k)
```

which transfers the cardinal value stored in k to an address value.

Because of the variety of addressing schemes available on different computer systems, questions may arise about the relationships between cardinal and address values. The preceding statements are true for the VAX and PDP-11 implementations of Modula-2. They are also true of address values on the IBM-PC, despite the internal representation of addresses in the paragraph-addressing scheme of the 8086/88 family of microprocessors.

The type PROCESS is described in detail in Chapter 10 on concurrent processing, along with the procedures NEWPROCESS and TRANSFER, which are also declared in SYSTEM. The revised definition of Modula-2 no longer supports the type PROCESS; every reference to it is replaced by ADDRESS.

The module SYSTEM also contains three function procedures. The declaration

```
PROCEDURE ADR (x : AnyType) : ADDRESS;
```

defines a function that returns the address of the variable x, where x may be of any type. This function procedure allows a program to determine, during its execution, the location of any data object.

The other two function procedures, SIZE and TSIZE, provide information about storage allocation. The declaration

```
PROCEDURE SIZE ( VAR x : AnyType ) : CARDINAL;
```

defines a function that returns the number of memory locations allocated to the data object x. x may be of any type. The declaration

```
PROCEDURE TSIZE ( t ) : CARDINAL;
```

defines a function that returns the number of memory locations allocated to each variable of type t. Note that t is the identifier corresponding to a type, not a variable. Since the capacity of a memory location is not specified in Modula-2, the value returned by TSIZE may represent the number of words or possibly bytes occupied by a type. These concepts and the types WORD and BYTE are discussed in Section 10:1.

The module SYSTEM may contain additional identifiers. For example, a VAX/VMS Modula-2 compiler declares the types BYTE (8 bits), SHORTWORD (16 bits), QUADWORD (8 bytes), and OCTAWORD (16 bytes). Anyone interested in accessing low-level features through Modula-2 should study the module SYSTEM and other low-level, system dependent modules.

7:7 Other Modules

Each Modula-2 implementation comes with a collection of modules to support a variety of features, such as I/O for real numbers, file processing, and memory management. Memory management is discussed in detail in Chapter 9. The VAX/VMS (Hamburg) Modula-2 compiler supports real I/O as part of the module InOut. The MRI Modula-2 compiler for the IBM-PC supports real I/O through a separate module named RealInOut. However, both implementations declare the procedures

```
PROCEDURE ReadReal ( x : REAL )
```

and

```
        PROCEDURE WriteReal ( x : REAL; n : CARDINAL )
```

which perform I/O for reals in a manner analogous to integer I/O, as explained for ReadInt and WriteInt.

Another standard module is Storage. It exports procedures that support dynamic storage allocation. Both VAX/VMS and IBM PC versions of Storage contain the procedure declarations

```
PROCEDURE ALLOCATE ( VAR a : ADDRESS; size : CARDINAL );
```

and

```
PROCEDURE DEALLOCATE ( VAR a : ADDRESS; size : CARDINAL );
```

These procedures support run time requests for memory management. A program using these procedures must contain an IMPORT statement of the form

```
    FROM Storage IMPORT ALLOCATE, DEALLOCATE;
```

The IBM-PC (and Lilith) versions of Storage also contain a procedure declaration,

```
    PROCEDURE Available ( size : CARDINAL ) : BOOLEAN;
```

which determines if enough free memory space is available to satisfy a certain size request. For example, a request to allocate space might appear in a statement sequence as

```
    IF Available (Size) THEN
        ALLOCATE (Pointer, Size);
      ELSE
        WriteString('---ERROR: No Memory Available');
        WriteLn;
        HALT
    END;
```

In many dynamic storage allocation situations, ALLOCATE and DEALLOCATE are not used directly. Instead, the standard procedures NEW and DISPOSE are used. All four of these procedures are discussed in greater detail in Chapter 9.

A variety of procedures and declarations are provided through various modules made available on different implementations of Modula-2. Appendix D contains a selected listing of the typical contents of these modules.

8 Module Structure

8:1 Overview

Chapter 7 contains descriptions of several standard modules available in various implementations of Modula-2. In all cases, regardless of the particular operating system or computer on which Modula-2 is implemented, the method of access to modules is always the same. This chapter introduces Modula-2's capabilities that allow programmers to create their own modules.

The three types of modules are as follows:

1. **Program Modules**: Every program is a module — the highest level of module. That is, other modules do not reference program modules, but program modules may reference other modules. Modules are referenced with the *Import Statement*.

2. **Library Modules**: The standard modules presented in Chapter 7 are examples of library modules. Programmers can create additional library modules. The creation of library modules is discussed in Section 8:3. They require the preparation of separate definition and implementation parts, a *Definition Module* and an *Implementation Module*, which together describe the library module. Hierarchies of modules may be created with library modules because a library module may import from lower-level modules and export to higher-level modules.

3. **Local Modules**: Sometimes a program needs the support provided by modules, but for one reason or another it is inappropriate to make the module into a library module. In this case a module may be completely contained in a program module. This

type of module is called a local module. Anything exported by a local module is automatically imported (that is, no *Import Statement* is required) to the program module containing the local module. Local modules may import from library modules or from other local modules contained within the library module. Therefore local modules may be nested. Local modules are discussed in detail in Section 8:2.

It is important to distinguish between modules and procedures. In addition to providing for separate compilation, modules provide certain facilities that are not supported by procedures. For example, the identifiers (constants, types, variables, and procedures) declared within a procedure cannot be made visible outside of that procedure, whereas the identifiers declared within a module may be exported. Three important facilities provided through modules and not through procedures are:

1. Data Abstraction: A module can export types while hiding the representation of the type within the module. A user of the module may declare and manipulate objects of the type and not know the exact representation of the type. This use of modules is also referred to as hiding detail or declaring hidden data types.

2. Own Variables: Variables declared within procedures are allocated when the procedure is called and deallocated when the procedure is terminated. Hence a procedure does not "own" variables; that is, a value cannot be left in a procedure's local variable between calls to the procedure with the assumption that the value will be there for the next procedure call. In fact, the variable might not be assigned to the same memory location for the next call to the procedure.

Variables declared within a module, regardless of whether they are exported or not, are allocated as part of the program module using the module. That is, the global variables in a program module and the global variables in all of the local modules and library modules directly and indirectly referenced by the program module are allocated before the beginning of the program module's execution.

The allocation of a module's variables occurs during the loading and initialization of the program module containing or referencing the module. Before the program module begins execution, a module's variables are bound to memory locations, and this relationship continues until the program module terminates. Hence the variables within a module are "own" variables.

3. Initialization: Both library modules and local modules may contain a statement sequence as part of their declaration. These statements execute once, before the program module begins execution. In this way each module may properly initialize itself. Procedures, on the other hand, must depend on statements elsewhere in the program module for their initialization.

Declaring and using a module is relatively easy. Local modules are created within a program and logically provide the same support that comes with library modules, but without the need to create separately compiled *Definition Modules* and corresponding *Implementation Modules*. Library modules and, sometimes, local modules are referenced using the *Import Statement*, whose syntax is presented in Figure 8-1.

The formal structure of modules is described in this chapter. To show its relationship to program structure, two examples are emphasized. One example collects the string-manipulating procedures presented in Section 6:5 and forms a library module. The other is an interesting problem described as follows:

> **The Birthday Problem**: Given a group of n people, what is the probability that at least two of these people have the same birthday? The same birthday means the same month and day, not necessarily the same year.

For someone familiar with the mathematical framework of this problem, it is easy to solve. Yet, it is an interesting problem in that the answer is not intuitive.

To estimate a solution to the Birthday Problem, we present a discrete simulation program. The solution uses a random number generator to simulate taking a survey of people's birthdays. For example, to estimate the probability that at least 2 of 30 people have the same birthday, the program simulates the experiment of asking 100 groups of 30 people the day of their birth and recording when a match occurs. The procedure in Figure 8-2 accomplishes this simulation, assuming that CardRandom is a random number generator satisfying

$$0 <= \text{CardRandom (N)} < N$$

Using the procedure BirthdaySimulation, an estimated solution is writ-

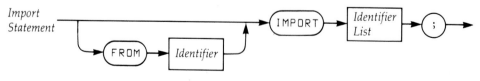

Import Statement

Figure 8-1   Syntax Diagram for *Import Statement*

```
1    PROCEDURE BirthdaySimulation (Group,
2                                 Number : CARDINAL) : REAL;
3        VAR     Bday    : ARRAY [ 1 .. 365 ] OF BOOLEAN;
4                Interview, I, SuccessCount, Day : CARDINAL;
5                Success : BOOLEAN;
6
7        BEGIN
8        SuccessCount := 0;
9        FOR Interview := 1 TO Number DO
10           FOR I := 1 TO 365 DO  Bday [I] := FALSE   END;
11           Success := FALSE;
12           FOR I := 1 TO Group DO
13               Day := CardRandom (365) + 1; (* One person's birthday *)
14               IF Bday [Day] (* If this birthday was recorded then   *)
15                  THEN Success := TRUE (* this is a common birthday  *)
16                  ELSE Bday [Day] := TRUE
17               END
18           END;
19           IF Success THEN  INC (SuccessCount)  END
20       END;
21       RETURN real (SuccessCount) / real (Number)
22       END BirthdaySimulation;
```

Figure 8-2   Procedure BirthdaySimulation

---

ten with the statement

```
WriteReal ( BirthdaySimulation (30, 100) );
```

However, a simulation of the Birthday Problem requires a good, uniform random number generator, which necessitates careful programming. Many computer systems might have uniform random number generators supplied with the system software. If we assume that such a random number generator is unavailable, Figure 8-3 presents the declaration of a good, uniform random number generator.

The problem of combining the random number generator with the simulation itself provides an example of some of the advantages of modules. For example, the function procedure RandomThree needs an own variable, Seed, to store the changing bit pattern, which helps generate random numbers. If the birthday simulation program inadvertently modified the values in the array Seed, the quality of the random number generator would be jeopardized. We should emphasize two other points. First, the details of generating random numbers might not be interesting to someone who simply wishes to solve the Birthday Problem; thus these two distinct subproblems should be kept separate. Second, a random

```
 1   CONST  Bound = 21845;  (*  Used by RandomThree  *)
 2
 3   VAR    Seed : ARRAY [ 1 .. 2 ] OF CARDINAL;
 4          Group, Number, I : CARDINAL;
 5
 6   PROCEDURE RandomThree () : CARDINAL;
 7                              (*  Returns a bit (0 or 1) *)
 8      VAR    Product, Carry, I : CARDINAL;
 9
10      BEGIN
11      LOOP
12         Carry := 0;
13         FOR I := 1 TO 2 DO
14            Seed [I] := Seed [I] + Carry;
15            Product  := 3 * Seed [I];
16            Carry    := Product DIV Bound;
17            Seed [I] := Product MOD Bound
18         END;
19         CASE Carry OF      (*  Return a zero or one  *)
20            0 : RETURN 0 |
21            1 : RETURN 1
22          ELSE             (* Or loop around and try again  *)
23         END
24      END
25      END RandomThree;
26
27   PROCEDURE InitSeed ( V1, V2 : CARDINAL );
28
29      BEGIN  (*  Make sure the seeds are within the bound  *)
30      Seed [1] := V1 MOD Bound;
31      Seed [2] := V2 MOD Bound
32      END InitSeed;
33
34   PROCEDURE CardRandom ( V : CARDINAL ): CARDINAL;
35                              (* V <= 32767 *)
36      VAR    Current, Answer : CARDINAL;
37
38      BEGIN
39      LOOP
40         Current := 1; Answer := 0;
41         REPEAT  (*  Form the random number a bit at a time  *)
42            IF RandomThree () = 1
43              THEN Answer := Answer + Current
44            END;
45            Current := 2 * Current
46         UNTIL Current > V;
47         IF Answer < V THEN  RETURN Answer  END
48      END  (*  If the number was too big, try again  *)
49      END CardRandom;
```

Figure 8-3   A Random Number Generator

number generator is a valuable tool in the solution of other discrete simulation problems and should be convenient to use and readily available.

Figure 8-4 presents a complete program module for simulating interviews with large numbers of people to estimate solutions to the Birthday Problem. A large portion of this program supports the random number generator, specifically, the constant BOUND, the ARRAY OF CARDINAL Seed, and three procedures. Someone unfamiliar with either the

```
1  MODULE BirthdayProblem;
2
3  FROM InOut      IMPORT WriteCard, WriteString, WriteLn, ReadCard;
4  FROM RealInOut IMPORT WriteReal;
5  FROM MathLib0  IMPORT real;
6
7  CONST  Bound = 21845;  (*  Used by RandomThree  *)
8
9  VAR    Seed : ARRAY [ 1 .. 2 ] OF CARDINAL;
10         Group, Number, I : CARDINAL;
11
12 PROCEDURE RandomThree (): CARDINAL;  (* Returns a bit (0 or 1) *)
13
14     VAR    Product, Carry, I : CARDINAL;
15
16     BEGIN
17     LOOP
18        Carry := 0;
19        FOR I := 1 TO 2 DO
20           Seed [I] := Seed [I] + Carry;
21           Product   := 3 * Seed [I];
22           Carry     := Product DIV Bound;
23           Seed [I] := Product MOD Bound
24        END;
25        CASE Carry OF                (*  Return a zero or one  *)
26           0 : RETURN 0 !
27           1 : RETURN 1
28          ELSE                (* Or loop around and try again *)
29        END
30     END
31     END RandomThree;
32
33 PROCEDURE InitSeed ( V1, V2 : CARDINAL );
34
35     BEGIN (*  Make sure the seeds are within the bound  *)
36     Seed [1] := V1 MOD Bound;
37     Seed [2] := V2 MOD Bound
38     END InitSeed;
39
40 PROCEDURE CardRandom ( V : CARDINAL ) : CARDINAL;
41                                   (* V <= 32768 *)
42     VAR    Current, Answer : CARDINAL;
```

```
43
44    BEGIN
45    LOOP
46       Current := 1; Answer := 0;
47       REPEAT  (*  Form the random number a bit at a time  *)
48          IF RandomThree () = 1
49             THEN Answer := Answer + Current
50          END;
51          Current := 2 * Current
52       UNTIL Current > V;
53       IF Answer < V THEN  RETURN Answer  END
54    END           (*  If the number was too big, try again  *)
55    END CardRandom;
56
57 PROCEDURE BirthdaySimulation (Group, Number : CARDINAL) : REAL;
58
59    VAR    Bday     : ARRAY [ 1 .. 365 ] OF BOOLEAN;
60           Interview, I, SuccessCount, Day : CARDINAL;
61           Success : BOOLEAN;
62
63    BEGIN
64    SuccessCount := 0;
65    FOR Interview := 1 TO Number DO
66       FOR I := 1 TO 365 DO  Bday [I] := FALSE  END;
67       Success := FALSE;
68       FOR I := 1 TO Group DO
69          Day := CardRandom (365) + 1;  (* One person's birthday *)
70          IF Bday [Day] (* If this birthday was recorded then     *)
71             THEN Success := TRUE (* this is a common birthday    *)
72             ELSE Bday [Day] := TRUE
73          END
74       END;
75       IF Success THEN  INC (SuccessCount)  END
76    END;
77    RETURN real (SuccessCount) / real (Number)
78    END BirthdaySimulation;
79
80 BEGIN
81 InitSeed ( 5AE3H, 4E7FH ); (* Initialize the Random Number Seed *)
82 FOR I := 1 TO 4 DO
83    WriteString ('Enter Number: ');     ReadCard (Group);  WriteLn;
84    WriteString ('How Many Groups? '); ReadCard (Number); WriteLn;
85    WriteString ('Probability ');
86    WriteReal (BirthdaySimulation (Group, Number),15);
87    WriteLn;  WriteLn
88 END
89 END BirthdayProblem.
```

Figure 8-4   Program Module BirthdayProblem

Birthday Problem or the construction of the random number generator will find it difficult to distinguish the roles played by identifiers used to solve the Birthday Problem from those supporting the random number generator.

Methods of logically partitioning this program into either a local module or a library module are discussed in Sections 8:2 and 8:3, respectively. Modules may play an important role in the design and maintenance of large programming systems. For example, having a module that contains the random number generator and its support may be useful when writing discrete simulation programs. The module hides the details of generating random numbers and allows the programmer to concentrate on the simulation. Modules also provide programmers with the necessary tools for creating hierarchies of modules, on which large programming systems are economically built and maintained.

Exercises

1. Write and test a program to approximate the area under a curve using one of the methods learned in calculus. Evaluate which components in the solution are dependent upon the function being used and which components are dependent upon simply finding an area, in general.

2. Write and test a program to solve a set of n linear equations in n unknowns. Evaluate your solution and separate those parts of the solution that are related to the specific set of equations under consideration from those parts that are concerned with working with equations, in general.

3. Write and test a program that reads in a collection of student grades, stores them in an array, and computes their mean, median, mode, variance, and standard deviation. Properly implement each statistical calculation as a procedure.

8:2 Local Modules

The program module given as a solution to the Birthday Problem in Figure 8-4 is essentially a program containing the solution of a nontrivial subproblem, the generation of random numbers. Since the implementation details associated with this random number generator may be irrelevant to someone interested only in the program, the random number generator should be separated from the remainder of the program. Modula-2 provides two methods of carrying out this separation: library mod-

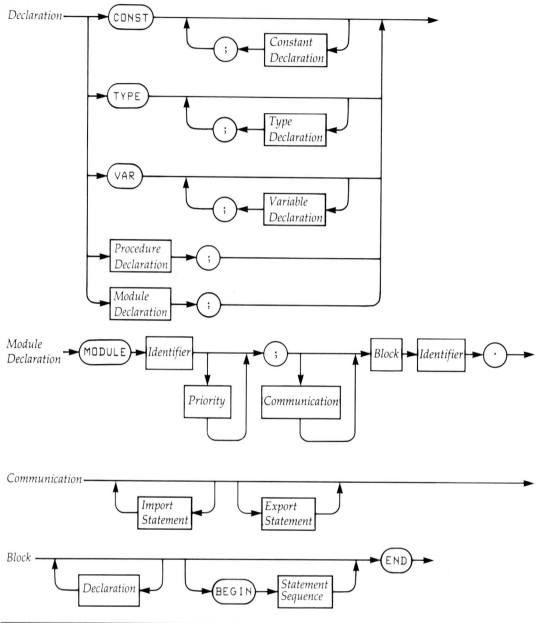

Figure 8-5   Syntax Diagrams for *Module Declaration*

ules and local modules. With local modules the separation is logical, whereas with library modules a more complete physical separation is obtained. A local module is still physically part of the program module that uses it, but its declaration logically separates it from the rest of the program.

The syntax diagrams in Figure 8-5 define the syntax for a local module. Note that the declaration of a local module appears as part of another module's declarations, thus creating an internal hierarchy.

A local module may contain its own identifiers, which represent constants, types, variables, procedures, and even other local modules. Additionally, it may include an optional *Statement Sequence*. The *Export Statement* of the module specifies those identifiers that may be referenced outside of the module. The local module's *Statement Sequence* is performed as an initialization before the program module begins execution. In this way the local module can guarantee its own initialization.

Figure 8-6 presents a program module skeleton containing two local modules. Note that the program module does not require an *Import Statement* for the identifiers imported from its local module. However, if one local module uses an identifier exported by another local module, then the identifier must be imported by the second local module. For example, the identifiers a and y are visible in the Program Module MainProgram,

```
MODULE   MainProgram;
MODULE Alpha;
         EXPORT a, b, c, d;
         IMPORT z;
         (*  a, b, c, d defined as identifiers *)

         (*  Access to a, b, c, d, and z        *)
END Alpha;

MODULE Beta;
         EXPORT x, y, z;
         IMPORT a, c;
         (*  x, y, z defined here               *)

         (* Access to a, c, x, y, and z here    *)


END Beta;

(*  Access to a, b, c, d, x, y, and z here *)


END MainProgram.
```

Figure 8-6   Example of Local Modules

but a must be imported from Alpha by Beta and y must be imported from Beta by Alpha.

To illustrate a use of local modules, Figure 8-7 contains a Birthday Problem simulation constructed with the random number generator declared in a local module. The local module partitions the program module into two major parts: (1) the program module containing the Birthday Problem simulator and (2) the local module containing the random number generator and its supporting identifiers. Only those identifiers that might be accessed, CardRandom and InitSeed, are exported from the local module. The constant Bound and the array Seed are **hidden** within the local module.

```
 1 MODULE BirthdayProblem2;
 2
 3 FROM InOut      IMPORT WriteString, WriteLn, ReadCard;
 4 FROM RealInOut IMPORT WriteReal;
 5 FROM MathLib0  IMPORT real;
 6
 7 VAR    Group, Number, I : CARDINAL;
 8
 9 (* -----------------------------------------------------------------*)
10 MODULE Random;
11
12    EXPORT  CardRandom, InitSeed;
13
14    CONST  Bound = 21845;  (*  Used by RandomThree  *)
15
16    VAR    Seed : ARRAY [ 1 .. 2 ] OF CARDINAL;
17
18    PROCEDURE RandomThree () : CARDINAL;
19                                 (* Returns a bit (0 or 1) *)
20       VAR    Product, Carry, I : CARDINAL;
21
22       BEGIN
23       LOOP
24          Carry := 0;
25          FOR I := 1 TO 2 DO
26             Seed [I] := Seed [I] + Carry;
27             Product := 3 * Seed [I];
28             Carry := Product DIV Bound;
29             Seed [I] := Product MOD Bound
30          END;
31          CASE Carry OF              (*  Return a zero or one  *)
32             0 : RETURN 0 ;
33             1 : RETURN 1
34           ELSE               (* Or loop around and try again  *)
35          END
36       END
```

```
37          END RandomThree;
38
39      PROCEDURE InitSeed ( V1, V2 : CARDINAL );
40
41          BEGIN      (*  Make sure the seeds are within the bound  *)
42          Seed [1] := V1 MOD Bound;
43          Seed [2] := V2 MOD Bound
44          END InitSeed;
45
46      PROCEDURE CardRandom ( V : CARDINAL ) : CARDINAL;
47                                            (* V <= 32768 *)
48          VAR    Current, Answer : CARDINAL;
49
50          BEGIN
51          LOOP
52            Current := 1; Answer := 0;
53            REPEAT  (*  Form the random number a bit at a time  *)
54              IF RandomThree () = 1 THEN
55                  Answer := Answer + Current
56              END;
57              Current := 2 * Current
58            UNTIL Current > V;
59            IF Answer < V THEN  RETURN Answer  END
60          END          (*  If the number was too big, try again  *)
61          END CardRandom;
62
63      BEGIN  (*  Initialize local module  *)
64      InitSeed ( 5AE3H, 4E7FH )
65
66      END Random;
67  (* -------------------------------------------------------------*)
68
69  PROCEDURE BirthdaySimulation (Group, Number : CARDINAL): REAL;
70
71      VAR    Bday    : ARRAY [ 1 .. 365 ] OF BOOLEAN;
72             Interview, I, SuccessCount, Day : CARDINAL;
73             Success : BOOLEAN;
74
75      BEGIN
76      SuccessCount := 0;
77      FOR Interview := 1 TO Number DO
78         FOR I := 1 TO 365 DO  Bday [I] := FALSE  END;
79         Success := FALSE;
80         FOR I := 1 TO Group DO
81            Day := CardRandom (365) + 1; (* One person's birthday  *)
82            IF Bday [Day]   (*  If this birthday was recorded then *)
83              THEN Success := TRUE   (* this is a common birthday  *)
84              ELSE Bday [Day] := TRUE
85            END
```

```
86          END;
87          IF Success THEN   INC (SuccessCount);   END
88       END;
89       RETURN real (SuccessCount) / real (Number)
90       END BirthdaySimulation;
91
92 BEGIN  (*  Birthday Problem  *)
93 FOR I := 1 TO 4 DO
94     WriteString ('Enter Number: ');    ReadCard (Group);   WriteLn;
95     WriteString ('How Many Groups? '); ReadCard (Number);  WriteLn;
96     WriteString ('Probability ');
97     WriteReal (BirthdaySimulation (Group, Number),15);
98     WriteLn;  WriteLn
99 END
100 END BirthdayProblem2.
```

Figure 8-7   Using the Local Module Random

Typically, creating a local module is the first step toward creating a library module. That is, in creating a local module, we isolate the contents of the module. The next step is described in Section 8:3.

Exercises

1. Rewrite one of the exercise problems at the end of Section 8:1 using a local module to separate and logically hide details.

2. Write and test a program module containing the local module Math-Lib1, which defines the hyperbolic and inverse hyperbolic functions.

3. Write and test a program module containing the local module Poly-Support. This module should support polynomials as a distinct data type and define procedures to perform polynomial arithmetic, integration, and differentiation. Refer to Exercise 6 in Section 5:1.

8:3 Library Modules

Library modules provide Modula-2 programmers with an external hierarchical structure of modules. Program modules are at the highest level of the hierarchy. They may import identifiers from library modules. Library modules export identifiers to higher-level modules and may import identifiers from lower-level library modules. Creating a library module re-

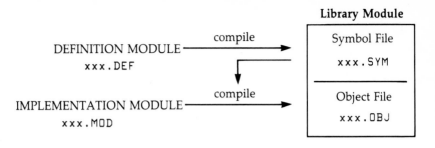

Figure 8-8   Forming a Library Module

quires the writing of two *Compilation Unit*s: a *Definition Module* and an *Implementation Module*. Normally, these files have the same file name but with different extensions. For example, ".DEF" may be used for *Definition Module*s and ".MOD" for *Implementation Module*s.

Each library module, once successfully compiled, is composed of two components: a symbol file and an object file. The symbol file, the result of compiling a *Definition Module*, contains necessary information about the identifiers exported by the module. When other modules access a library module during compilation, the language translator accesses the symbol file to obtain information about the identifiers exported by the library module. The object file, obtained by compiling an *Implementation Module*, contains the executable representation of the module.

The *Definition Module* is compiled first and produces a symbol file. With many systems the symbol file has the same file name as the *Definition Module* but with a different extension, such as ".SYM". The *Implementation Module* is then compiled to produce an object file. The object file usually has the same file name as the *Implementation Module* but with the file extension ".OBJ". Together the symbol and object files form a library module. Figure 8-8 illustrates the relationships between a *Definition Module* and an *Implementation Module* in forming a library module.

8:3:1 Definition Modules

Figure 8-9 presents the syntax diagrams that describe the structure of a *Definition Module*. The original definition of Modula-2 requires the use of *Export Statement*s in *Definition Module*s. *Export Statement*s specify the Identifiers made available by the module. In this statement an important option is the reserved word QUALIFIED. Although the use of QUALIFIED is optional, in normal practice it should always be used when creating modules.

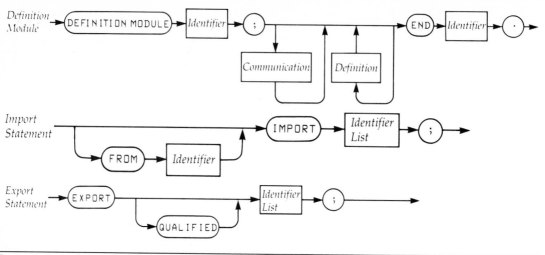

Figure 8-9   Syntax Diagrams for *Definition Module*

The reserved word QUALIFIED plays the following role: Suppose a programmer wishes to use two modules, A and B, and both modules contain an identifier X. That is, the program contains the statements

```
FROM A IMPORT X;
FROM B IMPORT X;
```

Furthermore, assume that both identifiers X are of the same type; hence Modula-2 cannot distinguish between them. Use of the reserved word QUALIFIED signifies that each of the identifiers may be accessed with its name qualified by the name of the module that exported it. For example, the two identifiers X are distinguished by accessing them as the qualified identifiers A.X and B.X. In fact, even if it is unnecessary to qualify the name of an identifier, as long as that identifier was exported QUALIFIED, the identifier can be accessed either with or without qualification.

In the original definition of Modula-2, exporting was necessary to specify those identifiers that may be imported by other modules. Exporting is unnecessary on newer Modula-2 implementations, because all identifiers declared in a definition module are implicitly exported. With the revised definition of Modula-2, all identifiers declared within a definition module are assumed to be exported and may be referenced either with or without qualification. This revision simplifies the exporting process, especially from complex modules. However, we recommend that users of new versions of Modula-2 consider placing a comment, where the export statement would have been, containing the names of the exported items.

```
 1 DEFINITION MODULE Random;
 2
 3 EXPORT QUALIFIED CardRandom, InitSeed;
 4
 5 PROCEDURE InitSeed ( V1, V2 : CARDINAL );
 6    (*  Transmit two cardinal numbers that seed the random number
 7     *  generator
 8     *  NOTE:  Both numbers should be odd and larger than 10000
 9     *)
10
11 PROCEDURE CardRandom ( V : CARDINAL ): CARDINAL;
12    (*  V must be <= 32768
13     *  Returns  0 <= CardRandom < V
14     *)
15
16 END Random.
```

Figure 8-10   Definition Module Random

Figure 8-10 presents the definition module for the library module Random, containing the random number generator used to solve the Birthday Problem presented earlier in this chapter. This definition module contains an *Export Statement* specifying those identifiers being exported. Note that the identifiers RandomThree, Bound, and Seed do not appear in the definition module because the details of their use are hidden within the corresponding implementation module. Optionally included in the definition module are comments. Comments are an important part of making a library module useful. They should provide sufficient information to assist users of the module.

As stated in Section 8:2, an important capability provided through modules is data abstraction. Data abstraction is accomplished by first declaring the type as an identifier in the definition module, without describing the structure of the type,

        TYPE AnIdentifier;

and then placing the description of the type,

        TYPE AnIdentifier = ... ;

in the corresponding implementation module. This technique effectively hides the structural details of the type from users of the module. A type declared in this way is often referred to as a **hidden type**. This concept is pursued in more detail in Section 8:4.

8:3:2 Implementation Modules

Finally, the details of a library module appear in its implementation module. Normally, a user of a module does not look at the implementation module. It hides the details. Typically, a user need only look at the definition module for information about the roles of the identifiers available through the module. When creating a module, the developer must first create and compile the definition module, which describes the identifiers exported by the library module. Then the corresponding implementation module is compiled.

Creating an *Implementation Module* is easy if the module was first created as a local module. Extract the local module from the program module to form a separate *Compilation Unit* with the reserved word IMPLEMENTATION placed before the word MODULE. From this *Compilation Unit* remove the declarations of any constants, types, or variables that are exported by the library module being created. These constants, types, and variables are declared in the corresponding *Definition Module*.

Figure 8-11 contains the implementation module for the Library Module Random, whose definition module appears in Figure 8-10. Since the library module imports no constants, identifiers, or variables, the implementation module is a clone of the local module presented in Figure 8-7.

```
1  IMPLEMENTATION MODULE Random;
2
3  CONST   Bound = 21845;   (*  Used by RandomThree  *)
4
5  VAR     Seed : ARRAY [ 1 .. 2 ] OF CARDINAL;
6
7  PROCEDURE RandomThree (): CARDINAL;   (* Returns a bit (0 or 1) *)
8
9      VAR     Product, Carry, I : CARDINAL;
10
11     BEGIN
12     LOOP
13        Carry := 0;
14        FOR I := 1 TO 2 DO
15           Seed [I] := Seed [I] + Carry;
16           Product   := 3 * Seed [I];
17           Carry     := Product DIV Bound;
18           Seed [I] := Product MOD Bound
19        END;
20        CASE Carry OF                        (*  Return a zero or one  *)
21           0 : RETURN 0 !
22           1 : RETURN 1
23          ELSE                               (* Or loop around and try again  *)
```

```
24          END
25      END
26      END RandomThree;
27
28  PROCEDURE InitSeed ( V1, V2 : CARDINAL );
29
30      BEGIN            (*  Make sure the seeds are within the bound  *)
31      Seed [1] := V1 MOD Bound;
32      Seed [2] := V2 MOD Bound
33      END InitSeed;
34
35  PROCEDURE CardRandom ( V : CARDINAL ): CARDINAL;   (* V <= 32768 *)
36
37      VAR    Current, Answer : CARDINAL;
38
39      BEGIN
40      LOOP
41         Current := 1;
42         Answer  := 0;
43         REPEAT     (*  Form the random number a bit at a time  *)
44            IF RandomThree () = 1
45              THEN Answer := Answer + Current
46            END;
47            Current := 2 * Current
48         UNTIL Current > V;
49         IF Answer < V THEN  RETURN Answer   END
50      END                (*  If the number was too big, try again  *)
51      END CardRandom;
52
53  BEGIN
54  InitSeed ( 5AE3H, 4E7FH )
55  END Random.
```

Figure 8-11   Implementation Module Random

A library module is created by first compiling the definition module and then compiling the corresponding implementation module. This library module may then be used by any other library module or program module that is compiled **after** the library module was created. The Birthday Problem solution can now be simulated with the program module that appears in Figure 8-12. This program module contains none of the details of the random number generator; it simply imports the identifier it needs, CardRandom, from the Library Module Random. With the details of the implementation of the random number generator hidden in this library module, the program module now describes only the simulation and not the random number generator. This arrangement makes it easier to verify the correctness of the simulation, assuming the random number

```
 1 MODULE BirthdayProblem3;
 2
 3 FROM InOut     IMPORT WriteString, WriteLn, ReadCard;
 4 FROM RealInOut IMPORT WriteReal;
 5 FROM MathLib0  IMPORT real;
 6 FROM Random    IMPORT CardRandom;
 7
 8 VAR    Group, Number, I : CARDINAL;
 9
10 PROCEDURE BirthdaySimulation (Group, Number : CARDINAL): REAL;11
12    VAR    Bday     : ARRAY [ 1 .. 365 ] OF BOOLEAN;
13           Interview, I, SuccessCount, Day : CARDINAL;
14           Success : BOOLEAN;
15
16    BEGIN
17    SuccessCount := 0;
18    FOR Interview := 1 TO Number DO
19       FOR I := 1 TO 365 DO
20          Bday [I] := FALSE
21       END;
22       Success := FALSE;
23       FOR I := 1 TO Group DO
24          Day := CardRandom (365) + 1; (* One person's birthday  *)
25          IF Bday [Day]   (*  If this birthday was recorded then *)
26             THEN Success    := TRUE (* this is a common birthday *)
27             ELSE Bday [Day] := TRUE
28          END
29       END;
30       IF Success THEN  INC (SuccessCount)  END
31    END;
32    RETURN real (SuccessCount) / real (Number)
33    END BirthdaySimulation;
34
35 BEGIN  (*  Birthday Problem  *)
36 FOR I := 1 TO 4 DO
37    WriteString ('Enter Number: ');    ReadCard (Group);   WriteLn;
38    WriteString ('How Many Groups? '); ReadCard (Number);  WriteLn;
39    WriteString ('Probability ');
40    WriteReal (BirthdaySimulation (Group, Number),15);
41    WriteLn;  WriteLn
42 END
43
44 END BirthdayProblem3.
```

Figure 8-12   Using the Library Module Random

generator is correct. Verifying the correctness of the random number generator would be a separate task, independent of the Birthday Problem.

There is one final observation concerning the Library Module Random. Note that the procedure InitSeed, exported from Random, is referenced in Random's initializing statement sequence. This reference provides the module with its own initialization, a default set of seeds. However, because InitSeed is exported, any user of Random may reinitialize the random number generator with different seeds and hence generate different random sequences.

8:4 Data Abstraction

Formally, an abstract data type is a data type along with a collection of operations that may be performed on objects of that type. Modula-2 is a programming language that allows for the effective declaration of abstract data types, primarily because of its facilities for the declaration of procedures, modules, and hidden types. Data abstraction involves the hiding of representational details of a data type. In Modula-2, abstraction is accomplished with library modules by hiding the details of a data type in the implementation module and exporting only the identifier declared as a hidden type, without any detail, in the definition module.

The following example should clarify this concept. Consider the procedures, developed in Section 6:5, that manipulate strings of characters. Users of these procedures do not have to be aware of the structure used to store strings. In fact, that knowledge could be harmful. A programmer with incomplete knowledge about how strings are represented and manipulated by these procedures could misuse the procedures. For example, these string-handling procedures store a count of the number of characters in the string in position 0 of the array in which the string is stored. If a user were not aware of this representation and bypassed the string initialization procedures, in particular STRFromCHARs, these string manipulation procedures could produce unpredictable results.

As this example shows, data abstraction is desirable. If the string-manipulating procedures were collected together to form a library module, then its definition module might appear as shown in Figure 8-13. Note that the type declaration,

    TYPE STR255;

hides the details of its structure, and the comment warns users that this structure must be used. The implementation module contains the declaration

$$\text{TYPE STR255 = ARRAY [0 .. 255] OF CHAR;}$$

which specifies the structure used to store strings.

```
 1 DEFINITION MODULE STRing;
 2
 3 FROM InOut IMPORT EOL, Read, Write;
 4
 5 EXPORT QUALIFIED
 6         STR255, STRXception, STRRead, STRWrite, STRFromCHARs,
 7         STRNull, STRCopy, STRConCat, STRLength,
 8         STRInsert, STRDelete, STRFindSub, STREqual, STRLess;
 9
10 CONST MaxSTRSize = 255;
11
12 TYPE  STR255;
13       (*  These procedures process character strings
14        *  containing 255 or fewer characters stored in a
15        *  special format. These structures must be used.
16        *)
17
18 VAR STRXception : BOOLEAN;
19     (*  STRXception is set as a side effect of all of the string
20      *  procedures
21      *     = FALSE, means the last procedure performed correctly
22      *               without any exception handling
23      *     = TRUE, means an exception was handled
24      *)
25
26 PROCEDURE STRNull ( VAR A : ARRAY OF CHAR );
27    (* But an empty string in the array A
28     * STRXception := FALSE
29     *)
30
31 PROCEDURE STRRead ( VAR A : ARRAY OF CHAR );
32    (* Read until a systems terminator or the array is filled
33     * Exception := TRUE if attempting to read more than
34                       255 characters *)
35
36 PROCEDURE STRFromCHARs ( VAR A : ARRAY OF CHAR;
37                              B : ARRAY OF CHAR;  Number : CARDINAL );
38    (* Convert an ARRAY OF CHARs to string format
39     * STRXception := TRUE if HIGH (A) > 255 or A too small for B
40     *)
41
42 PROCEDURE STRWrite ( VAR A : ARRAY OF CHAR );
43    (* Write string to output
44     * STRXception := FALSE
```

```
45     *)
46
47 PROCEDURE STRLength ( VAR A : ARRAY OF CHAR ): CARDINAL;
48    (*   Returns length of string
49    *   STRXception := FALSE
50    *)
51
52 PROCEDURE STRCopy ( VAR A, B : ARRAY OF CHAR );
53    (* Copy string from B to A
54    * STRXception := TRUE if A not large enough
55    *)
56
57 PROCEDURE STRConCat ( VAR A, B : ARRAY OF CHAR );
58    (* Attach the string in B onto A
59    * STRXception := TRUE if A not large enough
60    *)
61
62 PROCEDURE STRInsert ( VAR A, B : ARRAY OF CHAR;
63                                     Position : CARDINAL );
64    (*   Insert the string in B at the indicated Position in A
65    *   STRXception := TRUE if A not large enough
66    *)
67
68 PROCEDURE STRDelete ( VAR A : ARRAY OF CHAR;
69                                  Location, Size : CARDINAL );
70    (*   Delete the indicated piece from the string in A
71    *   STRXception := TRUE if attempt to delete more than is there
72    *)
73
74 PROCEDURE STRFindSub ( VAR A, B : ARRAY OF CHAR ): CARDINAL;
75    (*   Return the position of the first occurrence in A of the
76    *   string in B
77    *   STRXception := TRUE if B not found
78    *)
79
80 PROCEDURE STREqual ( VAR A, B : ARRAY OF CHAR ): BOOLEAN;
81
82 PROCEDURE STRLess ( VAR A, B : ARRAY OF CHAR ): BOOLEAN;
83
84 END  STRing.
```

Figure 8-13   Definition Module STRing

The writing of the corresponding implementation module is given as an exercise. After the definition and implementation modules are properly compiled, the Library Module STRing is accessible by other modules with an IMPORT statement, as in

```
MODULE UseSTRing;

FROM STRing IMPORT
            STR255, STRXception, STRRead, STRWrite,
            STRFromCHARs, STRNull, STRCopy, STRConCat,
            STRLength, STRInsert, STRDelete, STRFindSub,
            STREqual, STRLess;

(*  Other program declarations here *)

BEGIN
(*  Note that the STRXception initialization is not here  *)
(*  It should be in the IMPLEMENTATION MODULE             *)
(*  string processing program goes here                   *)
END UseSTRing.
```

In effect, three and one-half pages of procedure definitions are com-
pressed into five lines of references to the module.

Exercises

1. Create the Implementation Module STRings.

2. Create and test the Library Module StatLib0, consisting of procedures described in Exercise 3 in Section 8:1.

3. Create and test the Library Module PolySupport, described in the exercises in Section 8:2.

9 Dynamic Data Objects

9:1 Dynamic Storage Allocation

A common characteristic of the data structures presented thus far is that they are static. That is, once defined, arrays, sets, and records have a fixed size and cannot be expanded or shrunk to dynamically meet run time space requirements. This chapter presents dynamic data objects, that is, the use of pointers, through which the data space requirements of a module are determined and satisfied at run time.

Many programs manipulate a variety of logical structures and, during program execution, require space for these structures to expand and shrink. Typical examples of the need for dynamic storage allocation are found in the implementation of lists, stacks, queues, trees, and graphs.

The key to dynamic storage allocation is pointers. A pointer is a data object that stores the address of a location in memory. Pointers are declared in Modula-2 using *Pointer Type*s, whose syntax diagram appears in Figure 9-1. Note that this syntax requires the specification of the type of variable to be pointed to, as in

```
TYPE p = POINTER TO T
```

where T is the identifier of some type. Typically, in applications involving dynamic storage allocation, the data object being pointed to is a record. Although pointers are not limited to use with records, all dynamic allocation applications illustrated here utilize records. Records may have components that are pointers that, in turn, point to other records. In this way a large number of records may be allocated and accessed during the run time of a program.

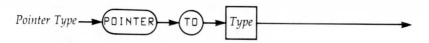

Figure 9-1   Syntax Diagram for *Pointer Type*

The standard module Storage contains the necessary support for dynamic storage allocation. The dynamically allocated memory space is referred to as the **heap**, and the module Storage manages the heap. When space is requested, either through the standard procedure NEW or the procedure ALLOCATE declared in Storage, a pointer variable is assigned the address of the space removed from the dynamic storage heap. Space is returned to the heap through either the standard procedure DISPOSE or the procedure DEALLOCATE declared by Storage.

Pointers are initialized in three ways. First, a pointer may be initialized with the reserved word NIL, as in the assignment statement

```
p := NIL;
```

The constant NIL represents a value indicating no address. Second, pointers may be initialized with the standard procedure NEW, as in the procedure call

```
NEW (p);
```

which stores in the pointer variable p the address of the memory area that has been allocated for a data object. Finally, if two pointers reference the same type, an assignment statement may be used,

```
p1 := p2
```

which results in both pointers, p1 and p2, pointing to the same object. Both variables store the address of the same memory area.

When a dynamically allocated data object is no longer required, its memory area can be returned to the storage heap with the standard procedure DISPOSE. The procedure call

```
DISPOSE (p)
```

returns the memory area pointed to by p to the heap, and p may no longer be validly used to access data unless p is reinitialized. Once dynamically allocated space is DISPOSEed, it is no longer available to the program. DISPOSE should assign the value NIL to the pointer p. Therefore any attempt to access that space after it has been disposed, or any attempt to use a pointer variable before it is properly initialized, can produce unpredictable results. When pointers are used, such attempts are responsible for many run time errors.

Any module that uses dynamic storage allocation must import the procedures ALLOCATE and DEALLOCATE from the module Storage:

```
FROM Storage  IMPORT ALLOCATE, DEALLOCATE;
```

Although the standard procedures NEW and DISPOSE perform dynamic storage allocation, they reference ALLOCATE and DEALLOCATE, respectively, to perform their tasks. This reference is necessary because the details of handling dynamic storage allocation may vary on different systems. NEW and DISPOSE provide programmers with high-level access to dynamic storage allocation, with the system dependent details hidden within the module Storage.

As an example of using dynamic allocation, consider the problem of performing complex arithmetic. Complex arithmetic may be performed with dynamically allocated records declared as

```
TYPE    Complex     = POINTER TO ComplexType;
        ComplexType = RECORD
                        Re, Im : REAL
                      END;

VAR    U, V, W, Z : Complex;
```

where U, V, W, and Z are pointer variables. The procedure call

```
NEW (Z);
```

dynamically allocates a record of type ComplexType, and Z is initialized as a pointer to that record.

Dynamically allocated objects are initialized and accessed through the **dereferencing operator**, which is indicated in Modula-2 by the carat symbol, "^". The use of the carat symbol, or some equivalent symbol, depends upon the collection of printable characters on a particular computer system. These characters may vary from one implementation to another. As an example of the use of the dereferencing operator, consider the variable Z declared and initialized above. The following statements are true:

1. Z is a pointer to a data object of type ComplexType.

2. Z^ (pronounced "Z dereferenced" or "Z points to") is the record of type ComplexType pointed to by the pointer stored in Z.

3. Z^.Re is the component Re in the record pointed to by Z, and Z^.Im is the component Im in that same record. Both Z^.Re and Z^.Im are of type REAL.

With these declarations two real numbers may be read from the current input device to initialize the real and imaginary parts of a complex number with the statements

```
ReadReal (Z^.Re);   ReadReal (Z^.Im)
```

The statements

```
NEW (Y);
Y^.Re := Z^.Re;
Y^.Im := Z^.Im
```

allocate and initialize a copy of the complex number pointed to by Z. Z^.Re and Z^.Im may appear in any Modula-2 statement where an identifier of type REAL appears. The reason for this fact should be clear from Item 3 in the preceding list: Z^.Re and Z^.Im identify data objects of type REAL. The syntax may appear a bit complicated. To clarify it, Z^ identifies a record, and .Re identifies a component; thus Z^.Re identifies the component Re in the record pointed to by Z. For example, the procedure call

```
sqrt (Z^.Re * Z^.Re  +  Z^.Im * Z^.Im)
```

computes the magnitude of the complex number stored in the record Z^.

In addition to its uses described in subsequent sections of this chapter, dynamic storage allocation overcomes a limitation of function procedures. Specifically, functions cannot return structured data values. That is, the value of a function cannot be an array, record, or set. On the surface this limitation looks severe. For example, if a programmer wishes to write a collection of procedures to support complex arithmetic using records of type ComplexType, these procedures could not be implemented directly as functions. Fortunately, functions can return pointer values; therefore pointers overcome this apparent limitation. The use of pointers is illustrated in the procedures declared in the library module ComplexArithmetic, presented in Figures 9-2 and 9-3.

Each function presented in the library module ComplexArithmetic bypasses the limitations on returning records by dynamically allocating a record, placing the mathematical result in a record, and returning the pointer to that record as the function's value. As a result complex arithmetic, implemented by this library module, may be performed in a fairly

```
1   DEFINITION MODULE ComplexArithmetic;
2
3   TYPE    Complex      = POINTER TO ComplexType;
4           ComplexType = RECORD
5                             Re, Im : REAL
6                         END;
7
8   PROCEDURE Initialize ( RealPart, ImaginaryPart : REAL ): Complex;
9
10  PROCEDURE ReadComplex ( Z : Complex );
11
12  PROCEDURE WriteComplex ( Z : Complex; n : CARDINAL );
13
14  PROCEDURE Add ( W, Z : Complex ) : Complex;
15
16  PROCEDURE Subtract ( W, Z : Complex ) : Complex;
17
18  PROCEDURE Multiply ( W, Z : Complex ) : Complex;
19
20  PROCEDURE Magnitude ( Z : Complex ) : REAL;
21
22  PROCEDURE Divide (W, Z : Complex ) : Complex;
23
24  END ComplexArithmetic.
```

Figure 9-2   Definition Module ComplexArithmetic

```
1   IMPLEMENTATION MODULE ComplexArithmetic;
2
3   FROM InOut      IMPORT Write, WriteString, WriteLn, Done;
4   FROM RealInOut IMPORT ReadReal, WriteReal;
5   FROM MathLib0  IMPORT sqrt;
6   FROM Storage   IMPORT ALLOCATE, DEALLOCATE;
7
8   PROCEDURE Initialize ( RealPart, ImaginaryPart : REAL ): Complex;
9
10     VAR    Temp : Complex;
11
12     BEGIN
13     NEW (Temp);
14     Temp^.Re := RealPart;
15     Temp^.Im := ImaginaryPart;
16     RETURN Temp
17     END Initialize;
18
19  PROCEDURE ReadComplex ( Z : Complex );
20
```

```
21        BEGIN
22        ReadReal (Z^.Re);
23        ReadReal (Z^.Im)
24        END ReadComplex;
25
26    PROCEDURE WriteComplex ( Z : Complex; n : CARDINAL );
27
28        BEGIN
29        WriteReal (Z^.Re, n );
30        IF Z^.Im < 0.0 THEN
31            Write (' ')
32          ELSE
33            WriteString (' +')
34        END;
35        WriteReal (Z^.Im, n);
36        WriteString ('I ')
37        END WriteComplex;
38
39    PROCEDURE Add ( W, Z : Complex ) : Complex;
40
41        VAR    Temp : Complex;
42
43        BEGIN
44        NEW (Temp);
45        Temp^.Re := W^.Re + Z^.Im;
46        Temp^.Im := W^.Im + Z^.Im;
47        RETURN Temp
48        END Add;
49
50    PROCEDURE Subtract ( W, Z : Complex ) : Complex;
51
52        VAR    Temp : Complex;
53
54        BEGIN
55        NEW (Temp);
56        Temp^.Re := W^.Re - Z^.Im;
57        Temp^.Im := W^.Im - Z^.Im;
58        RETURN Temp
59        END Subtract;
60
61    PROCEDURE Multiply ( W, Z : Complex ) : Complex;
62
63        VAR    Temp : Complex;
64
65        BEGIN
66        NEW (Temp);
67        Temp^.Re := W^.Re * Z^.Re - W^.Im * Z^.Im;
68        Temp^.Im := W^.Re * Z^.Im + W^.Im * Z^.Re;
```

```
69        RETURN Temp
70        END Multiply;
71
72    PROCEDURE Magnitude ( Z : Complex ) : REAL;
73
74        BEGIN
75        RETURN sqrt (Z^.Re * Z^.Re + Z^.Im * Z^.Im)
76        END Magnitude;
77
78    PROCEDURE Divide (W, Z : Complex ) : Complex;
79
80        VAR    Temp : Complex;
81               MagZ : REAL;
82
83        BEGIN
84        MagZ := Z^.Re * Z^.Re - Z^.Im * Z^.Im;
85        Temp^.Re := ( W^.Re * Z^.Re + W^.Im * Z^.Im) / MagZ;
86        Temp^.Im := ( W^.Re * Z^.Im - W^.Im * Z^.Re) / MagZ;
87        RETURN Temp
88        END Divide;
89
90    END ComplexArithmetic.
```

Figure 9-3   Implementation Module ComplexArithmetic

natural way with statements of the form

```
VAR    U, V, W, Z : Complex;

ReadComplex (U);   ReadComplex (V);
Z := Add (U, V);
WriteComplex (Z, 13);
```

It would be shortsighted not to note a problem with the approach suggested by the library module ComplexArithmetic presented in Figures 9-2 and 9-3. Since each call to one of these complex arithmetic functions allocates a record, a substantial number of calls could use up all of the available heap space. This situation could occur quite easily within a loop. This problem is not insurmountable, however, although its solution is a bit inconvenient. If space is a problem, the programmer would have to keep track of the pointers that have been initialized and dispose of the dynamically allocated ComplexType records before the pointers are reinitialized. For example, in a loop the single statement

```
Z := Multiply (U, V)
```

might be replaced by the statement sequence

```
DISPOSE (Z);
Z := Multiply (U, V)
```

which first deallocates the previous record pointed to by Z, then calls the function Multiply, which allocates a new dynamic data object. Thus the record pointed to by Z is returned to the heap before Z is reinitialized with a pointer to the record containing the result of the multiplication. We must take care in doing this manipulation, since not all calls to these arithmetic functions reinitialize pointers. Calls to DISPOSE must be carefully placed in a program so that the desired records are properly deallocated.

Exercises

1. Write a function procedure that tests to see if two complex numbers are almost equal. Develop

```
PROCEDURE AlmostEqual ( W, Z: Complex, Epsilon: REAL ) : BOOLEAN
```

where ¦Z¦ = Magnitude (Z) and

```
AlmostEqual = TRUE if ¦Z¦ < Epsilon and ¦W-Z¦ < Epsilon
            = TRUE if ¦Z¦ >= Epsilon and ¦W-Z¦/¦Z¦ < Epsilon
            = FALSE otherwise
```

2. Add the

```
PROCEDURE Copy (Z : Complex) : Complex;
```

to the library module ComplexArithmetic. What is the difference between the statement W := Z and the statement

```
W := Copy(Z)?
```

9:2 Lists

A list is a dynamic data structure similar to an array in some ways, but quite different in others. A list, like an array, is a sequential collection of data. However, unlike an array, whose elements are accessed directly

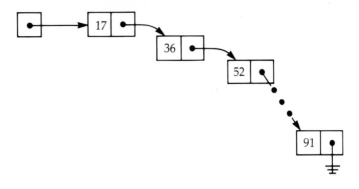

Figure 9-4 Illustration of a One-Way Grounded List

with subscripts, the elements in a list are accessed sequentially using pointers.

Each element in a list is represented as a record. The record must contain at least one pointer component. The pointers provide the sequential access to the list's elements. In the simplest form of a list, a one-way grounded list, each record contains a pointer that provides access to the next record in the list. The pointer in the last record contains the constant value NIL to indicate that no record follows.

A separate data object, a pointer, is kept to provide access to the first element in the list. This data object may be a distinct variable or part of another structure. Figure 9-4 illustrates an example of a one-way grounded list.

The primary difference between an array and a list is that array elements are stored physically adjacent to each other in the computer's memory. In a list, elements are logically adjacent to each other. The fact that array elements are stored in memory physically adjacent to each other means that a subscript may be used to directly locate each element in the array. This physical adjacency allows each element to be accessed quickly and directly without searching. Physical adjacency is not the case with a list. The records in a list may be scattered throughout memory, with pointers linking them in a logically sequential fashion, as shown in Figure 9-4.

As an example of the use of lists, consider the problem of registering students for classes at a college or university. Classes are defined with each class having its own class list. Students enroll in the classes by being included in the corresponding class lists. Figure 9-5 presents the definition module StudentLists, a proposed solution to this problem.

Each StudentRecord consists of an identification number, ID, and a Name component. ID is a cardinal value and provides an easy way of dis-

```
1    DEFINITION MODULE StudentLists;
2
3    FROM STRing IMPORT STR255;      (* See Figure 8.13 *)
4
5    EXPORT QUALIFIED StudentRecord, StudentList, Status, Create,
6                 Destroy, Insert, Delete, Retrieve, Advance, Access;
7
8    TYPE    StudentRecord  = RECORD
9                             ID    : CARDINAL;
10                            Name  : STR255
11                          END;
12
13          StudentList;    (* Hidden Type *)
14
15   VAR     Status : CARDINAL;      (* Result of last procedure call *)
16                                   (*  0 = all Ok
17                                       1 = Can't Delete; not found
18                                       2 = Can't Retrieve; not found
19                                       3 = Can't Advance; end of list
20                                       4 = Can't Access; end of list *)
21
22   PROCEDURE Create ( VAR Students : StudentList );
23
24   PROCEDURE Destroy ( VAR Students : StudentList );
25
26   PROCEDURE Insert ( StudentData : StudentRecord;
27                                   VAR Students : StudentList );
28   PROCEDURE Delete ( TheKey : CARDINAL;
29                                   VAR Students : StudentList );
30   PROCEDURE Retrieve ( TheKey : CARDINAL;  Students : StudentList;
31                              VAR StudentData : StudentRecord );
32
33   PROCEDURE Advance ( Current : StudentList ) : StudentList;
34
35   PROCEDURE Access ( Current : StudentList;
36                              VAR StudentData : StudentRecord );
37   END StudentLists.
```

Figure 9-5   Definition Module StudentLists

tinguishing between students. Name is a character string of type STR255, imported from the library module STRing developed in Chapter 8. The data type StudentList, which appears without a specific definition in the definition module, is a hidden type. Hidden types are discussed in Section 8:4. StudentList's exact definition is in the corresponding implementation module. Readers of the definition module know that StudentList is the type that represents a collection of StudentRecords,

```
IMPLEMENTATION MODULE StudentLists;

FROM Storage IMPORT ALLOCATE, DEALLOCATE;

TYPE    StudentList = POINTER TO ListElement;
        ListElement = RECORD
                          Element : StudentRecord;
                          Link    : StudentList
                      END;

(*  Implementation of procedures here  *)


BEGIN
Status := 0
END StudentLists.
```

Figure 9-6   Declarations and Initialization for StudentLists

---

but do not know the exact representation of this type. Since the declared procedures provide all the operations necessary to manipulate this structure, the user does not need to know the exact representation. Thus Figure 9-6 contains the declaration of the abstract data type StudentList.

The declarations in the implementation module, shown in Figure 9-6, reveal the exact representation of StudentList. StudentList is a pointer to a ListElement. One record of type ListElement exists for each student, and elements of this type form the class list. The first component in ListElement is of type StudentRecord, which is declared in the definition module. The data type StudentList not only is the list type but also locates each ListElement. Thus in this list representation each record in the list consists of data for one student and a pointer to the sublist of the remaining students in the class. In this way the pointer to the first element may refer to the entire class list.

Of course, each class list could have been stored in an array of records, but the array approach has the following disadvantages:

1. The array would have to be declared with a fixed number of student records. Since the number of students enrolled in a class may change over time, this fixed number is usually too high or too low. When it is too high, memory is wasted because not all array positions are occupied. When it is too low, all the data cannot be stored.

2. Keeping the class list in some order usually requires that a considerable amount of data be physically moved from one position in the array to another. For example, adding a new student to an

ordered class list may require that many, possibly all, of the elements in the array be moved to free the desired position for the new student's data. Likewise, removing a student from the array requires that all elements be moved down one position in the array to avoid an empty position.

Storing this data in a list structure avoids both of these disadvantages for arrays. This does not imply that a list is always superior to an array. However, lists are advantageous in certain applications, especially those involving unknown quantities of data or frequent additions and deletions.

The process of building this list structure is not difficult. Initially, the list pointer is assigned the value NIL, indicating that the class list contains no elements. As each student's data is obtained, the procedure NEW is

```
PROCEDURE Create ( VAR Students : StudentList );

   BEGIN
   Status := 0;
   Students := NIL
   END Create;

PROCEDURE Destroy ( VAR Students : StudentList );

   VAR    Current : StudentList;

   BEGIN
   Status := 0;
   WHILE Students # NIL DO
      Current := Students;
      Students := Students^.Link;
      DISPOSE ( Current )
   END
   END Destroy;

PROCEDURE Add ( TheData : StudentRecord;
                               VAR Students : StudentList );
   VAR    Location : StudentList;

   BEGIN
   NEW ( Location );
   Location^.Element := TheData;
   Location^.Link := Students;
   Students := Location
   END Add;
```

Figure 9-7   Procedures Create, Destroy, and Add

called to dynamically allocate a ListElement. Values are assigned to the corresponding ID and Name components of this record, and the pointers are adjusted to include the record in the list. Figure 9-7 presents the procedures for creating an empty list, destroying a list, and adding elements to a list. Note that the most recent element added is the new first element in the list. Thus the list's elements are accessible in the reverse order in which they were added.

Unfortunately, the procedure Add does not order the student records based on the ID number. The component used to order a collection of data is referred to as the **key**. In this problem the component ID is the key. A separate sorting procedure is unnecessary because the procedure Insert, presented in Figure 9-8, accomplishes the sorting. This procedure differs from the procedure Add in that as each element is added to the list, a search is performed to determine the position where the element belongs; then the pointers are adjusted to insert the element. In this way the list is kept in ascending order based on the key.

```
PROCEDURE Locate ( TheKey : CARDINAL;  Students : StudentList;
                            VAR Previous, Current : StudentList );
   BEGIN
   Previous := NIL;
   Current := Students;
   WHILE ( Current # NIL ) AND  ( TheKey > Current^.Element.ID ) DO
      Previous := Current;
      Current  := Current^.Link
   END
   END Locate;

PROCEDURE Insert ( TheData : StudentRecord;
                                 VAR Students : StudentList );
   VAR    Location, Previous, Current : StudentList;

   BEGIN
   Status := 0;
   NEW ( Location );
   Location^.Element := TheData;
   Locate ( TheData.ID, Students, Previous, Current );
   Location^.Link := Current;
   IF Previous = NIL THEN
       Students := Location
     ELSE
       Previous^.Link := Location
   END
   END Insert;
```

Figure 9-8   Procedures Locate and Insert

The procedure Locate in Figure 9-8 performs the search. Specifically, this procedure initializes two pointers, the parameters Current and Previous. Current points to the first element whose key is greater than or equal to TheKey. Previous points to the list element preceding the element pointed to by Current. Previous is NIL when Current points to the first element in the list or when the list is empty.

The loop in Locate searches the list until it encounters either a NIL pointer or an element whose key is greater than or equal to the key of the new element. Locate sets two pointers. Current points to the element satisfying the search criterion. The pointer Previous points to the element preceding the element that satisfies the search criterion. After these elements are determined, a decision statement handles the special case when the new element becomes the new first element in the list. This case is special because in all other cases the Link component in the record preceding the new element is modified. Inserting elements at the beginning of the list requires that the pointer for the list itself be modified. Recursion could have also been used to search through the list, but that procedure is left as an exercise. A properly written recursive procedure overcomes the need to treat the insertion at the beginning of the list as a special case.

The problem of deleting an element from a list has a similar solution. Specifically, first a search is performed for the desired element by the procedure Locate; then the element is removed. Removing the element involves modifying the Link component of the preceding element.

```
PROCEDURE Delete ( TheKey : CARDINAL;  VAR Students : StudentList );

    VAR    Previous, Current : StudentList;

    BEGIN
    Status := 0;
    Locate ( TheKey, Students, Previous, Current );
    IF  ( Current = NIL ) OR  ( Current^.Element.ID # TheKey ) THEN
        Status := 1
      ELSE
        IF Previous = NIL THEN
            Students := Current^.Link
          ELSE
            Previous^.Link := Current^.Link
        END;
        DISPOSE ( Current )
    END
    END Delete;
```

Figure 9-9   Procedure Delete

The record removed from the list is then returned to the heap with the procedure DISPOSE. Figure 9-9 presents the procedure Delete, which accomplishes this removal.

Figure 9-10 presents the procedures Retrieve, Advance, and Access. Retrieve provides direct access to any element in the class list whose key is known. Advance and Access sequentially access the elements in a class list. Use of the procedures Advance and Access is illustrated in Figure 9-11, which contains procedures that produce a printout of the data in a class list.

```
PROCEDURE Retrieve ( TheKey : CARDINAL;  Students : StudentList;
                                      VAR StudentData : StudentRecord );

    VAR    Previous, Current : StudentList;      BEGIN
    Status := 0;
    Locate ( TheKey, Students, Previous, Current );
    IF ( Current = NIL ) OR ( Current^.Element.ID # TheKey ) THEN
        Status := 2
      ELSE
        StudentData := Current^.Element
    END
    END Retrieve;

PROCEDURE Advance ( Current : StudentList ) : StudentList;

    BEGIN
    IF Current^.Link = NIL THEN
        Status := 3
      ELSE
        Status := 0
    END;
    RETURN Current^.Link
    END Advance;

PROCEDURE Access ( Current : StudentList;
                                      VAR StudentData : StudentRecord );
    BEGIN
    IF Current = NIL THEN
        Status := 4
      ELSE
        Status := 0;
        StudentData := Current^.Element
    END
    END Access;
```

Figure 9-10   Procedures Retrieve, Advance, and Access

```
1    MODULE UseStudentLists;
2
3    FROM InOut          IMPORT Done, OpenInput, CloseInput,
4                              OpenOutput, CloseOutput,
5                              Read, ReadCard, Write,
6                              WriteCard, WriteString, WriteLn;
7
8    FROM StudentLists IMPORT StudentRecord, StudentList,
9                              Status, Create, Destroy, Insert,
10                             Delete, Retrieve, Advance, Access;
11
12   FROM STRing         IMPORT STRRead, STRWrite; (* See Figure 8.13 *)
13
14   PROCEDURE WriteHeading;
15
16      BEGIN
17      WriteString ( 'ID    Name                      ' );   WriteLn;
18      WriteString ( '----- --------------------' );   WriteLn
19      END WriteHeading;
20
21   PROCEDURE WriteStudent ( Data:StudentRecord );
22
23      CONST  Blank = ' ';
24
25      BEGIN
26      WriteCard ( Data.ID,5 );
27      Write ( Blank );
28      STRWrite ( Data.Name )
29      END WriteStudent;
30
31   PROCEDURE WriteStudents ( Students:StudentList );
32
33      VAR    Student : StudentList;
34             Data    : StudentRecord;
35
36      BEGIN
37      WriteHeading;
38      Student := Students;
39      REPEAT
40         Access ( Student,Data );
41         IF Status = 0 THEN
42            WriteStudent ( Data );
43            WriteLn;
44            Student := Advance ( Student )
45         END
46      UNTIL Status # 0;
47      Status := 0
48      END WriteStudents;
49
50   END UseStudentLists.
```

Figure 9-11   Using Procedures Advance and Access

Exercises

1. Complete the implementation module for StudentLists presented in Figure 9-6.

2. The procedure Locate given in Figure 9-8 may be written recursively instead of having a loop in its body. Rewrite this procedure using recursion, but be sure that both output parameters return their correct values in all cases.

3. Rewrite the procedure Delete recursively.

4. Using the declarations given in Figure 9-5, write the procedure

   PROCEDURE tsiL (VAR Students:StudentList);

   which reverses the elements in the given class list. Thus if we assume that the list is originally kept in ascending order, this procedure rearranges the elements so that the list is now in descending order.

5. A **two-way grounded list** is a structure in which each element contains two pointers, one to the following element and the other to the preceding element.

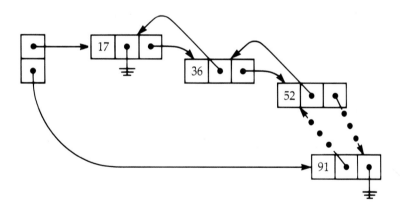

   a. Modify the implementation module StudentLists given in this section so that the class list is represented by a two-way grounded list. Which representation do you feel is more appropriate? Why?

   b. Write a procedure Retreat, similar to Advance, but which returns a pointer to the preceding record.

6. Using the declarations given in Figure 9-5 and the procedures given in Figure 9-7, write a complete library module that implements a list

structure in which elements are only added to and only removed from the beginning of the list.

9:3 Stacks

A **stack** is a sequential data structure in which elements must be added and removed from only one end, which is referred to as the **top.** Figure 9-12 illustrates a stack as a structure anchored at one end and unbounded at the other. A stack is conceptually infinite, meaning that any number of elements may be stored in the stack by placing elements on the top. Storing an element in a stack is termed the **push** operation. The new element becomes the new top of the stack. Removing an element from a stack is termed the **pop** operation. The only element that may be removed is the element currently stored at the top of the stack. Thus the first element removed from the stack is the last element that was stored.

A stack is a useful data structure because it stores data in a **last-in-first-out** fashion. The solutions to many problems require stacks. Computer systems and programming languages rely heavily upon stacks to

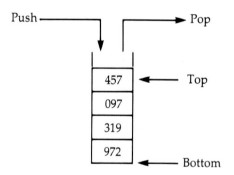

Figure 9-12   Visualization of a Stack

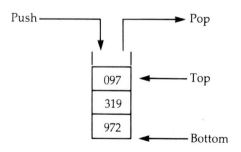

Figure 9-13   The Stack in Figure 9-12 After Several Operations

perform certain tasks. For example, recursion, which is supported by Modula-2 and several other programming languages, requires a stack to support the programming language's environment both during the translation and the execution of programs. These stacks, which are usually inaccessible to the programmer, store the return addresses, parameter addresses or values, and the local variables during procedure calls.

The stack in Figure 9-12 appears as shown in Figure 9-13 after the following operations are performed:

Push the element 200.

Pop an element.

Pop an element.

Push the element 150.

Pop an element.

Figure 9-14 contains the definition module CharStacks, which maintains a stack whose elements are character values. The variable StatusStack indicates the success or failure of each procedure call. Figure 9-15 presents the corresponding implementation module.

```
1   DEFINITION MODULE CharStacks;
2
3   EXPORT QUALIFIED StackItem, StackType, StatusStack, CreateStack,
4                    Push, Pop, EmptyStack, DestroyStack;
5
6   CONST   StackLimit = 100;
7
8   TYPE    StackItem = CHAR;
9           StackType;
10
11  VAR     StatusStack : CARDINAL; (*  0 = All Ok
12                                      1 = Can't Push; Stack Full
13                                      2 = Can't Pop ; Stack Empty *)
14
15  PROCEDURE CreateStack ( VAR Stack : StackType );
16
17  PROCEDURE Push ( Item : StackItem;  VAR Stack : StackType );
18
19  PROCEDURE Pop ( VAR Item : StackItem;  VAR Stack : StackType );
20
21  PROCEDURE EmptyStack ( Stack : StackType ) : BOOLEAN;
22
23  PROCEDURE DestroyStack ( VAR Stack : StackType )
24
25  END CharStacks.
```

Figure 9-14   Definition Module CharStacks

```
1    IMPLEMENTATION MODULE CharStacks;
2
3    FROM Storage IMPORT ALLOCATE,DEALLOCATE;
4
5    TYPE    StackType = POINTER TO StackRecord;
6            StackRecord = RECORD
7                              Top  : CARDINAL;
8                              Data : ARRAY[1..StackLimit] OF StackItem
9                          END;
10
11   PROCEDURE CreateStack ( VAR Stack : StackType );
12
13      BEGIN
14      StatusStack := 0;
15      NEW ( Stack );
16      Stack^.Top := 0
17      END CreateStack;
18
19   PROCEDURE Push ( Item : StackItem;  VAR Stack : StackType );
20
21      VAR    NewTop : CARDINAL;
22
23      BEGIN
24      NewTop := Stack^.Top + 1;
25      IF NewTop > StackLimit THEN
26          StatusStack := 1
27        ELSE
28          StatusStack := 0;
29          Stack^.Data[NewTop] := Item;
30          Stack^.Top := NewTop
31      END
32      END Push;
33
34   PROCEDURE Pop ( VAR Item : StackItem;  VAR Stack : StackType );
35
36      BEGIN
37      IF Stack^.Top = 0 THEN
38          StatusStack := 2
39        ELSE
40          StatusStack := 0;
41          Item := Stack^.Data[Stack^.Top];
42          Stack^.Top := Stack^.Top - 1
43      END
44      END Pop;
45
46   PROCEDURE EmptyStack ( Stack : StackType ) : BOOLEAN;
47
```

```
48       BEGIN
49       StatusStack := 0;
50       IF Stack^.Top = 0 THEN
51          RETURN TRUE
52        ELSE
53          RETURN FALSE
54       END
55       END EmptyStack;
56
57   PROCEDURE DestroyStack ( VAR Stack : StackType );
58
59       BEGIN
60       StatusStack := 0;
61       DISPOSE ( Stack )
62       END DestroyStack;
63
64   END CharStacks.
```

Figure 9-15   Implementation Module CharStacks

Arithmetic expressions may be evaluated using a stack. Usually, arithmetic expressions involving the binary operators, indicated by "+", "-", "*", and "/", are written in infix form; that is, with the operator placed between the two operands. The infix form of arithmetic expressions is taught throughout elementary and secondary mathematics education. Unfortunately, unless one learns the rules for evaluation, the infix form of arithmetic expressions is ambiguous. Consider the expression

A + B * C

Except for the notion of operator precedence, which we've learned, it is unclear just by looking at the expression whether the addition or multiplication operation is to be performed first. One way of clarifying this ambiguity is with parentheses, which are placed around each operation. The following result is termed a **fully parenthesized expression**.

((A + B) * C)

Fully parenthesized expressions may become quite cumbersome. Fortunately, **postfix form**, also called **Reverse Polish Notation**, is a way of writing arithmetic expressions so that the exact order of operations is unambiguous. Specifically, a postfix expression is an expression in which the two operands are immediately followed by the operator, and the expression is evaluated by scanning the expression from left to right and applying each operator to the two operands immediately to its left. Thus the postfix form expression

A B + C *

is equivalent to the fully parenthesized infix expression

((A + B) * C

In this form,

A B +

is a subexpression, representing the addition of A and B, which is then multiplied by C to compute the final result.

Another method of evaluating a postfix expression is with a push down stack. The expression is scanned from left to right. When an operand is scanned, it is pushed onto the stack. When an operator is scanned, two operands are popped from the stack, the operation is performed on the operands, and the result is pushed onto the stack. When the scan of the expression is complete, only one value is in the stack, the value of the expression.

The procedure for translating a fully parenthesized infix expression into a postfix expression also involves a stack. If each operand is identified by a single letter and, in addition, the symbols "+", "-", "*", and "/" serve as the operators, then the translation is accomplished as follows:

1. Create a new empty stack, which temporarily stores the operators during the process.

2. Scan the infix expression left to right, ignoring all blanks.

    a. If the character scanned is a left parenthesis, then ignore it.

    b. If the character is an operand, immediately place it in the postfix string.

    c. If the character is an operator, then push it onto the stack.

    d. If the character is a right parenthesis, then pop an operand from the stack and place it in the postfix string.

Figure 9-16 presents the program module UseCharStacks, which uses the library module CharStacks to implement the translation process, from infix to postfix, as just described.

```
 1   MODULE UseCharStacks;
 2
 3   FROM InOut       IMPORT Read, Done, EOL, Write,
 4                           WriteString, WriteCard, WriteLn;
 5
 6   FROM CharStacks IMPORT StackType, StatusStack,
 7                           CreateStack, DestroyStack, Push, Pop;
 8
 9   CONST   STRINGMax = 80;
10
11   TYPE    STRING = ARRAY [ 1..STRINGMax ] OF CHAR;
12
13   VAR     InFix    : STRING;
14           IFLen    : CARDINAL;
15           PostFix  : STRING;
16           PFLen    : CARDINAL;
17           Result   : CARDINAL;
18
19   PROCEDURE ReadSTRING ( VAR It : STRING; VAR Length : CARDINAL);
20
21       VAR    AChar : CHAR;
22
23       BEGIN
24       Length := 0;
25       REPEAT
26          Read ( AChar);
27          IF ( AChar # EOL) AND ( Length < STRINGMax) THEN
28              INC ( Length);
29              It [Length] := AChar
30          END
31       UNTIL AChar = EOL
32       END ReadSTRING;
33
34   PROCEDURE WriteSTRING ( It : STRING; Length : CARDINAL);
35
36       VAR    I : CARDINAL;
37
38       BEGIN
39       FOR I := 1 TO Length DO
40          Write ( It[I])
41       END
42       END WriteSTRING;
43
44   PROCEDURE InfixToPostfix ( InFix : STRING; IFLen : CARDINAL;
45                        VAR PostFix : STRING; VAR PFLen : CARDINAL;
46                        VAR Result  : CARDINAL);
47
```

```
48       CONST   Blank = ' ';
49               Left  = '(';
50               Right = ')';
51
52       VAR     OpStack   : StackType;
53               Balance   : CARDINAL;
54               I         : CARDINAL;
55               AnOperator : CHAR;
56
57       PROCEDURE ValidOperator ( Symbol : CHAR) : BOOLEAN;
58
59          BEGIN
60          CASE Symbol OF
61              '+','-','*','/' : RETURN TRUE
62            ELSE
63               RETURN FALSE
64          END
65          END ValidOperator;
66
67       BEGIN
68       PFLen := 0;
69       CreateStack (OpStack);
70       IF StatusStack = 0 THEN
71           Balance := 0;
72           FOR I := 1 TO IFLen DO
73               IF StatusStack = 0 THEN
74                   IF ValidOperator ( InFix[I]) THEN
75                       Push ( InFix[I], OpStack )
76                     ELSIF InFix[I] = Left  THEN
77                       INC ( Balance )
78                     ELSIF InFix[I] = Right THEN
79                       DEC ( Balance );
80                       Pop ( AnOperator, OpStack);
81                       INC ( PFLen );
82                       PostFix [PFLen] := AnOperator
83                     ELSIF InFix [I] # Blank THEN
84                       INC ( PFLen );
85                       PostFix [PFLen] := InFix [I]
86                   END
87               END
88           END
89       END;
90       IF Balance # 0 THEN
91          Result := 101      (* Indicates Mis-matched parentheses *)
92         ELSE
93          Result := StatusStack
94       END;
95       DestroyStack (OpStack)
96       END InfixToPostfix;
```

```
 97
 98  BEGIN
 99  REPEAT
100     ReadSTRING ( InFix, IFLen);
101     IF IFLen > 0 THEN
102         InfixToPostfix ( InFix, IFLen, PostFix, PFLen, Result);
103         IF Result = 0 THEN
104             WriteSTRING ( InFix, IFLen);
105             WriteString ( ' ===> ');
106             WriteSTRING ( PostFix, PFLen)
107           ELSE
108             WriteString ( '---ERROR: ('); WriteCard ( Result, 3);
109             WriteString ( ') Unable to perform translation')
110         END;
111         WriteLn
112     END
113  UNTIL IFLen = 0
114  END UseCharStacks.
```

Figure 9-16   Program Module UseCharStacks

Exercises

1. Draw an illustration of the following stack after each of the specified operations is performed.

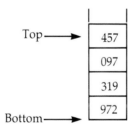

a. Pop an element.

b. Push the element 514.

c. Push the element 91.

d. Pop an element.

e. Pop an element.

f. Pop an element.

2. Given the following fully parenthesized infix expression, illustrate each step in the translation process given in this section.

$$(F - (((A - B) * (C + D)) + E))$$

3. Write a program module to use the library module CharStacks to translate conventional (not fully parenthesized) infix expressions to their postfix form equivalents. Assume the normal precedence of operators.

4. An advantage of postfix form is the simple set of rules for evaluating postfix expressions. Once again, a stack is required. Given a postfix expression, such as

45 13 − 5 *

we evaluate it by scanning the expression left to right using the following rules:

a. If scanning an operand, push it into the stack.

b. If scanning an operator, pop two values from the stack, perform the operation, and push the result onto the stack.

When the scanning is complete, one value should be left in the stack, and this value will represent the result. Write a library module to implement a stack whose elements are integer values; then use this module to develop a program module to implement the evaluation of postfix expressions.

9:4 Queues

As Section 9:2 illustrates, sequential data structures are considered sequential not necessarily because of their physical representation in memory but because of the logical way in which elements are accessed. Arrays and lists are not the only commonly used sequential structures. Queues, discussed in this section, and stacks, presented in the previous section, are two other commonly used sequential data structures. In fact, queues and stacks are forms of lists with restricted access.

A **queue** is a structure in which elements are added only to one end, called the **rear**, and removed from the other end, called the **front**. Figure 9-17 illustrates a queue as a structure that is conceptually unbounded at both ends. New elements are added by storing them in the position following the current rear of the queue. The only element that may be removed from a queue is the element currently at the front of it.

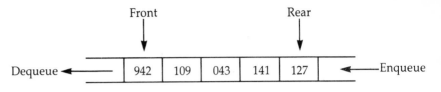

Figure 9-17   Visualization of a Queue

The operation of storing an element in a queue is called the **enqueue** operation. Removing an element is termed the **dequeue** operation.

The queue in Figure 9-17 appears as shown in Figure 9-18, after all of the following operations are performed:

Enqueue the element 200.
Dequeue an element.
Dequeue an element.
Enqueue the element 150.
Dequeue an element.

Many examples of queues exist in everyday life. In a bank, for example, customers form lines in front of teller windows, waiting their turn for service. Courtesy requires that newly arriving customers place themselves at the end of a line rather than attempting to cut into the middle. Likewise, tellers always service the customer at the front of the line. Essentially, each teller line is a queue.

The example involving students enrolling in classes introduced in Section 9:2 may be expanded to illustrate a use of queues. Frequently, schools set limits on class sizes. Students who attempt to enroll after the limit has been reached are placed on a waiting list and enrolled in the class only if some currently enrolled students drop the class. This waiting list functions exactly like a queue. The first student placed on the waiting list becomes the first student allowed to enroll in the class when some student drops the class. The second student placed on the waiting list is enrolled in the class when a second student drops the class. Figure 9-19 contains the definition module StudentQueues for maintaining a waiting list of students.

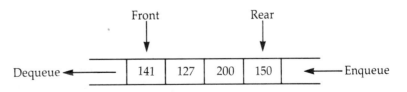

Figure 9-18   The Queue in Figure 9-17 After Several Operations

```
1   DEFINITION MODULE StudentQueues;
2
3   FROM StudentLists IMPORT StudentRecord;
4
5   EXPORT QUALIFIED StudentQueue, StatusQ, CreateQ, DestroyQ,
6                      Enqueue, Dequeue, LengthQ;
7
8   TYPE    StudentQueue;
9
10  VAR     StatusQ : CARDINAL;      (* Result of last procedure call *)
11                                   (*   0 = all Ok
12                                        1 = Can't Destroy; not empty
13                                        2 = Unable to Dequeue         *)
14
15  PROCEDURE CreateQ ( VAR Students : StudentQueue );
16
17  PROCEDURE DestroyQ ( VAR Students : StudentQueue );
18
19  PROCEDURE Enqueue ( StudentData : StudentRecord;
20                                    VAR Students : StudentQueue );
21  PROCEDURE Dequeue ( VAR StudentData : StudentRecord;
22                                    VAR Students : StudentQueue );
23
24  PROCEDURE LengthQ ( Students : StudentQueue ) : CARDINAL
25
26  END StudentQueues.
```

Figure 9-19   Definition Module StudentQueues

The data, of type StudentRecord, is kept in a StudentQueue. StudentRecord is imported from the module StudentLists presented in Section 9:2. StudentQueue is declared as a hidden type, so that users of this module need not concern themselves with the specific representation of the queue. Thus the definition module StudentQueues effectively defines StudentQueue as an abstract data type. This definition is appropriate from the applications point of view because the collection of operations performed on this type is more important than the type's representation. The available operations correspond to the declared procedures. In addition to the enqueue and dequeue operations, entire queues may be dynamically created and destroyed. This module also specifies the procedure LengthQ. LengthQ is a function that determines the number of elements currently stored in the specified queue. In most applications involving queues, knowing whether or not a queue contains any elements is necessary information. Finally, in the event that an invalid operation is attempted, the variable StatusQ conveys this information.

A queue can be represented in many ways, but the two most common approaches use either an array or a list. Using an array to represent

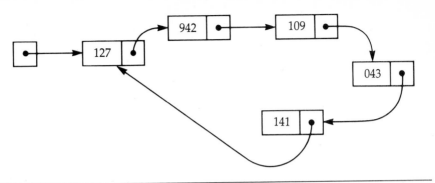

Figure 9-20   Visualization of a One-Way Circular List

a queue is given as an exercise at the end of this section. Figure 9-20 illustrates the use of a **one-way circular list** to represent a queue. A one-way circular list is a list in which a pointer variable defines the location of the first record in the list, and each record contains a pointer to the following record. The last record in the list contains a pointer to the first record.

Figure 9-20 not only illustrates a one-way circular list but also represents the queue in Figure 9-17. The first element in this circular list corre-

```
IMPLEMENTATION MODULE StudentQueues;

FROM StudentLists IMPORT StudentRecord;
FROM Storage      IMPORT ALLOCATE, DEALLOCATE;

TYPE    QueueList    = POINTER TO QueueElement;
        QueueElement = RECORD
                          Element : StudentRecord;
                          Link    : QueueList
                       END;

        StudentQueue = POINTER TO QueueDescriptor;

        QueueDescriptor  = RECORD
                              Rear   : QueueList;
                              Length : CARDINAL
                           END;

        (*   Implementations of the procedures   *)

BEGIN
StatusQ := 0
END StudentQueues.
```

Figure 9-21   Declarations and Initialization for StudentQueues

sponds to the element at the **rear** of the queue. The pointer in the record containing the rear element points to the record containing the front element, and the front element points to the next element, and so on. The queue is maintained in this way to allow an efficient implementation of the enqueue and dequeue operations. Figure 9-21 presents the declarations for the implementation module StudentQueues.

Variables of type StudentQueue point to records of type QueueDescriptor, and each QueueDescriptor contains two components. The first component, Rear, of type QueueList is the pointer to a one-way circular list. The second component, Length, stores the count of the number of elements in the queue. Each QueueElement represents an element in the queue. Each QueueElement also contains two components: (1) a pointer to the adjacent QueueElement and (2) Element, which is a student's data.

Figure 9-22 presents the procedures CreateQ, DestroyQ, and LengthQ. Creating a queue involves allocating a QueueDescriptor with the standard procedure NEW and initializing its components. Initially, the

```
PROCEDURE CreateQ ( VAR Students : StudentQueue );

   BEGIN
   NEW ( Students );
   WITH Students^ DO
      Rear   := NIL;
      Length := 0
   END;
   StatusQ := 0
   END CreateQ;


PROCEDURE DestroyQ ( VAR Students : StudentQueue );

   BEGIN
   IF Students^.Length > 0 THEN
         StatusQ := 1
      ELSE
         DISPOSE ( Students );
         StatusQ := 0
   END
   END DestroyQ;


PROCEDURE LengthQ ( Students : StudentQueue ) : CARDINAL;

   BEGIN
   RETURN Students^.Length
   END LengthQ;
```

Figure 9-22   Procedures CreateQ, DestroyQ, and LengthQ

list is empty and LengthQ is 0. Destroying a queue is only allowed when the queue is empty. This rule is usually not a limitation, since queues typically empty before their usefulness ends. Rewriting the procedure DestroyQ to allow nonempty queues to be destroyed requires a loop to dequeue each element in the queue before disposing of the QueueDescriptor. This task is left as an exercise.

Hidden types hide the exact representation of certain data types within implementation modules. This **information hiding** is generally desired and, in Modula-2, is accomplished using hidden types. Unfortunately, hidden types may not be structured; therefore they are frequently pointer types, as illustrated in the examples in this text. This limitation is not severe because, in most cases, dynamically creating and destroying instances of such types is required. This dynamic allocation is conveniently accomplished with pointers.

Figure 9-23 presents the procedures Enqueue and Dequeue. Note the IF statement in the procedure Enqueue, which handles the special case when the first element is being stored in a queue. Since each queue is represented in a one-way circular list, this single element is both the front and rear element in the queue. It must point to itself, which is logically consistent. Similarly, the IF statement in the procedure Dequeue handles the special case when the last element is removed from the queue and the queue becomes empty.

Figure 9-24 contains the framework of a program module that illustrates a use of the modules StudentLists and StudentQueues to register students in classes with waiting lists.

Using a list to represent another data structure, a queue, illustrates a common situation in programming. Often a hierarchy of structures and representations exists, with procedures implementing the mappings. Ultimately, all data objects and structures are mapped onto computer memory, which is really an array of memory locations. In most applications there is no need to manipulate data at this low level, but Modula-2 does allow low-level programming, which is discussed in Section 10:1.

```
PROCEDURE Enqueue ( StudentData : StudentRecord;
                    VAR Students : StudentQueue );

   VAR    Location : QueueList;

   BEGIN
   NEW ( Location );
   Location^.Element := StudentData;
   IF Students^.Length = 0 THEN
      Location^.Link :=  Location
      ELSE
      Location^.Link := Students^.Rear^.Link;
      Students^.Rear^.Link := Location
   END;
```

```
            Students^.Rear := Location;
            INC ( Students^.Length );
            StatusQ := 0
            END Enqueue;

        PROCEDURE Dequeue ( VAR StudentData : StudentRecord;
                                VAR Students : StudentQueue );

            VAR    Front : QueueList;      BEGIN

            IF Students^.Length = 0 THEN
               StatusQ := 2
             ELSE
               Front := Students^.Rear^.Link;
               StudentData := Front^.Element;
               IF Students^.Length = 1 THEN
                   Students^.Rear := NIL
                ELSE
                   Students^.Rear^.Link := Front^.Link
               END;
               DISPOSE ( Front );
               DEC ( Students^.Length );
               StatusQ := 0
            END
            END Dequeue;
```

Figure 9-23   Procedures Enqueue and Dequeue

```
MODULE UseStudentQueues;

FROM StudentLists  IMPORT StudentRecord, StudentList,
                          Status, Create, Destroy,
                          Insert, Delete, Retrieve, Advance, Access;

FROM StudentQueues IMPORT StudentQueue, StatusQ, CreateQ, DestroyQ,
                          Enqueue, Dequeue, LengthQ;

FROM STRing        IMPORT STR255, STRRead, STRWrite;

TYPE   Class = RECORD
                  Title      : STR255;
                  Instructor : STR255;
                  Limit      : CARDINAL;
                  Size       : CARDINAL;
                  Enrolled   : StudentList;
                  Waiting    : StudentQueue
               END;
```

```
VAR      CMPS001 : Class;

BEGIN
STRRead (CMPS001.Title);
STRRead (CMPS001.Instructor);
CMPS001.Limit := 30;
CMPS001.Size  := 0;
Create ( CMPS001.Enrolled );
CreateQ ( CMPS001.Waiting );
IF ( Status = 0 ) AND ( StatusQ = 0 ) THEN

   . . .

END;
Destroy ( CMPS001.Enrolled );
DestroyQ ( CMPS001.Waiting )

END UseStudentQueues.
```

| Figure 9-24 | Using Library Modules StudentLists and StudentQueues |

Exercises

1. Draw the representation of the following queue after each of the given operations are performed.

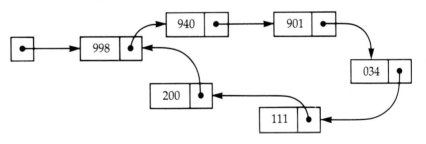

  a. Dequeue an element.

  b. Enqueue the element 700.

  c. Dequeue an element.

  d. Dequeue an element.

  e. Enqueue the element 111.

2. A basic approach to representing a queue uses an array with two subscripts, one identifying the front element and the other identifying the rear element. Using the definition module StudentQueues given in

Figure 9-19, write the implementation module that corresponds to this representation.

3. Rewrite the procedure `DestroyQ` given in Figure 9-22 to allow nonempty queues to be destroyed.

4. Evaluate the use of a one-way grounded list instead of a one-way circular list to represent a queue. Give special thought to the handling of the "special cases" and the timing of the enqueuing and dequeuing operations.

9:5 Trees

A tree is a logical structure encountered in many disciplines, including mathematics, computer science, and linguistics. Formally, a **tree** is a type of directed graph. We assume that the reader is familiar with the basic concepts and terminology of graphs, directed graphs (digraphs), and trees. Figure 9-25 illustrates an example tree. The nodes are labeled for reference with letters of the alphabet. Node A is the **root** of the tree. For any node, the node connected to it by an arc from above is called its **parent node**. A node directly connected below is called a **child node**. A node with no children is called a **leaf node** or **terminal node**. Nodes with at least one child are called **nonterminal nodes**. In Figure 9-25, for example, node C has A as its parent node and E and F as its children nodes.

Figure 9-25 is an example of a binary tree. A **binary tree** is a tree in which each node has **at most** two children nodes. Binary trees may be represented using dynamic allocation, with one record corresponding to each node in the tree. Each record contains two components, both pointers, that point to the children nodes. Additional components for storing the information associated with each node are normally declared as part of the record.

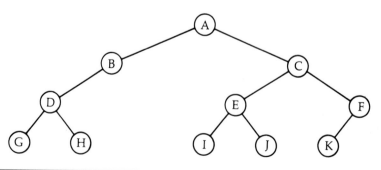

Figure 9-25   Visualization of a Tree Structure

As an example consider the use of a binary tree to logically sort a collection of integer values. Each node in the tree corresponds to a record containing a number and two pointers. These pointers point to nodes satisfying the following relationships: The first, or left, pointer points to a node containing a smaller number. The second, or right, pointer points to a node containing a larger value. An example of this appears in Figure 9-26.

Before inserting a number into this type of binary tree, we must locate an appropriate position for the number. This position is located by following the appropriate pointers representing the "less than" and "greater than" relationships. For example, if the number 85 is to be placed in the tree, a comparison is made between the number 85 and the value at the root node, 55. Since 85 is larger, the right branch is followed to the node 83. Next, a comparison is made between the value at this node, 83, and the number 85. Since 85 is larger, the right branch is followed down to the node 92. Here, 85 is smaller, and the left branch is followed to 89. Since 85 is smaller than 89, the left branch of 89 is followed. Since there is no left branch coming from the node containing 89, a child node with the value 85 may be connected to the left branch of 89, as shown in Figure 9-27.

The binary tree structure just described could be implemented with the support of the declarations

```
TYPE    TreePointer  = POINTER TO TreeRecord;
        TreeRecord   = RECORD
                        NodeValue     : INTEGER;
                        LessThan      : TreePointer;
                        GreaterThan   : TreePointer;
                        Multiplicity  : INTEGER
                       END;
```

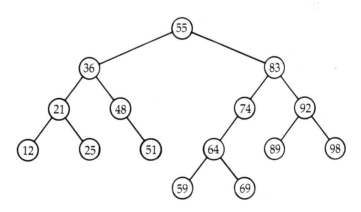

Figure 9-26   Visualization of a Less/Greater Binary Tree

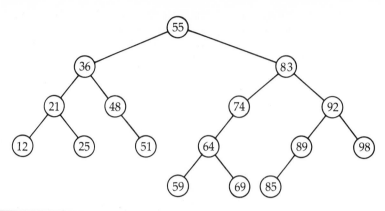

Figure 9-27   The Binary Tree in Figure 9-26 After Adding the Value 85

The four components in each record store the value at the node, two children pointers, and a multiplicity value. Rather than storing several nodes with the same value in the tree, each value appears, at most, once in the tree, and the node's multiplicity value indicates the number of appearances of the value in the tree.

Figure 9-28 presents a program module that performs the tree-sorting process just described. The main loop in the program module reads a number entered from the current input device, stores it in a record, ini-

```
 1    MODULE TreeSort;
 2
 3    FROM InOut    IMPORT Done, OpenInput, CloseInput, ReadInt,
 4                         WriteLn, WriteInt, Write;
 5
 6    FROM Storage IMPORT ALLOCATE, DEALLOCATE;
 7
 8    TYPE    TreePointer = POINTER TO TreeRecord;
 9            TreeRecord  = RECORD
10                            LessThan, GreaterThan   : TreePointer;
11                            NodeValue, Multiplicity : INTEGER;
12                          END;
13
14    VAR     Tree, NodePointer : TreePointer;
15            Number : INTEGER;
16
17    PROCEDURE TreeInsert (VAR Tree : TreePointer;
18                               NodePointer : TreePointer);
19       BEGIN
20       IF Tree = NIL THEN
21            Tree := NodePointer
```

```
22        ELSIF NodePointer^.NodeValue < Tree^.NodeValue THEN
23           TreeInsert (Tree^.LessThan, NodePointer)
24        ELSIF NodePointer^.NodeValue > Tree^.NodeValue THEN
25           TreeInsert (Tree^.GreaterThan, NodePointer)
26        ELSE
27           INC (Tree^.Multiplicity);  DISPOSE (NodePointer)
28     END;
29     END TreeInsert;
30
31  PROCEDURE TreePrint (VAR Tree : TreePointer;
32                                  VAR Count : INTEGER);
33     VAR    I : INTEGER;
34
35     BEGIN
36     IF Tree^.LessThan # NIL THEN
37          TreePrint (Tree^.LessThan, Count)
38     END;
39     FOR I := 1 TO Tree^.Multiplicity DO
40        WriteInt (Tree^.NodeValue, 8);
41        INC (Count);
42        IF  (Count MOD 10) = 0  THEN  WriteLn  END;
43     END;
44     IF Tree^.GreaterThan # NIL THEN
45          TreePrint (Tree^.GreaterThan, Count)
46     END;
47     END  TreePrint;
48
49  BEGIN
50  Tree := NIL;
51  Write (']');  ReadInt (Number);
52  WHILE Done DO
53     WriteLn;
54     NEW (NodePointer);
55     WITH NodePointer^ DO
56         LessThan    := NIL;
57         GreaterThan := NIL;
58         NodeValue   := Number;
59         Multiplicity := 1
60     END;
61     TreeInsert (Tree, NodePointer);
62     Write (']');  ReadInt (Number)
63  END;
64  WriteLn;
65  Number := 0;
66  TreePrint (Tree, Number);
67  IF (Number MOD 10) # 0 THEN  WriteLn  END;
68  END TreeSort.
```

Figure 9-28   Program Module TreeSort

tializes the record, then calls the procedure TreeInsert to place the record into the tree. The tree pointer, Tree, is initially assigned the value NIL. When the first value is added to the tree, by TreeInsert, Tree is initialized to point to it and this node becomes the root. Thus Tree points to the entire tree by pointing to the root node.

TreeInsert is a recursive procedure that places nodes into the tree. This procedure recursively searches down the tree until a NIL pointer is encountered. The position of the NIL pointer is the appropriate position where the node must be added. In the special case where a node in the tree has the same value as the value to be inserted, the multiplicity of the node in the tree is incremented and the new node is returned, using DISPOSE, to the heap.

Lines 31 through 47 print the numbers in the tree in ascending order. A call to the recursive procedure TreePrint, on line 66, initiates the printing process. This procedure recursively calls itself on line 37 to be certain that all the smaller numbers are printed first. Lines 39 through 43 print each number according to its multiplicity; then the recursive call on line 45 ensures that larger numbers are printed next. The IF statement on line 42 guarantees that at most 10 numbers are printed on each line. The IF statement on line 67 ensures that if the last line of numbers contain less than 10 numbers, a WriteLn is performed to print this line of numbers.

Trees with more than two children per node are not typically represented by expanding on this method of representing binary trees. A tree

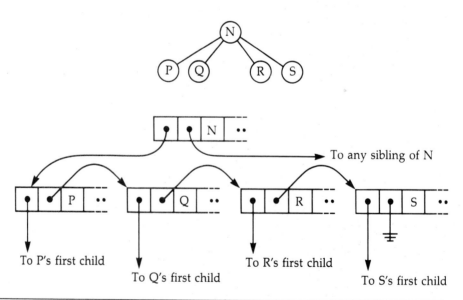

Figure 9-29   Visualization of a Two-Pointer Tree Representation

with no prespecified limit on the number of children for any node is often termed an **n-ary tree**. One method of representing n-ary trees is with two pointers per node. To illustrate this alternative representation, consider the node N with several children nodes P, Q, R, and S, shown in Figure 9-29. This representation uses records with two pointers as follows: The first pointer in each record points to the leftmost child. The second pointer is a pointer to the next sibling and may be thought of as forming a list of sibling nodes.

To illustrate an n-ary tree, consider the problem of alphabetizing an arbitrary list of words. It is desirable to have a program that accepts a list of words,

mom
knew
after
zebra
mommy
zoo
quit
quiet
momma
quite

and prints them in alphabetic order:

after
knew
mom
momma
mommy
quiet
quit
quite
zebra
zoo

One method of performing this alphabetization is with a program module that stores the representation of words in an n-ary tree. Figure 9-30 illustrates a tree structure containing the 10 words given above. Each word in the tree is represented by one letter per node along the path from the root node to the appropriate marked node. The root node contains a character value that is not part of any word; it serves only as a placeholder.

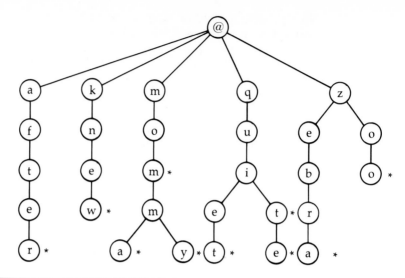

Figure 9-30   Visualization of an Alphaberized n-ary Tree

The program in Figure 9-31 reads a collection of words and creates an alphabetized n-ary tree, as illustrated in Figure 9-30. The procedure TreeProbe does more than just add words to the tree; it adds words in such a way that the tree is alphabetized. Since each node represents a single letter, TreeProbe adds letters as needed in ascending order within the sibling lists. For any node the letters of its children nodes appear in ascending alphabetic order.

```
 1 MODULE NaryTree;
 2
 3 FROM InOut   IMPORT  ReadString, Write, WriteLn;
 4 FROM Storage IMPORT  ALLOCATE, DEALLOCATE;
 5
 6 CONST  MaxWordSize = 20;
 7
 8 TYPE   TreePointer = POINTER TO TreeRecord;
 9        TreeRecord  = RECORD
10                         FirstChild  : TreePointer;
11                         NextSibling : TreePointer;
12                         Letter      : CHAR;
13                         EndWord     : BOOLEAN
14                      END;
15
16 VAR    WordSize : CARDINAL;
17        Word : ARRAY [ 1 .. MaxWordSize ] OF CHAR;
```

```
18          Tree, Node : TreePointer;
19
20  PROCEDURE TreeProbe (VAR Tree   : TreePointer;
21                       VAR Word   : ARRAY OF CHAR;
22                       WordSize   : CARDINAL;
23                       Index      : CARDINAL;
24                       BuildMode : BOOLEAN
25                        (* = TRUE means build if neccessary
26                           = FALSE means just search *)
27                                        ) : TreePointer;
28
29     (* SIDE EFFECT WARNING
30      * When BuildMode = TRUE, the procedure might build nodes
31                         into the Tree                    *)
32
33     VAR    Node : TreePointer;
34
35     BEGIN
36     IF (Tree = NIL) OR (Tree^.Letter > Word [Index-1]) THEN
37        IF BuildMode THEN
38           NEW (Node);
39           Node^.FirstChild := NIL;
40           Node^.NextSibling := Tree;
41           Tree             := Node;
42           Node^.Letter     := Word [Index-1];
43           Node^.EndWord    := FALSE;
44           RETURN TreeProbe (Tree, Word, WordSize,
45                                 Index, BuildMode)
46        ELSE
47           RETURN NIL
48        END
49     ELSIF Tree^.Letter < Word [Index-1] THEN
50        RETURN TreeProbe (Tree^.NextSibling, Word, WordSize,
51                                    Index, BuildMode);
52     ELSIF Index = WordSize THEN
53        RETURN Tree
54     ELSE
55        RETURN TreeProbe (Tree^.FirstChild, Word, WordSize,
56                                 Index+1, BuildMode);
57     END;
58     END  TreeProbe;
59
60  PROCEDURE ReadAWord (VAR Word: ARRAY OF CHAR;
61                                 VAR WordSize : CARDINAL);
62
63     BEGIN
64     FOR WordSize := 0 TO HIGH (Word) DO
65        Word [WordSize] := CHR (0)
```

```
66      END;
67      ReadString (Word);
68      WordSize := 0;
69      WHILE (WordSize <= HIGH (Word)) &
70             (Word [WordSize] # CHR (0) ) DO
71        INC (WordSize)
72      END;
73      END ReadAWord;
74
75  PROCEDURE Alphabetize (Tree : TreePointer;
76                                    VAR Word : ARRAY OF CHAR;
77                                       VAR Index : CARDINAL);
78
79      VAR    I : CARDINAL;
80
81      BEGIN
82      IF Tree # NIL THEN
83          INC (Index);
84          Word [Index-1] := Tree^.Letter;
85          IF Tree^.EndWord THEN
86              FOR I := 0 TO Index-1 DO  Write (Word [I])  END;
87              WriteLn;
88          END;
89          IF Tree^.FirstChild # NIL THEN
90              Alphabetize (Tree^.FirstChild, Word, Index)
91          END;
92          DEC (Index);
93          IF Tree^.NextSibling # NIL THEN
94              Alphabetize (Tree^.NextSibling, Word, Index)
95          END;
96      END;
97      END Alphabetize;
98
99  BEGIN
100 Tree := NIL;
101 Write (']');  ReadAWord (Word, WordSize);
102 WHILE Word [1] # '/' DO
103    Node          := TreeProbe (Tree, Word, WordSize, 1, TRUE);
104    Node^.EndWord := TRUE;
105    WriteLn;
106    Write (']');  ReadAWord (Word, WordSize)
107 END;
108 WriteLn;  WriteLn;  WriteLn;
109 WordSize := 0;
110 Alphabetize (Tree, Word, WordSize)
111 END NaryTree.
```

Figure 9-31   Program Module NaryTree

The procedure Alphabetize performs a **natural order traversal** of trees created by TreeProbe. A tree may be traversed in a number of organized ways. A natural order traversal of a tree begins at the root and always follows the path to the leftmost child that has not yet been visited. When a leaf is visited, the traversal continues with the next sibling of that node. When all children of a node have been visited, the traversal moves up a level in the tree and continues with the siblings of the parent node.

To print an alphabetized listing of the words in the tree, a natural order tree traversal is performed. An array is used to store the characters appearing along the path from the root to the current node. Immediately after each character value is placed in the array, the component EndWord in the current node is checked to determine if this node represents the last character of a word. If it does, then the contents of the array are printed.

The auxiliary procedure, ReadAWord, uses the procedure Read-String from InOut to read words from the input device. Additionally, this procedure counts the number of characters in the word just read and returns this count in its second parameter. This counting is accomplished by initially storing the character value CHR (0) in each position in the array parameter Word and then later counting the number of leading positions in the array until CHR (0) is encountered.

The procedure TreeProbe is a function with a side effect. Side effects are generally considered to be undesirable. TreeProbe not only searches for a word in the tree but builds the tree as required. This tree building is the side effect; nodes must be added to include the word in the tree. Building the tree only occurs when the parameter BuildMode has the value TRUE. Thus the statement sequence

```
Node := TreeProbe (Tree, Word, WordSize, 1, FALSE);
IF (Node = NIL) OR (NOT Node^.EndWord) THEN
    WriteString ('The word IS NOT in the tree')
  ELSE
    WriteString ('The word IS in the tree')
END;
```

causes the tree pointed to by Tree to be searched and an appropriate message to be printed indicating the result of the search.

Exercises

1. Write a procedure to translate from Morse code assuming input of the form

   .-//-.-./.-/-// ...

where dots and dashes play their normal Morse code roles and the slashes separate the letters. A double slash separates words. A binary tree can assist in the translation in the following manner: Dots represent traversing the left branch of a node, and dashes represent traversing the right branch. A letter is placed at a node in the tree such that the dots and dashes associated with the path from the root to the node containing the letter form the Morse code for the letter. The blank character is stored at the root, and the first level of the tree appears as illustrated in the following tree.

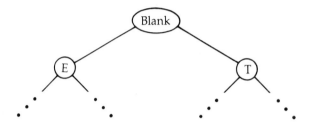

2. Use the n-ary tree structure discussed in this section to implement a program module that produces concordance listings of programs. A **concordance listing** is a printout that shows every identifier used in a program along with the line numbers on which that identifier appears. The component EndWord of each record may be replaced by a pointer to a list of line numbers. Each element in the list contains the number of a line in the program on which the identifier appears.

9:6 Directed Graphs

Graphs and directed graphs, often referred to as digraphs, are frequently represented using dynamic storage allocation. Once again, we assume readers are familiar with the basic concepts and terminology of graphs. Any representation for a digraph may also be used to represent a graph. Although an efficient digraph representation may not necessarily be an efficient graph representation, a separate discussion of graph representations is beyond the scope of this text. Figure 9-32 illustrates a digraph with six nodes, labeled A, B, C, D, E, and F, and eleven directed arcs, where the arrowheads indicate the direction of the arcs.

A digraph may be represented by a list of records, one record for each node in the directed graph. Each record contains the information specific to that node, which includes information about the arcs associated with the node. One general representation uses two lists of arcs.

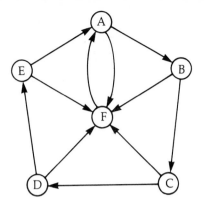

Figure 9-32   Visualization of a Digraph

One list identifies the arcs entering the node (arrowhead toward the node), and the other list identifies the arcs leaving the node.

Figure 9-33 illustrates the two distinct record structures used here to represent a digraph. This representation uses one NodeRecord for each node in the digraph. Each NodeRecord contains a pointer component that forms the list of nodes. The other two pointers form lists identifying the arcs leaving (OutArcList) and entering (InArcList) the node. Additional information about the node may be stored by adding additional components to the records. Similarly, each arc is represented with an ArcRecord. Each ArcRecord is an element in two lists. That is, each arc record is linked with the OutArcList pointer of one node and with the InArcList pointer of another. Additional components may be added to the ArcRecords to store data about the arcs.

Figure 9-34 illustrates the representation of the digraph shown in Figure 9-32 using the record structures illustrated in Figure 9-33. The list of nodes appears down the left-hand side of the figure, linked together with the pointers in the first component in each of these records. Each

Nodelink pointer	NodeName	OutArcList pointer	InArcList pointer

NodeRecord

OutLink pointer	OutNode pointer	InLink pointer	InNode pointer	

ArcRecord

Figure 9-33   Visualization of NodeRecord and ArcRecord

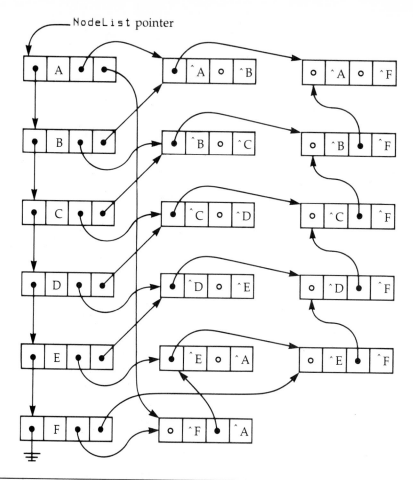

Figure 9-34   Representation of the Digraph in Figure 9-32

NodeRecord contains two additional pointers, one to the list of arcs leaving the node and one to the list of arcs entering the node. Each ArcRecord is an element of two lists. To simplify the figure and reduce the number of lines drawn, the notations ^A, ^B, and so forth appear in several instances instead of the line to the appropriate NodeRecord.

The program module in Figure 9-35 creates the graph representations illustrated in Figure 9-34. The input to this program module consists of the name of a node followed by the names of the nodes at the other end of the arcs leaving the node. For example, the data to create the representation of the graph shown in Figure 9-34 are

```
A    B    F
B    C    F
C    D    F
D    E    F
E    A    F
F    A
     /
```

The procedure BuildGraph processes input of this format with the help of the procedures ReadName and LocateNode. The procedure LocateNode is a function procedure with a side effect. LocateNode's side effect builds the list of nodes in the graph. By relegating this process to LocateNode, the procedure Buildgraph handles the creation of the arc lists, which is accomplished by the statement sequence appearing on lines 89 through 95, inclusive.

```
 1 MODULE DiGraph;
 2
 3 FROM InOut    IMPORT EOL, termCH, ReadString, OpenInput,
 4                      CloseInput, Write, WriteLn, WriteString;
 5
 6 FROM Storage IMPORT ALLOCATE;
 7
 8 CONST  MaxNameSize = 10;
 9        CR = 15C;
10
11 TYPE   ArcPointer  = POINTER TO ArcRecord;
12        NodePointer = POINTER TO NodeRecord;
13        NameType    = ARRAY [ 1 .. MaxNameSize ] OF CHAR;
14        NodeRecord  = RECORD
15                        NodeLink : NodePointer;
16                        NodeName : NameType;
17                        OutArcList, InArcList : ArcPointer;
18                      END;
19 TYPE   ArcRecord   = RECORD
20                        OutLink : ArcPointer;
21                        OutNode : NodePointer;
22                        InLink : ArcPointer;
23                        InNode : NodePointer;
24                      END;
25
26 VAR    NodeList : NodePointer;
27
28 PROCEDURE LocateNode (VAR Name: NameType) : NodePointer;
29
30     (*  POSSIBLE SIDE EFFECT - Builds node list  *)
31
32     VAR    NodeIndex : NodePointer;
33
```

```
34     PROCEDURE NoMatch (VAR  N1, N2 : NameType) : BOOLEAN;
35
36        VAR    I : CARDINAL;
37
38        BEGIN
39        FOR I := 1 TO MaxNameSize DO
40           IF N1 [I] # N2 [I] THEN RETURN TRUE  END;
41        END;
42        RETURN FALSE
43        END  NoMatch;
44
45     BEGIN
46     NodeIndex := NodeList;
47     WHILE (NodeIndex # NIL) &
48           NoMatch (Name, NodeIndex^.NodeName) DO
49        NodeIndex := NodeIndex^.NodeLink
50     END;
51     IF NodeIndex = NIL THEN
52        NEW (NodeIndex);
53        WITH NodeIndex^ DO
54           NodeLink    := NodeList;
55           OutArcList := NIL;
56           InArcList  := NIL;
57           NodeName    := Name
58        END;
59        NodeList := NodeIndex
60     END;
61     RETURN NodeIndex
62     END  LocateNode;
63
64 PROCEDURE ReadName (VAR Word: ARRAY OF CHAR);
65
66     VAR    I : CARDINAL;
67
68     BEGIN
69     FOR I := 0 TO HIGH (Word) DO  Word [I] := CHR (0)  END;
70     ReadString (Word)
71     END ReadName;
72
73 PROCEDURE BuildGraph;
74
75     VAR    FromNode : NodePointer;
76            ToNode   : NodePointer;
77            Arc      : ArcPointer;
78            Name     : NameType;
79
80     BEGIN
81     NodeList := NIL;
82     OpenInput ('.DAT');
```

```
 83       ReadName (Name);
 84       WHILE Name [1] # '/' DO
 85          FromNode := LocateNode (Name);
 86          ReadName (Name);
 87          WHILE termCH # EOL DO
 88             ToNode := LocateNode (Name);
 89             NEW (Arc);
 90             WITH Arc^ DO
 91                OutLink  := FromNode^.OutArcList;
 92                OutNode  := FromNode;
 93                InLink   := ToNode^.InArcList;
 94                InNode   := ToNode
 95             END;
 96             FromNode^.OutArcList := Arc;
 97             ToNode^.InArcList    := Arc;
 98             ReadName (Name)
 99          END;
100          ReadName (Name)
101       END;
102       CloseInput
103       END  BuildGraph;
104
105 BEGIN
106 BuildGraph
107 END  DiGraph.
```

Figure 9-35   Program Module DiGraph

The function LocateNode, with its side effect, performs two processes. First, as its name implies, LocateNode locates the record associated with a particular node in the node list. Second, if a record does not
exist in the node list, the side effect adds a node with the specified name.

Note that some programmers might find this particular method of
representing digraphs more general than necessary for certain applications and thus somewhat inefficient. An advantage of this representation
is that, in addition to representing digraphs, it may also represent graphs
in a reasonably efficient manner. Furthermore, many digraph applications
require access to the arcs coming into a node as well as the arcs going out
of a node. In such situations this representation is appropriate.

In those applications where only one of the arc lists is needed, the
record components corresponding to the unnecessary list could be removed. For example, if only the OutArcList were needed, the records
may be reduced as shown in Figure 9-36, and the corresponding representation for the graph in Figure 9-32 is reduced to the linked structure illustrated in Figure 9-37.

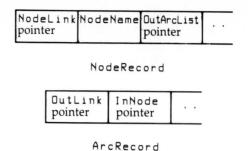

NodeRecord

ArcRecord

Figure 9-36   Visualization of the Reduced Form of **NodeRecord** and **ArcRecord**

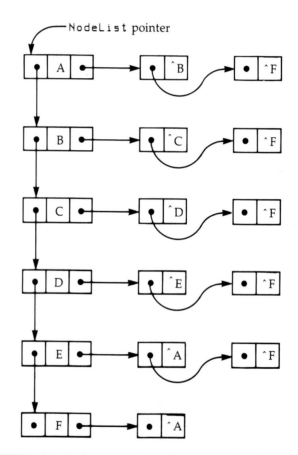

Figure 9-37   Reduced Form Representation of the Digraph in Figure 9-32

Removing the `InArcLists` from this representation requires the removal of the corresponding statements referencing the eliminated components. The procedures presented in Figure 9-35 may be easily modified to accommodate these changes. There are no structural changes; simply remove the statement

```
InArcList := NIL;
```

in `LocateNode`, and remove the statements

```
OutNode  :=  FromNode;
InLink   :=  ToNode^.InArcList;
```

in `BuildGraph`.

Exercises

1. Write a library module to create a graph representation of the United States or any other similar map.

2. Write a program module to solve the **border-crossing problem** on maps represented using the library module written for Exercise 1. The border-crossing problem requires the determination of the fewest number of borders that must be crossed to proceed from one state to another.

3. Write a program that "four colors" a map.

4. Write a program that determines if a Eulerian path exists in a map and, if one does exist, prints the path.

5. Write a program that determines if a Hamiltonian path exists in a map and, if one exists, prints it.

9:7 Variant Records in Dynamic Allocation

Variant records were introduced in Section 5:2, in the context of statically allocated records. Variant records play a much richer role with dynamic storage allocation. Many Modula-2 implementations of the standard procedures NEW and DISPOSE efficiently allocate and deallocate variant records. For example, consider the declarations

```
TYPE    PayType = ( Salaried, Hourly, PieceRate );
        DVRPointer = POINTER TO DynamicVariantRecord;
        DynamicVariantRecord = RECORD
                            Link          : DVRPointer;
                            Name          : STR255;
                            AddressLine1  : STR255;
                            AddressLine2  : STR255;
                            GrossPay, Taxes, NetPay : REAL;

                            CASE PayMethod : PayType OF
                                    Salaried  : Salary          : REAL
                                  ! Hourly    : Rate, Hours   : REAL
                                  ! PieceRate : Rate, Pieces  : REAL
                            END;

                        END;
```

which declare a variant record type for an element in a list of employees. The type DynamicVariantRecord consists of seven nonvarying components followed by a variant part. The variant part corresponds to the case structure and handles three different payment schemes. Given the declaration

```
VAR    AnEmployee : DVRPointer;
```

the statements

```
NEW ( AnEmployee, Hourly );
AnEmployee.PayMethod := Hourly
```

dynamically allocate a data object of type DynamicVariantRecord, which contains nine components, the last two of which are Rate and Hours. A variation of the standard procedures NEW and DISPOSE allows the specification of tag components as optional parameters, as in the preceding example. Likewise, the statement

```
DISPOSE ( AnEmployee, Hourly )
```

dynamically deallocates the data object pointed to by AnEmployee. A tag component in a dynamically allocated variant record helps determine the exact memory requirements of a record at execution time. The variant record need only be large enough to accommodate the components required by the desired tag component values. We must take care when using variant dynamically allocated records. The values of the tag components specified when the record is allocated **must** be the same values that are eventually stored in the record. Furthermore, these values must remain in the record until it is disposed. Since different variants may have different memory requirements, unpredictable results might occur if an attempt is made to manipulate components of a variant different from the one that was used to allocate the record. Thus, if we use our current example, the following statement sequence is incorrect:

```
NEW (AnEmployee, Salaried);
AnEmployee^.PayMethod := PieceRate;
AnEmployee^.Rate       := 0.75;
AnEmployee^.Pieces     := 41
```

Another use of variant records is to permit components within records to be accessed using aliases. To illustrate, consider the binary tree sort in Figure 9-28 of Section 9:5. The time required to access a number within the tree depends upon the length of the path from the root to the number's node. Several procedures were developed to restructure binary trees to minimize the length of the longest path in the tree, while maintaining the "less than" and "greater than" relations between nodes.

One method uses the **AVL tree-restructuring** algorithms. A few simple definitions are necessary before these AVL algorithms may be presented. The binary tree in Figure 9-38 illustrates these terms. The **length of a path** between two nodes is the number of arcs in the path. The **balance of a node** is the length of the longest path from the node to a terminal node down its left, or "less than," branch minus the length of the longest path down its right, or "greater than," branch. Figure 9-38 shows a binary tree in which each node satisfies the relationship that each left child is less than its parent and each right child is greater than its parent. Alongside each node value is the balance of that node. For example, the

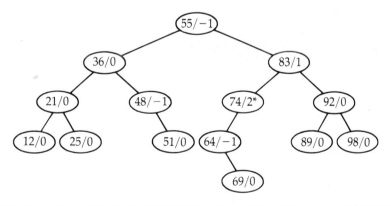

Figure 9-38   Visualization of a Less/Greater Binary Tree with Balances

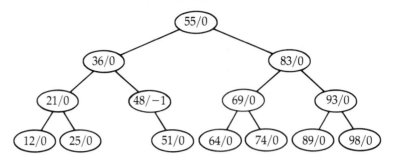

Figure 9-39   The Tree in Figure 9-38 After AVL Restructuring

root node has a balance of −1, obtained as 3 − 4, indicating the length of the longest left path minus the length of the longest right path.

The AVL restructuring algorithms allow nodes to have only balances of −1, 0, and 1. Thus the binary tree in Figure 9-38 is not considered to be AVL balanced. To make it balanced, some restructuring must occur. As the AVL algorithm checks the balance of each node, starting at the node containing 69 and working up the tree toward the root, the first node whose balance would exceed the allowable range is the node containing the value 74. The AVL algorithm would then restructure the tree as shown in Figure 9-39.

There are two distinct AVL tree-restructuring algorithms. When a restructuring is performed, the choice of algorithm depends upon the position of the node just placed in the tree and the position of the first node whose balance has gone out of the allowable range. Figure 9-40 illustrates the two cases and their corresponding restructurings. In both cases, once a restructuring occurs, there is no need to rebalance any of the nodes between the restructuring and the root node. This approach to restructuring, in part, makes the AVL restructuring algorithms not only effective but also quite efficient. The second case requires a careful analysis of the actual position of the newly inserted node relative to the restructuring. This analysis is necessary to determine the actual balances of two of the nodes below the point where the restructuring occurs.

Each of the two AVL restructurings shown in Figure 9-40 can occur in two ways: either as illustrated or in mirror image. Since two restructuring algorithms are used and each appears in two forms, a left-branch and a right-branch form, as many as four procedures could be required to perform these tree restructurings. Rather than having four procedures, Figure 9-41 presents a method of implementing the AVL restructuring algorithms with just two procedures. This method is accomplished using a variant record and aliases.

The program module presented in Figure 9-41 is basically the tree sort program presented in Figure 9-28 in Section 9:5 with the addition of

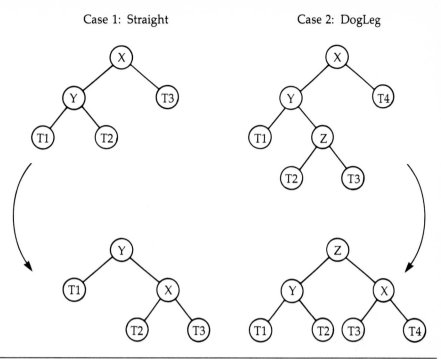

Figure 9-40   AVL Restructuring Illustrations

```
 1 MODULE AVLTreeSort;
 2
 3 FROM InOut IMPORT
 4         Done, OpenInput, CloseInput, ReadInt,
 5         WriteLn, WriteInt, Write;
 6
 7 FROM Storage IMPORT ALLOCATE, DEALLOCATE;
 8
 9 TYPE   TreePointer = POINTER TO TreeRecord;
10        TreeRecord  = RECORD
11                         CASE BOOLEAN OF
12                              TRUE :  LessThan    : TreePointer;
13                                      GreaterThan : TreePointer
14                          ! FALSE:  Arrow :
15                              ARRAY [ 1 .. 2 ] OF TreePointer
16                         END;
17                         NodeValue    : INTEGER;
18                         Balance      : INTEGER;
19                         Multiplicity : CARDINAL
20                         END;
21
22 VAR    Tree         : TreePointer;
```

```
23            NodePointer : TreePointer;
24            Number      : INTEGER;
25            Extra       : BOOLEAN;
26
27 PROCEDURE TreeInsert (VAR Tree : TreePointer;
28                           NodePointer : TreePointer) : BOOLEAN;
29
30 (* If result = TRUE then reblance otherwise no rebalancing *)
31
32    PROCEDURE AVL;
33
34        PROCEDURE StraightAVL (Direction: INTEGER);
35
36            VAR    XPoint, YPoint: TreePointer;
37
38            BEGIN
39            XPoint := Tree;
40            YPoint := Tree^.Arrow [Direction];
41            Tree^.Arrow [Direction] := YPoint^.Arrow [3-Direction];
42            YPoint^.Arrow [3-Direction] := Tree;
43            Tree   := YPoint;
44            XPoint^.Balance := 0;
45            YPoint^.Balance := 0
46            END  StraightAVL;
47
48        PROCEDURE DogLegAVL (Direction: INTEGER);
49
50            VAR    XPoint, YPoint, ZPoint: TreePointer;
51
52            BEGIN
53            XPoint := Tree;
54            YPoint := Tree^.Arrow [Direction];
55            ZPoint := YPoint^.Arrow [3-Direction];
56            YPoint^.Arrow [3-Direction] := ZPoint^.Arrow[Direction];
57            ZPoint^.Arrow [Direction]    := Tree^.Arrow [Direction];
58            Tree^.Arrow [Direction]   := ZPoint^.Arrow [3-Direction];
59            ZPoint^.Arrow [3-Direction] := Tree;
60            Tree := ZPoint;
61            ZPoint^.Balance := 0;
62            IF NodePointer^.NodeValue < Tree^.NodeValue THEN
63                CASE Direction OF
64                     1: XPoint^.Balance := -1;
65                        YPoint^.Balance :=  0
66                   ! 2: XPoint^.Balance :=  0;
67                        YPoint^.Balance := -1
68                END
69            ELSIF NodePointer^.NodeValue > Tree^.NodeValue THEN
70                CASE Direction OF
71                     1: XPoint^.Balance :=  0;
72                        YPoint^.Balance :=  1
```

```
 73                         ! 2: XPoint^.Balance :=  1;
 74                             YPoint^.Balance :=  0
 75                 END
 76               ELSE
 77                 XPoint^.Balance :=  0;
 78                 YPoint^.Balance :=  0
 79           END
 80           END  DogLegAVL;
 81
 82      BEGIN (*  AVL  *)
 83      IF NodePointer^.NodeValue < Tree^.NodeValue THEN
 84          IF NodePointer^.NodeValue < Tree^.LessThan^.NodeValue
 85            THEN
 86               StraightAVL (1)
 87            ELSE
 88               DogLegAVL (1)
 89          END;
 90        ELSE
 91          IF NodePointer^.NodeValue > Tree^.GreaterThan^.NodeValue
 92            THEN
 93               StraightAVL (2)
 94            ELSE
 95               DogLegAVL (2)
 96          END
 97      END
 98      END AVL;
 99
100    BEGIN (*  TreeInsert  *)
101    IF Tree = NIL THEN
102       Tree := NodePointer;
103       RETURN  TRUE
104     ELSIF NodePointer^.NodeValue < Tree^.NodeValue THEN
105         IF TreeInsert (Tree^.LessThan, NodePointer) THEN
106             INC (Tree^.Balance);
107             CASE Tree^.Balance OF
108                  0:  RETURN FALSE
109                ! 1:  RETURN TRUE
110                ! 2:  AVL;  RETURN FALSE
111             END
112           ELSE
113             RETURN FALSE
114         END;
115     ELSIF NodePointer^.NodeValue > Tree^.NodeValue THEN
116         IF TreeInsert (Tree^.GreaterThan, NodePointer) THEN
117             DEC (Tree^.Balance);
118             CASE Tree^.Balance OF
119                  0: RETURN FALSE
120                !-1: RETURN TRUE
121                !-2: AVL;  RETURN FALSE
122             END
```

```
123              ELSE
124                  RETURN FALSE
125              END;
126          ELSE
127              INC (NodePointer^.Multiplicity);
128              RETURN FALSE
129      END
130      END TreeInsert;
131
132 PROCEDURE TreePrint (VAR Tree : TreePointer; VAR Count : INTEGER);
133
134      VAR    I : INTEGER;
135
136      BEGIN
137      IF Tree^.LessThan # NIL THEN
138          TreePrint (Tree^.LessThan, Count)
139      END;
140      FOR I := 1 TO Tree^.Multiplicity DO
141          WriteInt (Tree^.NodeValue, 8);
142          Write ('['); WriteInt (Tree^.Balance, 2);   Write (']');
143          INC (Count);
144          IF  (Count MOD 6) = 0   THEN   WriteLn   END
145      END;
146      IF Tree^.GreaterThan # NIL THEN
147          TreePrint (Tree^.GreaterThan, Count)
148      END
149      END  TreePrint;
150
151 BEGIN
152 Tree := NIL;
153 Write (']');   ReadInt (Number);
154 WHILE Done DO
155      WriteLn;
156      NEW (NodePointer);
157      WITH NodePointer^ DO
158        LessThan     := NIL;
159        GreaterThan  := NIL;
160        NodeValue    := Number;
161        Multiplicity := 1;
162        Balance      := 0
163      END;
164      Extra := TreeInsert (Tree, NodePointer);
165      Write (']');   ReadInt (Number)
166 END;
167 WriteLn;
168 Number := 0;   TreePrint (Tree, Number);
169 IF (Number MOD 10) # 0 THEN   WriteLn   END
170 END AVLTreeSort.
```

Figure 9-41   AVL Tree Restructuring

a variant record and the two AVL procedures. The variant record allows the two tree pointer fields in the records to be accessed as an array. The reason for having array access to the pointers is that manipulating array subscripts makes it possible to easily implement the four AVL restructurings with just two procedures.

The two AVL restructuring cases are implemented by the procedures StraightAVL and DogLegAVL. Each procedure accepts a parameter, whose value indicates the form: 1 indicates the left form, and 2 indicates the right form. The restructurings are performed as follows: The procedure TreeInsert recursively traverses down the tree until the new node is inserted. When a value of TRUE is returned from a recursive call, the node at the particular position in the tree must be rebalanced. Whenever the balance of the node goes out of the allowed range, −1 to 1, the procedure AVL is called. This procedure determines which particular AVL restructuring is necessary and calls the appropriate procedure with the proper parameter value.

The procedures StraightAVL and DogLegAVL make extensive use of the variant declarations. Each procedure handles two forms by treating the pointer values as an array of elements. Since pointer arrays are used within the records, simple index calculations eliminate the need for four restructuring procedures.

10 Advanced Features

10:1 Low-Level Programming

Although Modula-2 is a high-level programming language with strong type checking, it contains features that provide access to low-level facilities. Because of these features Modula-2 may be an effective systems programming tool. However, note that whenever these machine dependent facilities are referenced and used within Modula-2 programs, the resulting program may then become machine dependent.

To a certain extent some low-level programming features compromise the strong type checking done within the language. For example, type transfer functions are necessary so that Modula-2's type-checking rules are not violated, but their use allows data of one type to be assigned to an object of another type. We must take care when using type transfer functions.

The module SYSTEM declares the essential types and procedures for low-level programming support. This module is an exception among modules because, although its definition module exists and may be viewed, its implementation module is machine dependent and may not be viewed. The implementation module for SYSTEM is best thought of as part of the language implementation itself. For this reason SYSTEM is often referred to as a **pseudomodule**.

Memory consists of a collection of locations, each of a certain size and each identified by a unique number, termed an address. The size of a memory location is expressed in terms of the number of bits, or binary digits, it contains. On some computer systems the smallest unit of memory, which may be individually referenced with an address, is eight bits in length and referred to as a byte. On other computer systems the smallest unit of memory that may be addressed is more than 8 bits in length, frequently 16 or 32 bits. Thus the size of a memory location is machine dependent and not assumed in Modula-2. However, the types WORD and ADDRESS, exported from SYSTEM, form the definition of memory for low-level programming.

The data type WORD identifies an individually addressable location of memory. This identification does not imply that an object of type WORD corresponds to the smallest individually addressable unit of memory, only that such an object may be referenced using an address. Usually, the amount of memory occupied by a WORD is the same as the amount of memory occupied by data objects of type INTEGER and CARDINAL. The amount of memory required for a data object of any data type is determined with the standard function TSIZE. TSIZE is a function procedure that accepts a single argument, a type identifier, and returns a value of type CARDINAL, indicating the amount of memory needed to represent an object of the specified type. TSIZE is discussed in more detail later in this section.

The type ADDRESS is a numeric type whose values are the addresses of data objects. We may consider ADDRESS to be declared as

```
TYPE
   ADDRESS = POINTER TO WORD;
```

No operations, except assignment, may be performed on objects of type WORD. Also, because of strong type checking, type transfer functions are necessary when transferring data to and from objects of this type. For example, given the declaration

```
TYPE Where : ADDRESS;
```

the statements

```
WriteCard (CARDINAL (Where^), 12);

WriteInt (INTEGER (Where^), 12);
```

print two numbers. The first number is the cardinal value corresponding to the bit pattern in Where^. The second number printed is the integer value corresponding to that same bit pattern.

Likewise, a type transfer function is required to place a value into memory with an ADDRESS variable. For example, the statement

```
Where^ := WORD (-117)
```

places the integer value −117 into memory at the location pointed to by Where. The type transfer function, WORD, is necessary because Where is

```
 1    MODULE IntegerToCardinal;
 2
 3    FROM SYSTEM  IMPORT WORD, ADDRESS, TSIZE;
 4    FROM Storage IMPORT ALLOCATE;
 5    FROM InOut   IMPORT WriteInt, WriteCard, WriteString, WriteLn;
 6
 7    VAR  Where : ADDRESS;
 8
 9    BEGIN
10    ALLOCATE (Where, TSIZE (CARDINAL) );
11    Where^ := WORD (-117);
12    WriteString ('Where is the address of the Integer  ');
13    WriteInt (INTEGER (Where^), 12);  WriteLn;
14    WriteString ('Where is the address of the Cardinal ');
15    WriteCard (CARDINAL (Where^), 12); WriteLn
16    END IntegerToCardinal.
```

Figure 10-1   Program Module IntegerToCardinal

of type ADDRESS, a POINTER TO WORD. The program module in Figure 10-1 illustrates how the data type WORD is used to view the contents of memory in a type independent manner. This program module places a value of type INTEGER in memory, then retrieves this value as a CARDINAL and prints it.

Objects of type ADDRESS are compatible with all pointer types. In addition, on many computer systems the type ADDRESS is also compatible with the type CARDINAL. In the revised syntax of Modula-2, the type ADDRESS is compatible with all pointer types and with either CARDINAL or LONGCARD. In either case any operation available for cardinals may be performed with addresses. The interpretation of addresses as numbers is implementation dependent.

Implementors of Modula-2 may declare additional types and procedures in SYSTEM corresponding to specifics in their computer system. For example, some implementations in which the smallest individually addressable unit of memory is eight bits in length define the data type BYTE. However, the definitions of WORD and ADDRESS usually remain consistent with the description given earlier. ADDRESS is always declared to be a POINTER TO WORD.

The procedures ADR, SIZE, and TSIZE are declared in SYSTEM. ADR is a one-argument function that returns the address of the argument. The value returned is of type ADDRESS, but the argument may be of any data type. As an example of this situation, consider the statement

    Same := ADR (Where^)

which results in the variables Same and Where having the same value, an address.

The procedures TSIZE and SIZE are both one-argument functions that return cardinal values representing the amount of memory occupied by their arguments. The argument passed to TSIZE must be the identifier of a type. TSIZE determines the amount of memory required for objects of a particular type. On line 10 in Figure 10-1, TSIZE returns the size of the memory area required to represent the type CARDINAL.

The function SIZE determines the amount of memory occupied by a data object of any type. SIZE accepts an argument, which may be a data object of any type, and it returns the size of the memory area required to represent the object.

Examples of the use of these two functions appear in the program module Determine presented in Figure 10-2. This program module declares several data types and objects of these types. The program lists the amount of memory occupied by each data object. In every case the two values printed for each type are the same. This program module may be run on any implementation of Modula-2 to determine some of the specifics of that implementation. Note that on some implementations of Modula-2, the values returned by SIZE and TSIZE indicate the number of BYTEs occupied rather than the number of WORDs. This implementation detail may be important in certain low-level programming situations.

The identifiers PROCESS, NEWPROCESS, and TRANSFER are also exported from the module SYSTEM. They are discussed in Section 10:4 on coroutines and concurrent programming.

Another feature that supports low-level programming is **hard addressing**, the ability to associate a variable to a specific address. This procedure is accomplished in a *Variable Declaration* by placing the address, within brackets, immediately following the variable's name. Figure 10-3 contains the corresponding syntax diagram for such a declaration. Note that this feature is not required of all Modula-2 implementation, but it is useful for low-level programming, especially on microcomputers.

```
 1 MODULE Determine;
 2
 3 FROM SYSTEM IMPORT WORD, ADDRESS, TSIZE, SIZE;
 4 FROM InOut IMPORT WriteCard, WriteString, WriteLn;
 5
 6 TYPE    BYTE = WORD;
 7
 8 CONST   Max = 3;
 9
10 VAR     Size : CARDINAL;
11
12 VAR                        (* Example simple data objects *)
13    Address  : ADDRESS;
14    Bitset   : BITSET;
15    Boolean  : BOOLEAN;
```

```
16    Byte     : BYTE;
17    Cardinal : CARDINAL;
18    Char     : CHAR;
19    Integer  : INTEGER;
20    Real     : REAL;
21    Word     : WORD;
22
23 TYPE                    (* Example data types *)
24    CHARARRAY    = ARRAY [ 1 .. Max ] OF CHAR;
25    BITSETARRAY  = ARRAY [ 1 .. Max ] OF BITSET;
26    BYTEARRAY    = ARRAY [ 1 .. Max ] OF BYTE;
27    INTEGERARRAY = ARRAY [ 1 .. Max ] OF INTEGER;
28    WORDARRAY    = ARRAY [ 1 .. Max ] OF WORD;
29
30 VAR                    (* Example objects of the example types *)
31    CharArray    : CHARARRAY;
32    BitsetArray  : BITSETARRAY;
33    ByteArray    : BYTEARRAY;
34    IntegerArray : INTEGERARRAY;
35    WordArray    : WORDARRAY;
36
37
38 TYPE                    (* Example structured data types *)
39    CHARRECORD    = RECORD Char    : CHAR END;
40    INTEGERRECORD = RECORD Integer : INTEGER END;
41    RECORD1       = RECORD Field1  : BITSET;
42                           Field2  : WORD     END;
43
44 VAR                    (* Example structured data objects *)
45    CharRecord    : CHARRECORD;
46    IntegerRecord : INTEGERRECORD;
47    Record1       : RECORD1;
48
49 TYPE
50    ENUMERATION    = ( Red, Green, Blue );
51    ENUMERATIONSET = SET OF ENUMERATION;
52    SUBRANGE       = [ 0 .. 15 ];
53    SUBRANGESET    = SET OF SUBRANGE;
54
55 VAR
56    Enumeration    : ENUMERATION;
57    EnumerationSet : ENUMERATIONSET;
58    Subrange       : SUBRANGE;
59    SubrangeSet    : SUBRANGESET;
60
61 BEGIN
62 WriteString ('Data Type       (      Memory Units    )'); WriteLn;
63 WriteString ('                       TSIZE       SIZE'); WriteLn;
64 WriteString ('--------------- ----------- -----------'); WriteLn;
```

```
 65 WriteLn;
 66
 67 WriteString ('ADDRESS          ');
 68 WriteCard (TSIZE (ADDRESS        ), 12);
 69 WriteCard (SIZE (Address         ), 12);   WriteLn;
 70
 71 WriteString ('BITSET           ');
 72 WriteCard (TSIZE (BITSET         ), 12);
 73 WriteCard (SIZE (Bitset          ), 12);   WriteLn;
 74
 75 WriteString ('BOOLEAN          ');
 76 WriteCard (TSIZE (BOOLEAN        ), 12);
 77 WriteCard (SIZE (Boolean         ), 12);   WriteLn;
 78
 79 WriteString ('BYTE             ');
 80 WriteCard (TSIZE (BYTE           ), 12);
 81 WriteCard (SIZE (Byte            ), 12);   WriteLn;
 82
 83 WriteString ('CARDINAL         ');
 84 WriteCard (TSIZE (CARDINAL       ), 12);
 85 WriteCard (SIZE (Cardinal        ), 12);   WriteLn;
 86
 87 WriteString ('CHAR             ');
 88 WriteCard (TSIZE (CHAR           ), 12);
 89 WriteCard (SIZE (Char            ), 12);   WriteLn;
 90
 91 WriteString ('INTEGER          ');
 92 WriteCard (TSIZE (INTEGER        ), 12);
 93 WriteCard (SIZE (Integer         ), 12);   WriteLn;
 94
 95 WriteString ('REAL             ');
 96 WriteCard (TSIZE (REAL           ), 12);
 97 WriteCard (SIZE (Real            ), 12);   WriteLn;
 98
 99 WriteString ('WORD             ');
100 WriteCard (TSIZE (WORD           ), 12);
101 WriteCard (SIZE (Word            ), 12);   WriteLn;
102
103 WriteString ('-------------------------------------');
104 WriteLn;
105
106 WriteString ('CHARARRAY        ');
107 WriteCard (TSIZE (CHARARRAY      ), 12);
108 WriteCard (SIZE (CharArray       ), 12);   WriteLn;
109
110 WriteString ('BITSETARRAY      ');
111 WriteCard (TSIZE (BITSETARRAY    ), 12);
112 WriteCard (SIZE (BitsetArray     ), 12);   WriteLn;
113
```

```
114 WriteString ('BYTEARRAY        ');
115 WriteCard (TSIZE (BYTEARRAY      ), 12);
116 WriteCard (SIZE (ByteArray       ), 12);   WriteLn;
117
118 WriteString ('INTEGERARRAY     ');
119 WriteCard (TSIZE (INTEGERARRAY   ), 12);
120 WriteCard (SIZE (IntegerArray    ), 12);   WriteLn;
121
122 WriteString ('WORDARRAY        ');
123 WriteCard (TSIZE (WORDARRAY      ), 12);
124 WriteCard (SIZE (WordArray       ), 12);   WriteLn;
125
126 WriteString ('------------------------------------');  WriteLn;
127
128 WriteString ('CHARRECORD       ');
129 WriteCard (TSIZE (CHARRECORD     ), 12);
130 WriteCard (SIZE (CharRecord      ), 12);   WriteLn;
131
132 WriteString ('INTEGERRECORD ');
133 WriteCard (TSIZE (INTEGERRECORD ), 12);
134 WriteCard (SIZE (IntegerRecord   ), 12);   WriteLn;
135
136 WriteString ('RECORD1          ');
137 WriteCard (TSIZE (RECORD1        ), 12);
138 WriteCard (SIZE (Record1         ), 12);   WriteLn;
139
140 WriteString ('------------------------------------');  WriteLn;
141
142 WriteString ('ENUMERATION      ');
143 WriteCard (TSIZE (ENUMERATION    ), 12);
144 WriteCard (SIZE (Enumeration     ), 12);   WriteLn;
145
146 WriteString ('ENUMERATIONSET ');
147 WriteCard (TSIZE (ENUMERATIONSET), 12);
148 WriteCard (SIZE (EnumerationSet), 12);   WriteLn;
149
150 WriteString ('SUBRANGE         ');
151 WriteCard (TSIZE (SUBRANGE       ), 12);
152 WriteCard (SIZE (Subrange        ), 12);   WriteLn;
153
154 WriteString ('SUBRANGESET      ');
155 WriteCard (TSIZE (SUBRANGESET    ), 12);
156 WriteCard (SIZE (SubrangeSet     ), 12);   WriteLn;
157
158 WriteLn
159
160 END Determine.
```

Figure 10-2   Program Module Determine

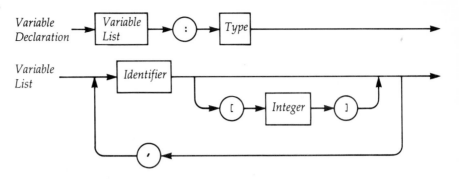

Figure 10-3   Optional Syntax Diagrams for *Variable Declaration*

For example, the declaration

```
VAR  Sample [1200] : CARDINAL;
```

not only defines Sample as a variable of type CARDINAL but also specifies that this data object corresponds to the location in memory whose address is 1200. Thus the statement

```
WriteCard (CARDINAL (ADR (Sample)), 12)
```

prints the cardinal value 1200.

This feature is very useful when a program requires access to certain memory locations corresponding to specific hardware features. To illustrate, consider one of the display modes supported by the color graphics adapter on the IBM PC. Figure 10-4 illustrates the correspondence of the 25-row-by-80-column character display to specific memory locations on

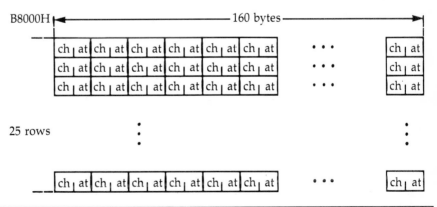

Figure 10-4   Memory Map for the IBM PC 25-by-80 Graphics Board Text Screen

the graphics adapter card in the IBM PC. Each character displayed on the screen is associated to two consecutive memory locations. The first memory location contains the extended ASCII code for the character, and the second location is interpreted as eight boolean switches that control the display attributes of the character. The purpose of each display attribute bit is described in a comment in the definition module appearing in Figure 10-5.

This text display reserves 4000 bytes of memory, starting at memory location B8000 (base 16). By placing the appropriate values in these 4000 bytes of memory, we may control the entire text display.

```
1    DEFINITION MODULE PCScreen;
2
3    (* Control for IBM PC Text screen using a graphics adapter *)
4
5    EXPORT QUALIFIED
6              DisplayString, ClearRectangle, ChangeDisplayMode;
7    CONST
8      RowMax = 25;
9      ColMax = 80;
10
11   PROCEDURE DisplayString (Row,Col : CARDINAL; It : ARRAY OF CHAR);
12
13   PROCEDURE ClearRectangle (TopRow,    LeftColumn,
14                             BottomRow, RightColumn : CARDINAL);
15
16   PROCEDURE ChangeDisplayMode (TopRow,    LeftColumn,
17                                BottomRow, RightColumn : CARDINAL;
18                                Mode : CHAR);
19
20      (*  The eight bits in Mode effect the screen as follows:
21       *  1 = turn on the feature, 0 = turns it off
22       *  +--------------- Blink
23       *  ¦ +------------- Red Background
24       *  ¦ ¦ +----------- Green Background
25       *  ¦ ¦ ¦ +--------- Blue Background
26       *  ¦ ¦ ¦ ¦ +------- Intensity
27       *  ¦ ¦ ¦ ¦ ¦ +----- Red Foreground
28       *  ¦ ¦ ¦ ¦ ¦ ¦ +--- Green Foreground
29       *  ¦ ¦ ¦ ¦ ¦ ¦ ¦ +- Blue Foreground
30       *  ¦ ¦ ¦ ¦ ¦ ¦ ¦ ¦
31       *  x x x x x x x x
32       *)
33
34   END PCScreen.
```

Figure 10-5   Definition Module PCScreen

The definition module PCScreen, presented in Figure 10-5, declares three procedures that support the direct manipulation of the 25-by-80 text screen on an IBM PC. The purpose of each procedure is self-explanatory. For example, the procedure call

```
ClearRectangle (1, 1, 25, 80)
```

clears the entire display. The procedure call

```
DisplayString (13, 36, 'I did it')
```

displays the specified string at the center of the screen.

The comment in the definition module PCScreen also shows how the eight bits in the display attribute bytes control the display of a character. For example, the procedure call

```
ChangeDisplayMode (8, 31, 18, 49, 340C)
```

displays a yellow (red-green) background with blinking black letters in the specified area.

The corresponding implementation module appears in Figure 10-6. The text screen layout is described as an array of records with each record

```
1    IMPLEMENTATION MODULE PCScreen;
2
3    CONST   Blank = ' ';
4
5    TYPE    CharRecord = RECORD
6                             Code, Attr : CHAR
7                             END;
8            TextScreen = ARRAY [1..RowMax], [1..ColMax] OF CharRecord;
9
10   VAR     Screen [0B8000H] : TextScreen;
11
12   PROCEDURE RowAdjust (Row : CARDINAL) : CARDINAL;
13
14       BEGIN
15       RETURN  (Row-1) MOD RowMax + 1
16       END RowAdjust;
17
18   PROCEDURE ColAdjust (Col : CARDINAL) : CARDINAL;
19
20       BEGIN
21       RETURN  (Col-1) MOD ColMax + 1
22       END ColAdjust;
23
```

```
24    PROCEDURE DisplayString (Row,Col : CARDINAL; It : ARRAY OF CHAR);
25
26       VAR    I : CARDINAL;
27
28       BEGIN
29       Row := RowAdjust (Row);  Col := ColAdjust (Col);
30       FOR I := 0 TO HIGH (It) DO
31          Screen [Row, Col+I].Code := It [I]
32       END
33       END DisplayString;
34
35    PROCEDURE ClearRectangle (TopRow,    LeftColumn,
36                                 BottomRow, RightColumn : CARDINAL);
37
38       VAR    I, J : CARDINAL;
39
40       BEGIN
41       TopRow      := RowAdjust (TopRow);
42       BottomRow   := RowAdjust (BottomRow);
43       LeftColumn  := ColAdjust (LeftColumn);
44       RightColumn := ColAdjust (RightColumn);
45       FOR I := TopRow TO BottomRow DO
46          FOR J := LeftColumn TO RightColumn DO
47             Screen [I, J].Code := Blank
48          END
49       END
50       END ClearRectangle;
51
52    PROCEDURE ChangeDisplayMode (TopRow,    LeftColumn,
53                                   BottomRow, RightColumn : CARDINAL;
54                                   Mode : CHAR);
55
56       VAR    I, J : CARDINAL;
57
58       BEGIN
59       TopRow      := RowAdjust (TopRow);
60       BottomRow   := RowAdjust (BottomRow);
61       LeftColumn  := ColAdjust (LeftColumn);
62       RightColumn := ColAdjust (RightColumn);
63       FOR I := TopRow TO BottomRow DO
64          FOR J := LeftColumn TO RightColumn DO
65             Screen [I, J].Attr := Mode
66          END
67       END
68       END ChangeDisplayMode;
69
70    END PCScreen.
```

Figure 10-6   Implementation Module PCScreen

containing two characters. This array is shown on lines 5 through 8. The *Variable Declaration* on line 10 binds the identifier Screen to the hardware address of the screen display. The procedures RowAdjust and Column-Adjust guarantee that the row and column values are within their respective bounds. The implementation of the three screen manipulation procedures is straightforward.

Exercises

1. Research the exact definition of the module SYSTEM for the implementation of Modula-2 you are using.

2. Run the program module Determine on the implementation of Modula-2 you are using and interpret the results.

10:2 Generics

The data structures introduced in Chapter 9 play important roles in solving many programming problems. For this reason and because many data structures have well-defined operations performed on them, programmers often find themselves writing separate procedures or modules that are identical except for the type of the data being manipulated. For example, the library module CharStacks developed in Section 9:3 implements stacks in which the elements **must** be characters. A library module to implement stacks of integers, bitsets, records, or arrays would differ only in the declaration of the type of elements being manipulated in the stack.

Other programming areas such as Input/Output and sorting require the same redefinition of procedures to accommodate data of different types. A data structure or an operation is said to be declared generically if it handles data of any type.

The low-level programming features of Modula-2 support the declaration of procedures and modules that operate generically. This support is accomplished through the coordinated use of several features. The types WORD and ADDRESS along with the procedures TSIZE and SIZE, imported from the pseudomodule SYSTEM, play a role. The procedures ALLOCATE and DEALLOCATE, imported from the module Storage, also play a role. A key feature in Modula-2 that makes the writing of generic procedures possible is **open array parameters**. An open array used in conjunction with the standard procedure HIGH is the key. Open array parameters and the standard procedure HIGH are discussed in Section 6:2.

An open array is the specification of a procedure parameter as an array in which no subscripting range is given. The standard procedure HIGH is a one-argument function that returns the subscript of the last element in the array, assuming the index range starts at 0. Thus the number of elements in an open array is determined at execution time with the function procedure HIGH.

When writing generic procedures, we must declare the formal parameter as an ARRAY OF WORD. In this way the parameter is looked at simply as a memory area whose actual size is determined at run time with the function procedure HIGH. Of course, passing a parameter this way hides the structure of the data from the procedure. The structure, if required within a procedure, must be determined in some other manner. However, many applications exist in which knowledge of the exact structure is unimportant.

Consider the task of writing a generic module for stacks in which the elements in the stack may be of any type. In the case of stacks, the structure of each element is unimportant. One question that might arise is, may elements of different types be stored in the same stack, or must all the elements in a stack be of the same type? The answer to this question depends upon the actual application at hand. However, allowing elements of different types to exist in the same structure is no more difficult than having a homogeneous stack.

The definition module Stacks is presented in Figure 10-7. This module is written generically so that elements of any type may be pushed onto and popped from a stack. Since dynamic allocation is used, this module supports the simultaneous existence of any number of stacks. The type Stack is a hidden type; its actual structure is hidden from the users of this module. The formal parameter ELEMENT, appearing in the parameter lists of the procedures Push, Pop, and TopElement, is declared as an open array of type WORD. This notation indicates that data of any type may be passed via this parameter. The function StatusStack returns a code that indicates the result of the last operation performed on the specified stack.

The implementation module Stacks is presented in Figure 10-8. It imports WORD, ADDRESS, and TSIZE from the module SYSTEM. In each of the three procedures Push, Pop, and TopElement, the data being processed is passed through an open array parameter. The size of the actual parameter is determined at execution time to allocate an area of memory sufficient to store the element. The data type StackObject utilizes a record template of the form

```
Link    Length          Data
┌─────┬─────┬──────────────────────┐         ┌─────┐
│     │     │                      │   ...   │     │
└─────┴─────┴──────────────────────┘         └─────┘
```

```
 1   DEFINITION MODULE Stacks;
 2
 3   FROM SYSTEM IMPORT WORD;
 4
 5   EXPORT QUALIFIED Stack,CreateStack, DestroyStack, StatusStack,
 6        SizeStack, Push, Pop, TopElement;
 7
 8   TYPE
 9     Stack;
10
11   PROCEDURE CreateStack (VAR STACK : Stack);
12
13   PROCEDURE DestroyStack (VAR STACK : Stack);
14
15   PROCEDURE StatusStack (STACK : Stack) : CARDINAL;
16     (* 0 = All Ok          *)
17     (* 1 = Can't Access Top Element; Stack Empty *)
18     (* 2 = Can't Pop; Stack Empty      *)
19     (* 3 = Actual Data longer than Element   *)
20     (* 4 = Element longer than Actual Data   *)
21
22   PROCEDURE SizeStack (STACK : Stack) : CARDINAL;
23
24   PROCEDURE Push (ELEMENT : ARRAY OF WORD; VAR STACK : Stack);
25
26   PROCEDURE Pop (VAR ELEMENT : ARRAY OF WORD; VAR STACK : Stack);
27
28   PROCEDURE TopElement (VAR ELEMENT : ARRAY OF WORD;
29                                            STACK : Stack);
30   END Stacks.
```

Figure 10-7   Definition Module **Stacks**

```
 1   IMPLEMENTATION MODULE Stacks;
 2
 3   FROM SYSTEM          IMPORT WORD, ADDRESS, TSIZE;
 4   FROM Storage         IMPORT ALLOCATE, DEALLOCATE;
 5
 6   CONST  MaxAddress = 32767;  (* The largest size of any element *)
 7
 8   TYPE   Object = POINTER TO StackObject;
 9          StackObject = RECORD
10                        Link   : Object;
11                        Length : CARDINAL;
12                        Data   : ARRAY [0..MaxAddress] OF WORD
13                      END;
14
```

```
15                Stack = POINTER TO StackRecord;
16                StackRecord = RECORD
17                           Top    : Object;
18                           Status : CARDINAL;
19                           Size   : CARDINAL
20                        END;
21
22   VAR    Overhead : CARDINAL;
23
24   PROCEDURE CreateStack (VAR STACK:Stack);
25
26      BEGIN
27      NEW (STACK);
28      WITH STACK^ DO
29        Top    := NIL;
30        Status := 0;
31        Size   := 0
32      END
33      END CreateStack;
34
35   PROCEDURE StatusStack (STACK:Stack) : CARDINAL;
36
37      BEGIN
38      RETURN STACK^.Status
39      END StatusStack;
40
41   PROCEDURE SizeStack (STACK:Stack) : CARDINAL;
42
43      BEGIN
44      RETURN STACK^.Size
45      END SizeStack;
46
47   PROCEDURE MoveData (From:ARRAY OF WORD; VAR To:ARRAY OF WORD;
48                                               High:CARDINAL);
49
50      VAR    I : CARDINAL;
51
52      BEGIN
53      FOR I := 0 TO (High-1) DO
54         To[I] := From[I]
55      END
56      END MoveData;
57
58   PROCEDURE Push (ELEMENT:ARRAY OF WORD; VAR STACK:Stack);
59
60      VAR    Actual   : CARDINAL;
61             NewTop   : Object;
62
63      BEGIN
```

```
 64        Actual := HIGH (ELEMENT) + 1;
 65        ALLOCATE (NewTop, (Actual+Overhead)); (* Only what's needed *)
 66        NewTop^.Link   := STACK^.Top;
 67        NewTop^.Length := Actual;
 68        MoveData (ELEMENT, NewTop^.Data, Actual);
 69        STACK^.Top := NewTop;
 70        INC (STACK^.Size);
 71        STACK^.Status := 0                        (* All Ok *)
 72     END Push;
 73
 74  PROCEDURE Pop (VAR ELEMENT:ARRAY OF WORD; VAR STACK:Stack);
 75
 76     VAR    OldTop      : Object;
 77            Actual      : CARDINAL;
 78            Available   : CARDINAL;
 79
 80     BEGIN
 81     IF STACK^.Size > 0 THEN
 82        OldTop     := STACK^.Top;
 83        STACK^.Top := OldTop^.Link;
 84        Actual     := OldTop^.Length;
 85        Available  := HIGH (ELEMENT) + 1;
 86        IF Available < Actual THEN
 87            STACK^.Status := 3  (* Actual Data > Element *)
 88          ELSIF Available > Actual THEN
 89            STACK^.Status := 4; (* Element > Actual Data *)
 90            Available := Actual
 91          ELSE
 92            STACK^.Status := 0    (* All Ok *)
 93        END;
 94        MoveData (OldTop^.Data, ELEMENT, Available);
 95        DEC (STACK^.Size);
 96        DEALLOCATE (OldTop, (Actual+Overhead))
 97      ELSE
 98        STACK^.Status := 2  (* Can't Pop; Stack empty *)
 99     END
100     END Pop;
101
102  PROCEDURE TopElement (VAR ELEMENT:ARRAY OF WORD; STACK:Stack);
103
104     VAR    OldTop      : Object;
105            Actual      : CARDINAL;
106            Available   : CARDINAL;
107
108     BEGIN
109     IF STACK^.Size > 0 THEN
110        OldTop     := STACK^.Top;
111        Actual     := OldTop^.Length;
112        Available  := HIGH (ELEMENT) + 1;
```

```
113              IF Available < Actual THEN
114                 STACK^.Status := 3  (* Actual Data > than Element  *)
115              ELSIF Available > Actual THEN
116                 STACK^.Status := 4; (* Element > than Actual Data  *)
117                 Available := Actual
118              ELSE
119                 STACK^.Status := 0    (* All Ok *)
120              END;
121              MoveData (OldTop^.Data, ELEMENT, Available)
122           ELSE
123              STACK^.Status := 1 (* Can't access; Stack empty *)
124        END
125        END TopElement;
126
127  PROCEDURE DestroyStack (VAR STACK:Stack);
128
129     VAR    Ignore : WORD;
130
131     BEGIN
132     WHILE STACK^.Size > 0 DO
133        Pop (Ignore, STACK)
134     END;
135     DISPOSE (STACK)
136     END DestroyStack;
137
138  BEGIN
139  Overhead := TSIZE (ADDRESS) + TSIZE (CARDINAL)
140  END Stacks.
```

Figure 10-8   Implementation Module Stacks

where the component Link is of type ADDRESS, Length is a CARDINAL, and Data is a contiguous collection of WORDs. Technically, Data is an extremely large ARRAY OF WORD, but since no data objects of type Stack-Object are ever allocated, this large array does not pose a problem. Generic stack records are obtained with the procedure ALLOCATE. Each record allocated is of sufficient size to hold the components Link and Length and the actual data. In this way only the required amount of memory is allocated.

Exercises

1. Write a generic module to support queues.

2. Write a generic module to support lists with the following characteristics:

a. A generic list type.

b. Procedures to create and destroy lists.

Consider and solve the following support problems:

   i.   Should the list be implemented as a two-way structure?
  ii.   Should all list procedures work with a pointer to the current item being processed, or should there be procedures Insert, Delete, and Read, which work on any item in the list?
 iii. Determine the pros and cons of each approach.

3. Write a generic AVL tree module.

4. Write a generic module to sort an array of values of any type. Declare a procedure type to convey the sorting criterion to the sort procedure.

10:3 Nontext Stream I/O

The standard module InOut provides support for text I/O. The word "text" implies that a translation occurs in the I/O process that converts numeric values between their internal representations and strings of characters. InOut also contains two procedures, ReadWrd and WriteWrd, that perform I/O transfer without translation.

ReadWrd and WriteWrd support I/O to peripheral storage devices, such as disks and tapes, where information is stored as bit patterns. Support for stream I/O may be built using ReadWrd and WriteWrd. Figure 10-9 presents the definition module GetPut, which supports nontext I/O for all data types, simple and structured. For example, a program might initialize an array or record and use the procedure Put to place data on some storage device. Later, another program could use the procedure Get to retrieve the data.

When storing and retrieving data on auxiliary devices, the procedures Get and Put offer two advantages over ReadInt, WriteInt, ReadCard, and so forth from InOut. Since Get and Put perform no translation, the I/O process should be faster and probably require less space for storage.

Another advantage of the library module GetPut is that data are stored in a consistent format. The procedure Put stores a value indicating the length of the data object, followed by that data object. This length must be stored because, later, when the data object is being read by Get, its size may not be known. A call to the procedure Get may specify a parameter whose size does not match the size of the next data value that is about to be read. The parameter's size may be either too big or too small. The variable IOFit is initialized by Get to indicate the relationship

```
 1   DEFINITION MODULE GetPut;
 2
 3   FROM SYSTEM   IMPORT WORD;
 4                 (*
 5                  * On some Modula-2 systems, BYTE, or its
 6                  * equivalent, should be IMPORTed from SYSTEM
 7                  *)
 8
 9   FROM InOut    IMPORT ReadWrd, WriteWrd;
10                 (*
11                  * If BYTE, or its equivalent, is IMPORTed from
12                  * SYSTEM, then ReadByte and WriteByte, or their
13                  * equivalents should be IMPORTed from InOut or
14                  * some I/O library module
15                  *)
16
17   EXPORT QUALIFIED IOFit, Okay, TooSmall, TooBig, IOSize, Get, Put;
18
19   VAR    IOFit  : (Okay, TooSmall, TooBig);
20          IOSize : CARDINAL;
21
22   PROCEDURE Get (VAR Buffer : ARRAY OF WORD);
23
24   PROCEDURE Put (VAR Buffer : ARRAY OF WORD);
25
26   END GetPut.
```

Figure 10-9   Definition Module GetPut

between the size of the parameter and the size of the data. In any case the variable ActualSize contains the size of the data that were transferred.

Figure 10-10 contains the corresponding implementation module GetPut. The procedure Put first transfers a value to the output device, indicating the size of the data object. This transfer is done with the statement

```
WriteWrd (IOSize);
```

Next, the data itself are transferred a WORD at a time.

Get is the more complex of the two procedures because it must determine the relationship between the size of the parameter and the size of the data. The variable IOFit is set accordingly on lines 25 through 34. Note that after the data read, if the parameter is too small, additional calls to ReadWrd skip over the remainder of the data and align the input stream with the beginning of the next data object. This is accomplished on lines 38 through 42.

```
1    IMPLEMENTATION MODULE GetPut;
2
3    FROM SYSTEM   IMPORT WORD;
4                 (*
5                  * On some Modula-2 systems, BYTE, or its
6                  * equivalent, should be IMPORTed from SYSTEM
7                  *)
8
9    FROM InOut    IMPORT ReadWrd, WriteWrd;
10                (*
11                 * If BYTE, or its equivalent, is IMPORTed from
12                 * SYSTEM, then ReadByte and WriteByte, or their
13                 * equivalents should be IMPORTed from InOut or
14                 * some I/O library module
15                 *)
16
17   PROCEDURE Get (VAR Buffer : ARRAY OF WORD);
18
19       VAR    I, BufferSize, GetSize : CARDINAL;
20              Temp : WORD;
21
22       BEGIN
23       ReadWrd (IOSize);
24       BufferSize := HIGH (Buffer);
25       IF IOSize = BufferSize THEN
26           GetSize := IOSize;
27           IOFit := Okay
28         ELSIF IOSize < BufferSize THEN
29           GetSize := IOSize;
30           IOFit := TooBig
31         ELSE
32           GetSize := BufferSize;
33           IOFit := TooSmall
34       END;
35       FOR I := 0 TO GetSize DO
36          ReadWrd (Buffer [I])
37       END;
38       IF IOFit = TooSmall THEN
39           FOR I := GetSize+1 TO IOSize DO
40               ReadWrd (Temp)
41           END;
42       END;
43       END Get;
44
45   PROCEDURE Put (VAR Buffer : ARRAY OF WORD);
46
47       VAR I : CARDINAL;
48
```

```
49        BEGIN
50        IOSize := HIGH (Buffer);
51        WriteWrd (IOSize);
52        IOFit := Okay;
53        FOR I := 0 TO HIGH (Buffer) DO
54            WriteWrd (Buffer [I])
55        END;
56        END  Put;
57
58    BEGIN
59    END GetPut.
```

Figure 10-10 Implementation Module GetPut

When working with system dependent features, a programmer must be careful. On some implementations of Modula-2, not only can the type WORD be imported but so can a smaller-sized addressable unit, referred to as a BYTE. If a programmer uses a system that declares the identifier BYTE, the library module GetPut presented in this system may have to be modified. To determine if the type BYTE must be used, place the following statements in a program module that references the module GetPut. First, include the declaration

        VAR Ch : CHAR;

then insert the procedure call

        Put (Ch);

into the program module. If an error message is generated during translation because of the parameter Ch in the call to Put, then GetPut must be modified as follows, using the identifier BYTE imported from the module SYSTEM. Modify the declarations of the parameter Buffer in the procedures Get and Put, changing ARRAY OF WORD to ARRAY OF BYTE. Then replace each procedure call of the form

        ReadWrd (Buffer [I]) and WriteWrd (Buffer [I])

by procedure calls of the form

        ReadByte (Buffer [I]) and WriteByte (Buffer [I])

respectively, or by whatever procedures are supplied in some standard module to support byte I/O.

Exercises

1. Thoroughly test the library module GetPut on the implementation of Modula-2 you are using.

2. If the data type BYTE is declared on the implementation of Modula-2 you are using, make the necessary modifications to the library module GetPut so that it works correctly in all cases.

3. Investigate FileSystem and other I/O support modules on your implementation of Modula-2 and determine which file structures are supported (ISAM, VSAM, B-Tree, and so forth).

4. The library module GetPut, as presented in this section, requires that users import and use Done, CloseInput, OpenInput, CloseOutput, and OpenOutput from the standard module InOut. Write and test a complete version of GetPut that internally imports these identifiers from InOut and declares and exports its own procedures to accomplish these same operations. What advantage, if any, do you see in doing it this way?

10:4 Coroutines

Concurrent programming and coroutines are important concepts that play a role in describing programming situations at the system level in a multiprogramming environment. A complete discussion of these concepts is beyond the scope of this text. However, the concepts of logical concurrency and coroutines are presented here. Coroutines are sequential processes that function in tandem by transferring control between each other, simulating concurrent processing in a well-defined way.

As an example of coroutines, consider the graph-building process described in Section 9:6. The program in Figure 9-35 creates a representation of a graph by building a list of the nodes in a graph with a record representing each node. Each record contains two pointers to lists of information about the arcs associated with the node. One list is a list of the arcs entering the node, and the other is a list of the arcs leaving the node. The process of building this representation depends upon a side effect of the function LocateNode. Since function side effects are undesirable, they should be removed.

Figure 10-11 presents an alternative to the program module DiGraph appearing in Figure 9-35. The side effect is removed from the function LocateNode by having the process of building the list of nodes implemented as a coroutine, identified as BuildNodeList. With this

```
 1 MODULE CoroutineExample;
 2
 3 FROM InOut    IMPORT EOL, termCH, ReadString, OpenInput,
 4                      CloseInput, Write, WriteLn, WriteString;
 5
 6 FROM Storage IMPORT ALLOCATE;
 7
 8 FROM SYSTEM  IMPORT WORD, ADR, PROCESS, NEWPROCESS, TRANSFER;
 9
10 CONST   MaxNameSize = 10;
11         CR          = 15C;
12         ScratchSize = 200;
13
14
15 TYPE    ArcPointer    = POINTER TO ArcRecord;
16         NodePointer   = POINTER TO NodeRecord;
17         NameType      = ARRAY [ 1 .. MaxNameSize ] OF CHAR;
18         NodeRecord    = RECORD
19                              NodeLink : NodePointer;
20                              NodeName : NameType;
21                              OutArcList, InArcList : ArcPointer;
22                         END;
23
24         ArcRecord     = RECORD
25                              OutLink : ArcPointer;
26                              OutNode : NodePointer;
27                              InLink : ArcPointer;
28                              InNode : NodePointer;
29                         END;
30
31         ScratchType = ARRAY [ 1 .. ScratchSize ] OF WORD;
32         ScratchPoint = POINTER TO ScratchType;
33
34 VAR     NodeList          : NodePointer;
35         ScratchArea       : ScratchType;
36         Name              : NameType;
37         Main, Coroutine   : PROCESS;
38         FromNode, ToNode  : NodePointer;
39         Arc               : ArcPointer;
40
41 PROCEDURE NoMatch (VAR  N1, N2 : NameType) : BOOLEAN;
42
43    VAR    I : CARDINAL;
44
45    BEGIN
46    FOR I := 1 TO MaxNameSize DO
47       IF N1 [I] # N2 [I] THEN
48            RETURN TRUE
49       END
```

```
50      END;
51      RETURN FALSE;
52      END  NoMatch;
53
54  PROCEDURE LocateNode (VAR Name: NameType) : NodePointer;
55
56      VAR    NodeIndex : NodePointer;
57
58      BEGIN
59      NodeIndex := NodeList;
60      WHILE (NodeIndex # NIL) &
61            NoMatch (Name, NodeIndex^.NodeName) DO
62         NodeIndex := NodeIndex^.NodeLink
63      END;
64      RETURN NodeIndex
65      END  LocateNode;
66
67  PROCEDURE ReadName (VAR Word: ARRAY OF CHAR);
68
69      VAR    I : CARDINAL;
70
71      BEGIN
72      FOR I := 0 TO HIGH (Word) DO
73         Word [I] := CHR (0)
74      END;
75      ReadString (Word)
76      END ReadName;
77
78  PROCEDURE BuildNodeList;
79
80      VAR    NodeIndex : NodePointer;
81
82      BEGIN
83      NodeList := NIL;                    (* Coroutine initialization *)
84      LOOP
85         NodeIndex := NodeList;
86         WHILE (NodeIndex # NIL) &
87               NoMatch (Name, NodeIndex^.NodeName) DO
88            NodeIndex := NodeIndex^.NodeLink
89         END;
90         IF NodeIndex = NIL THEN
91            NEW (NodeIndex);
92            WITH NodeIndex^ DO
93               NodeLink  := NodeList;   OutArcList := NIL;
94               InArcList := NIL;        NodeName := Name
95            END;
96            NodeList := NodeIndex
97         END;
98         TRANSFER (Coroutine, Main)
```

```
 99      END        (* of Coroutine loop *)
100      END   BuildNodeList;
101
102 BEGIN
103 NEWPROCESS (BuildNodeList, ADR (ScratchArea),
104                                    ScratchSize, Coroutine);
105 OpenInput ('DAT');
106 ReadName (Name);
107 WHILE Name [1] # '/' DO
108    WriteString (Name);
109    WriteString (' - ');
110    TRANSFER (Main, Coroutine);
111    FromNode := LocateNode (Name);
112    REPEAT
113       ReadName (Name);
114       WriteString (Name);  WriteString ('  ');
115       TRANSFER (Main, Coroutine);
116       ToNode := LocateNode (Name);
117       NEW (Arc);
118       WITH Arc^ DO
119          OutLink := FromNode^.OutArcList;  OutNode := FromNode;
120          InLink  := ToNode^.InArcList;     InNode   := ToNode
121       END;
122       FromNode^.OutArcList := Arc;
123       ToNode^.InArcList := Arc
124    UNTIL termCH = EOL;
125    WriteLn;
126    ReadName (Name)
127 END;
128 CloseInput
129
130 END   CoroutineExample.
```

Figure 10-11   Program Module CoroutineExample

modification the function LocateNode simply searches through the list of nodes, finds the record associated with the node whose name is passed as a parameter, and returns a pointer to that node.

The hidden type PROCESS and the procedures NEWPROCESS and TRANSFER, imported from SYSTEM, support the implementation of coroutines. In Figure 10-11 two variables of type process, Main and Coroutine, are declared. On line 103 NEWPROCESS associates the procedure BuildNodeList with the variable Coroutine of type PROCESS. The procedure NEWPROCESS requires four parameters to accomplish the initialization of a coroutine. The first parameter must be of type PROC. It specifies the parameterless procedure that embodies the coroutine. The second parameter must be of type ADDRESS or some pointer type. It passes to NEWPROCESS the address of a memory area where system dependent values are stored. The size of this area is implementation dependent and is passed to NEWPROCESS as the third parameter, of type CARDINAL. A size of 200 appears to be sufficient on most Modula-2 implementations. The fourth and final parameter is of type PROCESS and is initialized by NEWPROCESS to prepare for subsequent calls to the procedure TRANSFER.

The revised definition of Modula-2 no longer supports the type PROCESS. PROCESS's role is performed by the type ADDRESS. Since variables of type PROCESS are internally replaced by pointers, the type ADDRESS is sufficient. Thus on Modula-2 systems following the revised definition, all references to PROCESS are replaced by references to ADDRESS.

The loop on lines 107 through 127 builds the representation of the graph. In this loop, each time the name of a node is read, control is transferred to the process Coroutine. This transfer of control is accomplished with the procedure call

```
TRANSFER ( Main, Coroutine );
```

appearing on lines 110 and 115. The variable Main, of type PROCESS, maintains information about the state of the process, represented by Main, that is being suspended. This information is needed to transfer control back to the main process, on line 98.

The first transfer to the process Coroutine starts execution of the process at the beginning of the procedure BuildNodeList, which initializes the variable NodeList to NIL and enters the main loop of the coroutine, appearing on lines 84 through 99. Each time through the loop, the node list is searched, as shown on lines 86 to 89. If the node is not found, lines 90 to 97, a record to represent the new node is inserted in the node list. In either case, when this process is completed, line 98, the procedure TRANSFER transfers control back to the process Main. Note that this transfer is at the end of the loop so that the next coroutine transfer,

```
TRANSFER (Main, Coroutine)
```

continues execution of the coroutine BuildNodeList at this point. Coroutine transfers differ from procedure calls in that a procedure call always begins execution at the beginning of the procedure. In contrast, a coroutine continues execution with the statement following the previous transfer. Since the call to TRANSFER in Figure 10-11 is at the bottom of an **infinite loop**, each transfer to the process Coroutine performs a search through the node list for the node whose name is currently in the variable Name. This approach guarantees that the names of all nodes are in the node list and hence eliminates the side effect of the function LocateNode.

Another method of implementing coroutines is with the library module Processes. In this approach, processes coordinate their execution through the use of signals. The key to this approach is to have one or more processes initialized and waiting for particular signals. When a signal is transmitted, a process waiting for that signal resumes execution at the statement immediately following the statement that placed the process into a wait state. When a process completes its task, it may return to a wait state until the same or some other signal is sent. At that time, if other processes are waiting for the signal that was sent, one of them executes. This pattern continues until all processes waiting for the signal have executed and returned to wait states. Control is then returned to the statement following the statement that sent the signal.

All implementations of the library module Processes share the functionality of the identifiers exported by the library module Processes described in Niklaus Wirth's **Programming in Modula-2**. These identifiers are:

1. SIGNAL: A hidden type exported by Processes.

2. PROCEDURE StartProcess (P : PROC; n : CARDINAL): Initialize the parameterless procedure P with a workspace of size n.

3. PROCEDURE Init (VAR s : SIGNAL): Initialize the parameter s of type SIGNAL.

4. PROCEDURE SEND (VAR s : SIGNAL): Send the signal s.

5. PROCEDURE WAIT (VAR s : SIGNAL): Place the procedure currently executing into a wait state, waiting for the signal s.

6. PROCEDURE Awaited (s : SIGNAL) : BOOLEAN: Return a value of TRUE if there is at least one process waiting for the signal s; otherwise, return the value FALSE.

Signals must be initialized with Init before being used. If a signal is sent with SEND and no process is waiting for the signal, the result is a nonoperation. That is, program execution continues with the statement following the SEND statement.

Several processes may be initialized with StartProcess and be waiting for one or more signals. This situation includes the possibility of two or more processes waiting for the same signal. There is no presumed order of execution of processes waiting for the same signal. However, our experience indicates that many implementations use priority queues.

To illustrate a use of Processes, consider another implementation of the graph representation discussed in Section 9:6. This representation is implemented in various ways, including the program modules in Figures 9-35 and 10-11. A third approach appears in Figure 10-12. In this

```
 1 MODULE ProcessesExample;
 2
 3 FROM InOut      IMPORT EOL, termCH, ReadString, OpenInput,
 4                        CloseInput, Write, WriteLn, WriteString;
 5
 6 FROM Storage    IMPORT ALLOCATE;
 7
 8 FROM Processes IMPORT SIGNAL, Init, SEND, WAIT, StartProcess;
 9
10 CONST  MaxNameSize = 10;
11        CR          = 15C;
12        ScratchSize = 200;
13
14 TYPE   ArcPointer     = POINTER TO ArcRecord;
15        NodePointer    = POINTER TO NodeRecord;
16        NameType       = ARRAY [ 1 .. MaxNameSize ] OF CHAR;
17        NodeRecord     = RECORD
18                            NodeLink : NodePointer;
19                            NodeName : NameType;
20                            OutArcList, InArcList : ArcPointer;
21                         END;
22        ArcRecord      = RECORD
23                            OutLink : ArcPointer;
24                            OutNode : NodePointer;
25                            InLink : ArcPointer;
26                            InNode : NodePointer;
27                         END;
28
29 VAR    NodeList           : NodePointer;
30        Name               : NameType;
31        FromNode, ToNode : NodePointer;
32        Arc                : ArcPointer;
33        NameReady          : SIGNAL;
34
35 PROCEDURE NoMatch (VAR  N1, N2 : NameType) : BOOLEAN;
36
37    VAR I : CARDINAL;
38
39    BEGIN
40    FOR I := 1 TO MaxNameSize DO
41       IF N1 [I] # N2 [I] THEN
42            RETURN TRUE
43       END
44    END;
45    RETURN FALSE
46    END  NoMatch;
47
48 PROCEDURE LocateNode (VAR Name: NameType) : NodePointer;
49
```

```
50      VAR  NodeIndex : NodePointer;
51
52      BEGIN
53      NodeIndex := NodeList;
54      WHILE (NodeIndex # NIL) &
55            NoMatch (Name, NodeIndex^.NodeName) DO
56         NodeIndex := NodeIndex^.NodeLink
57      END;
58      RETURN NodeIndex
59      END  LocateNode;
60
61  PROCEDURE ReadName (VAR Word: ARRAY OF CHAR);
62
63      VAR I : CARDINAL;
64
65      BEGIN
66      FOR I := 0 TO HIGH (Word) DO
67         Word [I] := CHR (0)
68      END;
69      ReadString (Word)
70      END ReadName;
71
72  PROCEDURE BuildNodeList;
73
74      VAR  NodeIndex : NodePointer;
75
76      BEGIN
77      NodeList := NIL;                  (* Coroutine initialization *)
78      LOOP
79         WAIT (NameReady);
80         NodeIndex := NodeList;
81         WHILE (NodeIndex # NIL) &
82               NoMatch (Name, NodeIndex^.NodeName) DO
83            NodeIndex := NodeIndex^.NodeLink
84         END;
85         IF NodeIndex = NIL THEN
86            NEW (NodeIndex);
87            WITH NodeIndex^ DO
88               NodeLink  := NodeList;   OutArcList := NIL;
89               InArcList := NIL;        NodeName := Name
90            END;
91            NodeList := NodeIndex
92         END
93      END                             (* of Coroutine loop *)
94      END  BuildNodeList;
95
96  BEGIN
97  Init (NameReady);
98  StartProcess (BuildNodeList, ScratchSize);
```

```
 99 OpenInput ('DAT');
100 ReadName (Name);
101 WHILE Name [1] # '/' DO
102    WriteString (Name);
103    WriteString (' - ');
104    SEND (NameReady);
105    FromNode := LocateNode (Name);
106    REPEAT
107       ReadName (Name);
108       WriteString (Name);  WriteString ('  ');
109       SEND (NameReady);
110       ToNode := LocateNode (Name);
111       NEW (Arc);
112       WITH Arc^ DO
113          OutLink := FromNode^.OutArcList;  OutNode := FromNode;
114          InLink  := ToNode^.InArcList;      InNode  := ToNode
115       END;
116       FromNode^.OutArcList := Arc;
117       ToNode^.InArcList := Arc
118    UNTIL termCH = EOL;
119    WriteLn;
120    ReadName (Name)
121 END;
122 CloseInput
123 END  ProcessesExample.
```

Figure 10-12 Program Module ProcessesExample

implementation the signal NameReady is initialized in line 97. The procedure BuildNodeList is initialized in line 98, as a process waiting for the signal NameReady, in line 79.

When the signal NameReady is sent, in lines 104 and 109 of the program module, after the name of a node has been read into the array Name in lines 100, 107, and 120, the process BuildNodeList resumes execution on line 80, performs the actions contained in the loop of lines 78 through 93, and returns to the wait state in line 79.

In a more complex programming situation, where many signals are employed with a large number of processes, some questions might arise concerning the sending of a signal when no process is waiting. The function Awaited, which may be used in this circumstance, determines if a process is waiting for a particular signal. Awaited may be used to determine if a signal should be sent or if an alternative action should be performed. The

```
PROCEDURE Awaited ( s : SIGNAL ) : BOOLEAN
```

returns the value TRUE if at least one process is waiting for the signal s; otherwise, the value FALSE is returned. Hence tests may be made and signals sent or alternative actions performed, as in the statement sequence

```
IF  Awaited (XYZ) THEN
      SEND (XYZ)
      . . .
   ELSE
      (* alternate action when no
       * process is waiting
       *)
      . . .
   END;
```

Exercises

1. Rewrite the dictionary tree example presented in Section 9:5 using a coroutine.

2. Rewrite the AVL tree-restructuring example presented in Section 9:7 using a coroutine.

Appendixes

A   Modula-2 EBNF

The Modula-2 syntax as defined by Niklaus Wirth in **Programming in Modula-2** appears as follows. Some Modula-2 compilers might have variations from this standard. The syntax uses several syntactic symbols, which have the following interpretations:

.   Period: Terminates each production.

=   Replacement: The nonterminal symbol to the left can be replaced by the expression to the right.

{ .. }   Braces: The expression in the braces can appear an arbitrary number of times, including 0 times. For example,

     A = C { D }

means that each of the following can replace A:

     C, C D, C D D, C D D D, ...

| Or: One and only one of the options separated by this symbol can occur. For example,

     D = 0 | 1 | 2 | 3

means that D can be replaced by

     0, 1, 2, or 3

[..]   Brackets: Items within brackets are options. For example,

X = A [B ¦ C]

means that X can be replaced by

A, A B, or A C

(..)   Parentheses: A selection within parentheses must appear in the replacement. For example,

X = A (B ¦ C)

means that X can be replaced by

A B or A C

Syntax

```
1     ActualParameters = "(" [ ExpList ] ")".
2     AddOperator = "+" ¦ "-" ¦ OR.
3     ArrayType = ARRAY SimpleType { "," SimpleType } OF Type.
4     Assignment = Designator ":=" Expression.
5     Block = { Declaration } [ BEGIN StatementSequence ] END.
6*    Case = CaseLabelList ":" StatementSequence.
7     CaseLabelList = CaseLabels { "," CaseLabels }.
8     CaseLabels = ConstExpression [ ".." ConstExpression ].
9     CaseStatement = CASE Expression OF Case { "¦" Case }
10         [ ELSE StatementSequence ] END.
11    CompilationUnit = DefinitionModule ¦
12         [ IMPLEMENTATION ] ProgramModule.
13    ConstantDeclaration = Ident "=" ConstExpression.
14    ConstExpression = SimpleConstExpr [ Relation SimpleConstExpr ].
15*   ConstFactor = Qualident ¦ Number ¦ String ¦ Set ¦
16*        "(" ConstExpression ")" ¦ NOT ConstFactor.
17    ConstTerm = ConstFactor { MulOperator  ConstFactor }.
18    Declaration = CONST { ConstantDeclaration ";" } ¦
19         TYPE { TypeDeclaration ";" } ¦
20         VAR { VariableDeclaration ";" } ¦
21         ProcedureDeclaration ";" ¦ ModuleDeclaration ";".
22    Definition = CONST { ConstantDeclaration ";" } ¦
23         TYPE { Ident [ "=" Type ] ";" } ¦
24         VAR { VariableDeclaration  ";" } ¦
25         ProcedureHeading ";".
26*   DefinitionModule = DEFINITION  MODULE  Ident ";" { Import }
27*        [ Export ] { Definition } END Ident ".".
```

28 Designator = Qualident { "." Ident ⫶ "[" ExpList "]" ⫶ "∧" }.
29 Digit = OctalDigit ⫶ "8" ⫶ "9".
30* Element = ConstExpression [".." ConstExpression].
31 Enumeration = "(" IdentList ")".
32 ExpList = Expression { "," Expression }.
33 Export = EXPORT [QUALIFIED] IdentList ";".
34 Expression = SimpleExpression [Relation SimpleExpression].
35 Factor = Number ⫶ String ⫶ Set ⫶ Designator [ActualParameter] ⫶
36   "(" Expression ")" ⫶ NOT Factor.
37* FieldList = [IdentList ":" Type ⫶
38*   CASE [Ident ":"] Qualident OF Variant { "⫶" Variant }
39*   [ELSE FieldListSequence] END].
40 FieldListSequence = FieldList { ";" FieldList }.
41 FormalParameters =
42   "(" [FPSection { ";" FPSection }] ")" [":" Qualident].
43 FormalType = [ARRAY OF] Qualident.
44 FormalTypeList = "(" [[VAR FormalType
45   { "," [VAR] FormalType }] ")" [":" Qualident].
46 ForStatement = FOR Ident ":=" Expression TO Expression
47   [BY ConstExpression] DO StatementSequence END.
48 FPSection = [VAR] IdentList ":" FormalType.
49 HexDigit = Digit ⫶ "A" ⫶ "B" ⫶ "C" ⫶ "D" ⫶ "E" ⫶ "F".
50 Ident = Letter { Letter ⫶ Digit }.
51 IdentList = Ident { "," Ident }.
52 IfStatement = IF Expression THEN StatementSequence
53   { ELSIF Expression THEN StatementSequence }
54   [ELSE StatementSequence] END.
55 Import = [FROM Ident] IMPORT IdentList ";".
56 Integer = Digit { Digit } ⫶ OctalDigit { OctalDigit} ("B" ⫶ "C") ⫶
57   Digit {HexDigit} "H".
58 LoopStatement = LOOP StatementSequence END.
59 ModuleDeclaration =
60   MODULE Ident [Priority] ";" { Import } [Export] Block Ident.
61 MulOperator = "*" ⫶ "/" ⫶ DIV ⫶ MOD ⫶ AND ⫶ "&".
62 Number = Integer ⫶ Real.
63 OctalDigit = "0" ⫶ "1" ⫶ "2" ⫶ "3" ⫶ "4" ⫶ "5" ⫶ "6" ⫶ "7".
64 PointerType = POINTER TO Type.
65 Priority = "[" ConstExpression "]".
66 ProcedureCall = Designator [ActualParameters].
67 ProcedureDeclaration = ProcedureHeading ";" Block Ident.
68 ProcedureHeading PROCEDURE Ident [FormalParameters].
69 ProcedureType PROCEDURE [FormalTypeList].
70 ProgramModule =
71   MODULE Ident [Priority] ";" { Import } Block Ident ".".
72 Qualident = Ident { "." Ident }.
73 Real = Digit { Digit } "." {Digit} [ScaleFactor].
74 RecordType = RECORD FieldListSequence END.
75 Relation = "=" ⫶ "#" ⫶ "<>" ⫶ "<" ⫶ "<=" ⫶ ">" ⫶ ">=" ⫶ IN.
76 RepeatStatement = REPEAT StatementSequence UNTIL Expression.

77   ScaleFactor = "E" ["+" ∣ "-"] Digit { Digit }.
78   Set = [Qualident] "{" [Element { "," Element }] "}".
79   SetType = SET OF SimpleType.
80   SimpleConstExpr = ["+" ∣ "-"] ConstTerm { AddOperator
          ConstTerm }.
81   SimpleExpression = ["+" ∣ "-"] Term { AddOperator Term }.
82   SimpleType = Qualident ∣ Enumeration ∣ SubrangeType.
83   Statement = [Assignment ∣ ProcedureCall ∣
84   IfStatement ∣ CaseStatement ∣ WhileStatement ∣
85   RepeatStatement ∣ LoopStatement ∣ ForStatement ∣
86   WithStatement ∣ EXIT ∣ RETURN [Expression]].
87   StatementSequence = Statement { ";" Statement }.
88   String = "" { Character } "" ∣ '' { Character } ''.
89* SubrangeType = "[" ConstExpression ".." ConstExpression "]".
90   Term = Factor {MulOperator Factor }.
91   Type = SimpleType ∣ ArrayType ∣ RecordType ∣ SetType ∣
92   PointerType ∣ ProcedureType.
93   TypeDeclaration = Ident "=" Type.
94* Variant = CaseLabelList ":" FieldListSequence.
95   VariableDeclaration = IdentList ":" Type.
96   WhileStatement = WHILE Expression DO StatementSequence END.
97   WithStatement = WITH Designator DO StatementSequence END.

The EBNF productions marked with an "*" were contained in the original
form of the Modula-2 syntax and were revised in the new syntax. The
new versions of those productions are as follows:

6   Case = [CaseLabelList ":" StatementSequence].

15   ConstFactor = Qualident ∣ Number ∣ String ∣ Set ∣
16   "(" ConstExpression ")" ∣ NOT ConstFactor ∣ ConstSet.
16.1 ConstSet = [Qualident] "{" [ConstElement {"," ConstElement }] "}".
16.2 ConstElement = ConstExpression [".." ConstExpression].

26   DefinitionModule = DEFINITION MODULE Ident ";" { Import }
27   { Definition } END Ident ".".

30   Element = Expression [".." Expression].

37   FieldList = [IdentList ":" Type ∣
38   CASE [Ident] ":" Qualident OF Variant { "∣" Variant }
39   [ELSE FieldListSequence] END].

89   SubrangeType = [Ident] "[" ConstExpression ".." ConstExpression "]".

94   Variant = [CaseLabelList ":" FieldListSequence].

Modula-2 Syntax Diagrams

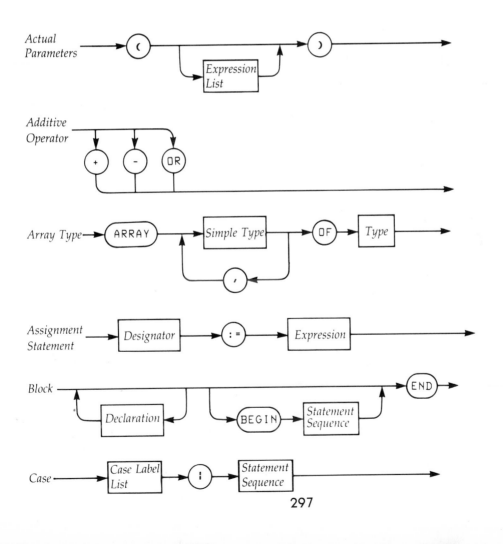

Actual Parameters

Additive Operator

Array Type

Assignment Statement

Block

Case

297

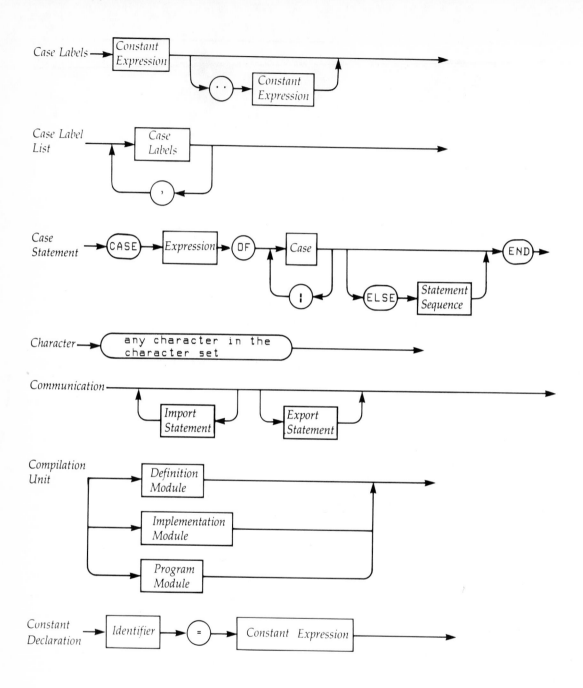

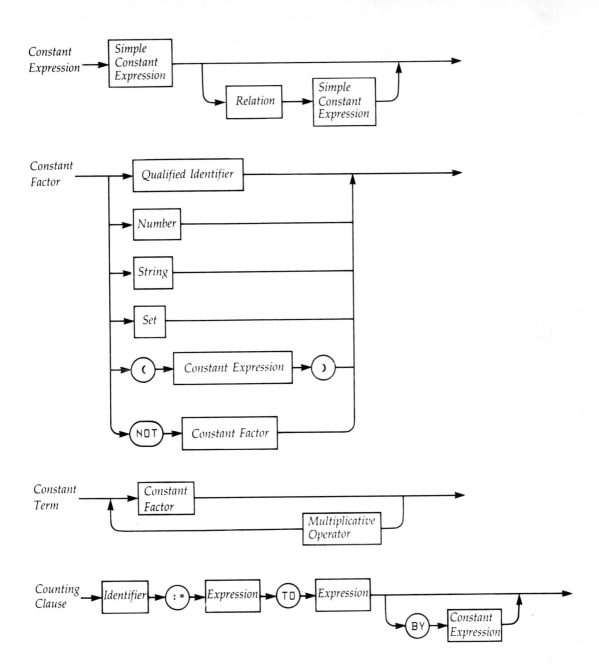

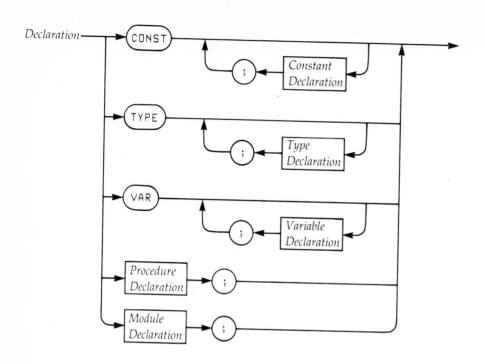

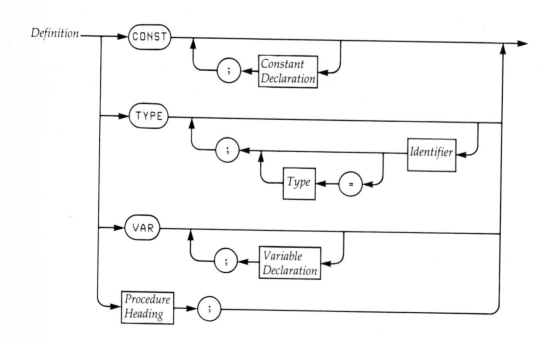

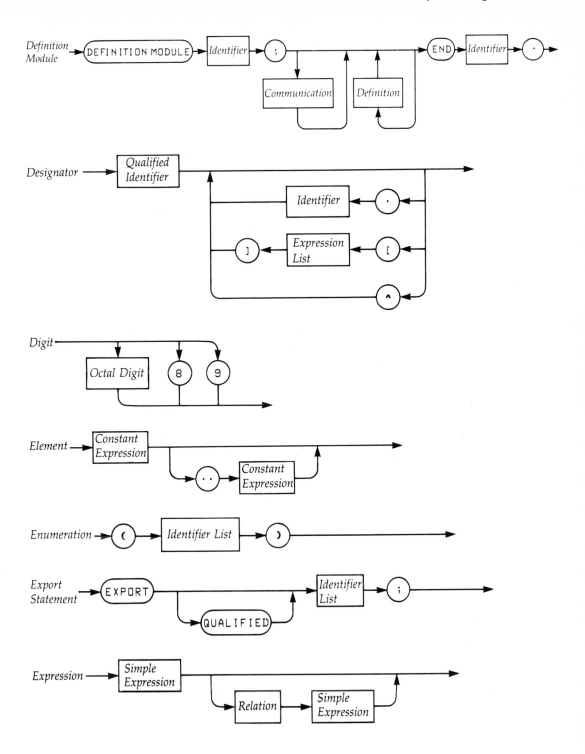

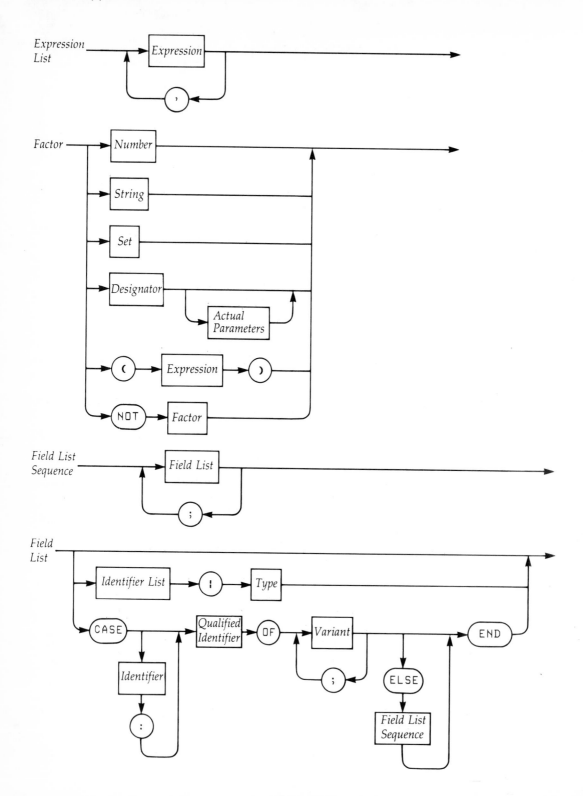

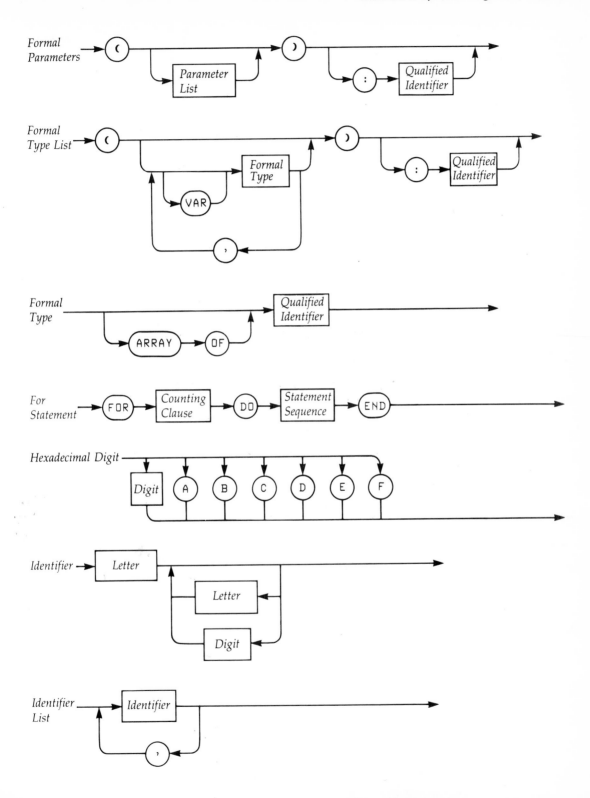

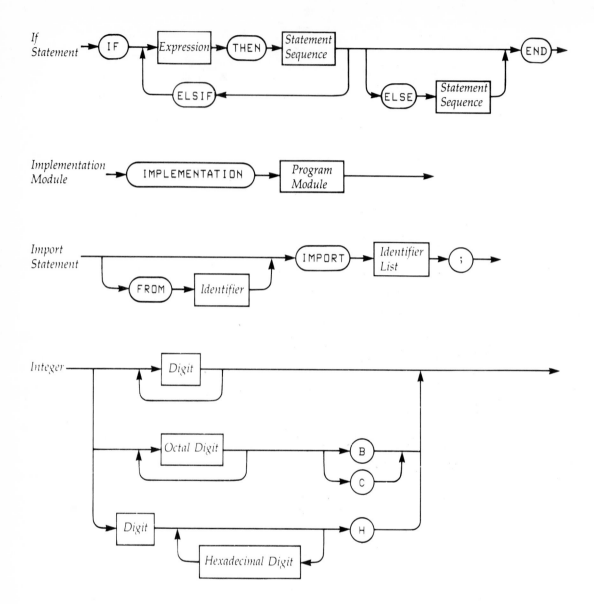

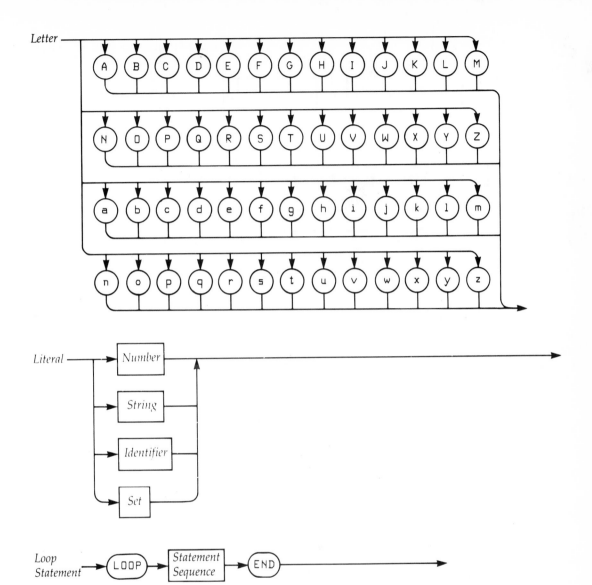

Letter

Literal

Loop Statement

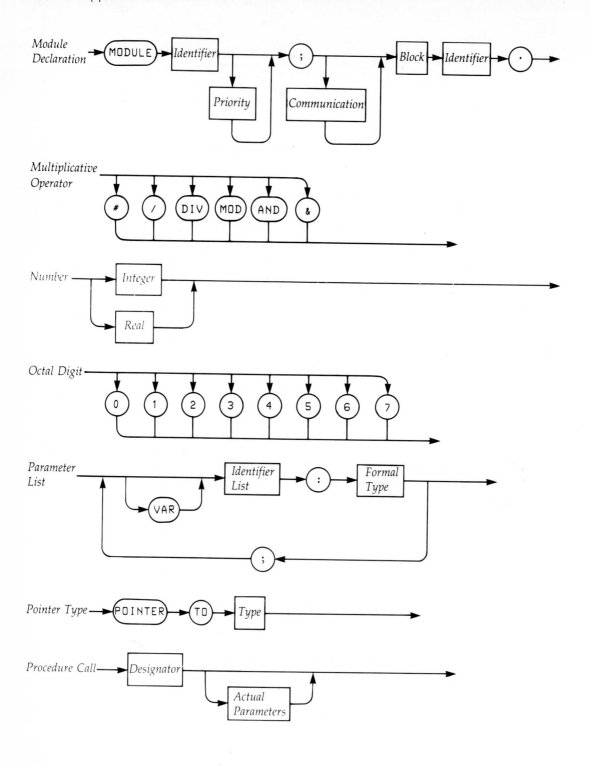

Module Declaration

Multiplicative Operator

Number

Octal Digit

Parameter List

Pointer Type

Procedure Call

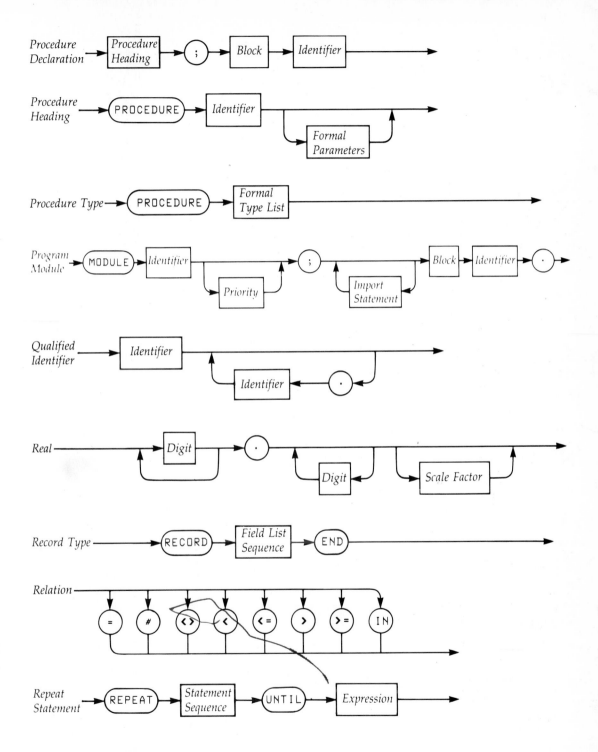

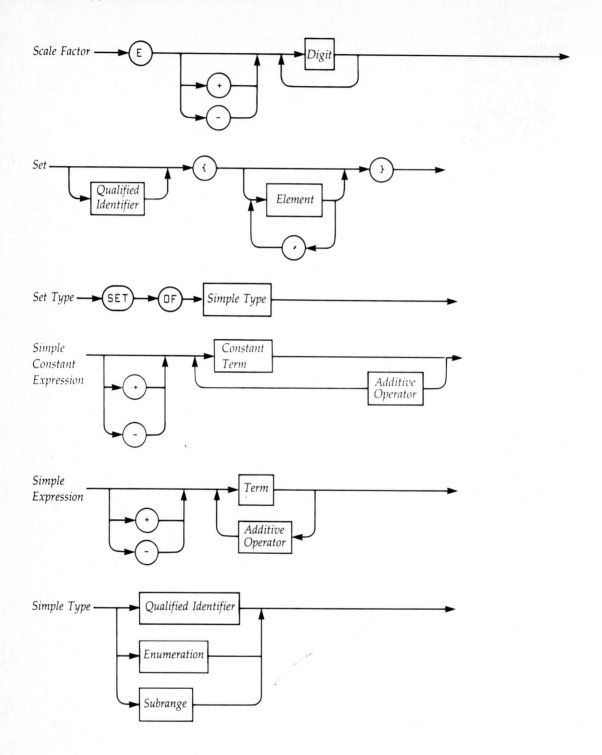

Scale Factor

Set

Set Type

Simple Constant Expression

Simple Expression

Simple Type

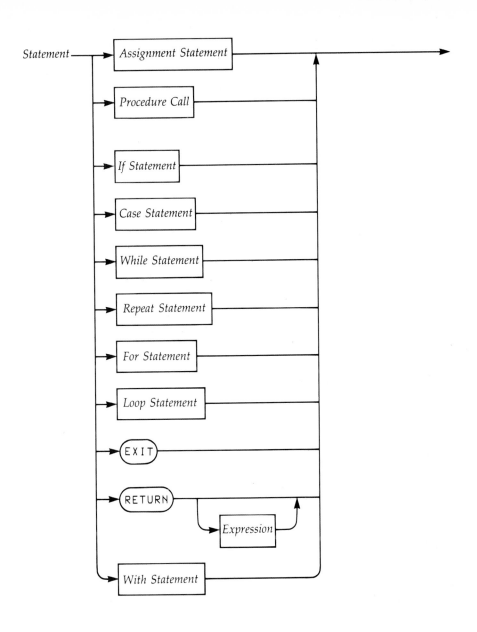

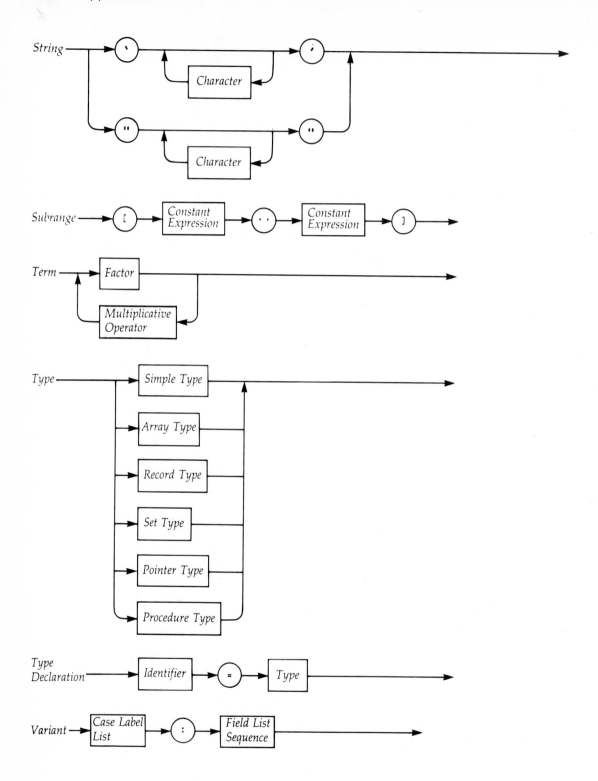

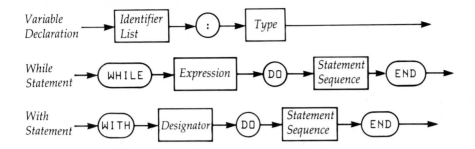

The preceding syntax diagrams describe the original definition of Modula-2. The following syntax diagrams describe the revised edition, put forth in 1984. Only those diagrams that have changed are presented; all of the others remain unchanged.

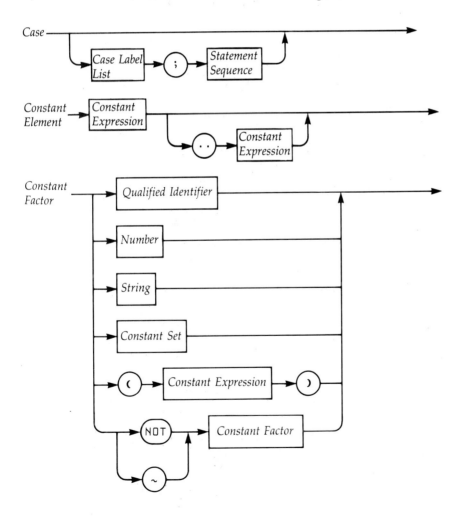

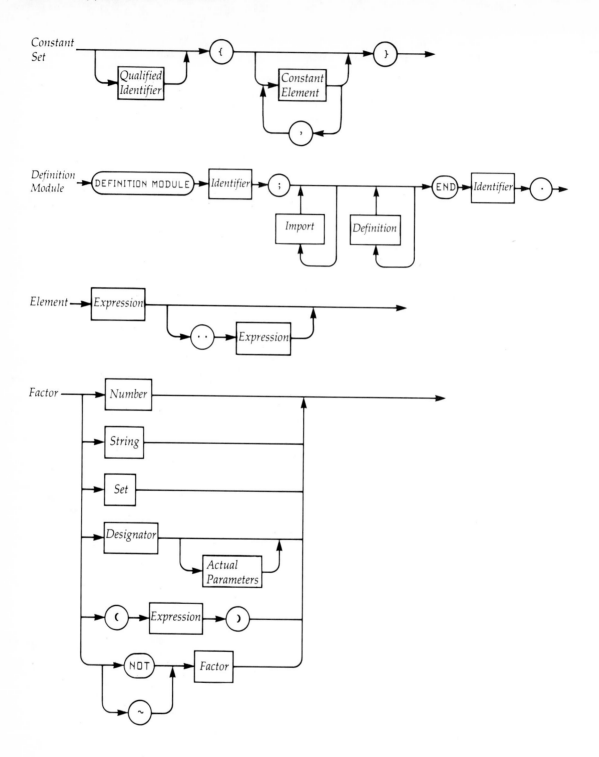

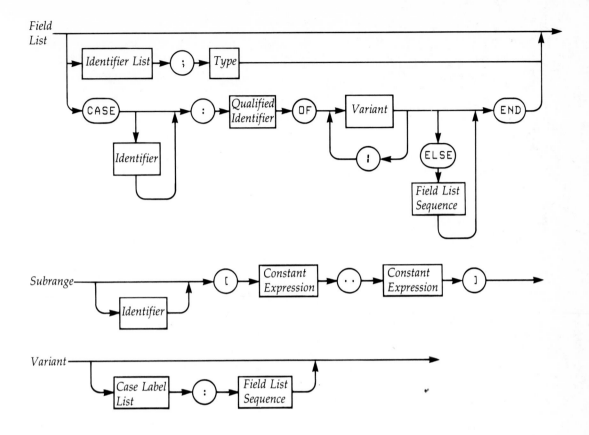

C

ASCII Character Set

Dec	Binary	Oct	Hex	Char	Dec	Binary	Oct	Hex	Char
000	0000000	000	00	nul	032	0100000	040	20	
001	0000001	001	01	soh	033	0100001	041	21	!
002	0000010	002	02	stx	034	0100010	042	22	"
003	0000011	003	03	etx	035	0100011	043	23	#
004	0000100	004	04	eot	036	0100100	044	24	$
005	0000101	005	05	enq	037	0100101	045	25	%
006	0000110	006	06	ack	038	0100110	046	26	&
007	0000111	007	07	bel	039	0100111	047	27	'
008	0001000	010	08	bs	040	0101000	050	28	(
009	0001001	011	09	ht	041	0101001	051	29	)
010	0001010	012	0A	lf	042	0101010	052	2A	*
011	0001011	013	0B	vt	043	0101011	053	2B	+
012	0001100	014	0C	ff	044	0101100	054	2C	,
013	0001101	015	0D	cr	045	0101101	055	2D	-
014	0001110	016	0E	so	046	0101110	056	2E	.
015	0001111	017	0F	si	047	0101111	057	2F	/
016	0010000	020	10	dle	048	0110000	060	30	0
017	0010001	021	11	dc1	049	0110001	061	31	1
018	0010010	022	12	dc2	050	0110010	062	32	2
019	0010011	023	13	dc3	051	0110011	063	33	3
020	0010100	024	14	dc4	052	0110100	064	34	4
021	0010101	025	15	nak	053	0110101	065	35	5
022	0010110	026	16	syn	054	0110110	066	36	6
023	0010111	027	17	etb	055	0110111	067	37	7
024	0011000	030	18	can	056	0111000	070	38	8
025	0011001	031	19	em	057	0111001	071	39	9
026	0011010	032	1A	sub	058	0111010	072	3A	:
027	0011011	033	1B	esc	059	0111011	073	3B	;
028	0011100	034	1C	fs	060	0111100	074	3C	<
029	0011101	035	1D	gs	061	0111101	075	3D	=
030	0011110	036	1E	rs	062	0111110	076	3E	>
031	0011111	037	1F	us	063	0111111	077	3F	?

Dec	Binary	Oct	Hex	Char	Dec	Binary	Oct	Hex	Char
064	1000000	100	40	@	096	1100000	140	60	'
065	1000001	101	41	A	097	1100001	141	61	a
066	1000010	102	42	B	098	1100010	142	62	b
067	1000011	103	43	C	099	1100011	143	63	c
068	1000100	104	44	D	100	1100100	144	64	d
069	1000101	105	45	E	101	1100101	145	65	e
070	1000110	106	46	F	102	1100110	146	66	f
071	1000111	107	47	G	103	1100111	147	67	g
072	1001000	110	48	H	104	1101000	150	68	h
073	1001001	111	49	I	105	1101001	151	69	i
074	1001010	112	4A	J	106	1101010	152	6A	j
075	1001011	113	4B	K	107	1101011	153	6B	k
076	1001100	114	4C	L	108	1101100	154	6C	l
077	1001101	115	4D	M	109	1101101	155	6D	m
078	1001110	116	4E	N	110	1101110	156	6E	n
079	1001111	117	4F	O	111	1101111	157	6F	o
080	1010000	120	50	P	112	1110000	160	70	p
081	1010001	121	51	Q	113	1110001	161	71	q
082	1010010	122	52	R	114	1110010	162	72	r
083	1010011	123	53	S	115	1110011	163	73	s
084	1010100	124	54	T	116	1110100	164	74	t
085	1010101	125	55	U	117	1110101	165	75	u
086	1010110	126	56	V	118	1110110	166	76	v
087	1010111	127	57	W	119	1110111	167	77	w
088	1011000	130	58	X	120	1111000	170	78	x
089	1011001	131	59	Y	121	1111001	171	79	y
090	1011010	132	5A	Z	122	1111010	172	7A	z
091	1011011	133	5B	[	123	1111011	173	7B	{
092	1011100	134	5C	\	124	1111100	174	7C	¦
093	1011101	135	5D	]	125	1111101	175	7D	}
094	1011110	136	5E	^	126	1111110	176	7E	~
095	1011111	137	5F	_	127	1111111	177	7F	del

Standard Modules

This appendix contains a description of typical modules found in most Modula-2 implementations. Each description concludes with information on major variations encountered with each module. Programmers should use this appendix only as a general reference and should carefully examine the definition modules on the particular implementation of Modula-2 they are using.

D:1 Files

This library module, along with `FileSystem`, usually provides access to the fundamental file support of the operating system. For this reason a great variety of implementations exists, each importing its own set of support procedures. Typical of these implementations are the procedures in the library module `Files`, presented in Niklaus Wirth's **Programming in Modula-2** and described as follows. If no library module named `Files` is available to you, its support might be provided through `FileSystem` or some other similarly named library module.

D:1:1 Types

`FILE [0 .. 15]`

Many implementations of Modula-2 import a hidden type named `File` or `file`.

`FileName ARRAY [0 .. 11] OF CHAR`

D:1:2 Procedures

`LookUp (f : FILE; fn : FileName; VAR reply : INTEGER);`

Look up file f in the current directory.

reply   >= 0 operation complete, reply = file length
= −1 channel used
= −2 file not found

`Create (f : FILE; fn : FileName; VAR reply : INTEGER);`

Create a new file, but not its directory entry. reply is the same as for LookUp.

`Delete (f : FILE; fn : FileName; VAR reply : INTEGER);`

Delete the file and its directory entry. reply is the same as for LookUp.

`Close (f : FILE);`

Close the file and record it in the directory.

`Release (f : FILE);`

Release file; make no directory entry.

`ReadBlock (f : FILE; p : ADDRESS; blknr, wcount : CARDINAL;`
`                                    VAR reply : INTEGER);`

Read from file f, where p is the buffer address, blknr is the first block to read, and wcount is the number of words to be read.

reply   >= 0 the number of words transferred
= −1 read error
= −2 channel not open

`WriteBlock (f : FILE; p : ADDRESS; blknr, wcount : CARDINAL;`
`                                    VAR reply : INTEGER);`

Write a block to a file using parameters, as in ReadBlock.

```
Rename (f : FILE; new, old : FileName; VAR reply : INTEGER);
```

Rename the file f, which must be opened.

reply   = 0 done
           = −1 channel used
           = −2 file not found

D:2 FileSystem

This library module contains low-level, systems dependent I/O support. The following module is from the Lilith system, as described in Niklaus Wirth's **Programming in Modula-2,** and, as such, should be considered representative of the typical support in FileSystem. However, it is not necessarily identical to the library module FileSystem that might be found in a particular implementation of Modula-2.

D:2:1 Types

File

Typically a hidden type that contains system dependent file control information.

Response

An enumeration of possible system dependent responses to an I/O operation.

D:2:2 Procedures

```
Create (VAR f : File; mediumname :ARRAY OF CHAR);
```

Create a temporary file on the indicated device.

```
Close (VAR f : File);
```

```
Lookup (VAR f :
            File; filename : ARRAY OF CHAR; new : BOOLEAN);
```

Search for the file indicated by filename. If the file does not exist and new is TRUE, a new file with the given name is created.

`Rename (VAR f : File; filename : ARRAY OF CHAR);`

Change the name of file f to `filename`. If `filename` is blank, make the file a temporary file.

`SetRead ( VAR f : File);`

Initialize the file so that it can be read.

`SetWrite (VAR f : File);`

Initialize the file so that it can be written.

`SetModify (VAR f : File);`

Initialize the file so that it can be modified.

`SetOpen (VAR f : File);`

Terminate any input or output operations on the file.

`Doio (VAR f : File);`

Used in conjunction with `SetRead`, `SetWrite`, and `SetModify` to read, write, or modify a sequential file.

`SetPos (VAR f : File; highpos, lowpos : CARDINAL);`

Set the current position of file f to the location

$$highpos * 2^{16} + lowpos$$

`GetPos (VAR f : File; VAR highpos, lowpos : CARDINAL);`

Return the current position of the file.

`Length (VAR f : File; VAR highpos, lowpos : CARDINAL);`

Return the length of the file.

`Reset (VAR f : File);`

Reset the file to the open state positioned at its beginning.

```
Again (VAR f : File);
```

The next call to ReadWord (or ReadChar) reads the same value that was read in the last ReadWord (or ReadChar).

```
ReadWord (VAR f : File; w : WORD);
```

Read from the file, at the current position.

```
WriteWord (VAR f : File; w : WORD);
```

```
ReadChar (VAR f : FILE; ch : CHAR);
```

```
WriteChar (VAR f : File; ch : CHAR);
```

D:2:3 Variations

Because the module FileSystem is very system dependent, practically every implementation of Modula-2 has a different version of it. However, there should be a great deal of similarity between the functionality of different implementations. Programmers should carefully examine this definition module before using it.

D:3 InOut

I/O support for INTEGER, CARDINAL, CHAR, and ARRAY OF CHAR is contained in the library module InOut. For INTEGER and CARDINAL values these procedures convert between the internal representation of the values and their external representations as numerals in base 10, base 8, or base 16.

D:3:1 Constants

EOL

End-of-line indicator.

D:3:2 Variables

Done

In several procedures this variable of type BOOLEAN is set to TRUE if the operation is successful; otherwise, it is set to FALSE.

`termCH`

>   Contains the character that terminated the value read by the last call
>   to `ReadString`, `ReadInt`, or `ReadCard`.

D:3:3 Procedures

`CloseInput;`

>   Close the current input file and accept further input from the ter-
>   minal.

`CloseOutput;`

>   Close the current output file and send all further output to the ter-
>   minal.

`OpenInput ( defext: ARRAY OF CHAR );`

>   Accept a file name from the terminal and open the file for input. If
>   the file name entered ends with a period, the value of `defext` (de-
>   fault extension) is appended to the name. If `OpenInput` is success-
>   ful, Done is set to TRUE.

`OpenOutput ( defext: ARRAY OF CHAR );`

>   Accept a file name from the terminal and open the file for output. If
>   the file name entered ends with a period, the value of `defext` (de-
>   fault extension) is appended to the name. If `OpenOutput` is success-
>   ful, Done is set to TRUE.

`Read ( VAR ch: CHAR );`

>   Read the next character into `ch`. Done is TRUE unless the end of file
>   is encountered.

`ReadCard ( VAR x: CARDINAL );`

>   Read an unsigned decimal number into `x`. Done is set to TRUE if suc-
>   cessful, and `termCH` contains the terminating character.

`ReadInt ( VAR x: INTEGER );`

>   Read an integer value into `x`. Done is set to TRUE if successful, and
>   `termCH` contains the terminating character.

ReadString (VAR s: ARRAY OF CHAR);

Leading blanks are ignored, but all characters following leading blanks until another blank or control character is read are placed into s. If s is not large enough, the input is truncated. termCH contains the character that terminated the input.

Write (ch: CHAR);

Write ch to the output device.

WriteLn;

Terminate the current output line. If output is buffered, all data written since the last call to this procedure are now printed.

WriteString (s: ARRAY OF CHAR);

Write the array s, a string of characters to the output device.

WriteInt (x: INTEGER; n: CARDINAL);

Write the integer value stored in x, right justified, in a field of n characters. If x is negative, the output includes a minus sign. If more than n characters are necessary, the field is expanded as needed. Leading blanks are used to pad the field if fewer than n characters are needed to print the value.

WriteCard (x,n: CARDINAL);

Write the cardinal number stored in x similarly to WriteInt.

WriteOct (x,n: CARDINAL);

Similar to WriteCard except the number is printed in base 8 rather than base 10.

WriteHex (x,n: CARDINAL);

Similar to WriteOct except the number is printed in base 16.

D:3:4 Variations

The VAX/VMS Hamburg and Logitech compilers contain the procedures ReadReal, WriteReal, and WriteRealOct, described in RealInOut, as well as the following procedures. See Section D:8 for a description of DFLOATING, GFLOATING, and HFLOATING.

> ReadDFloating (d : DFLOATING);

> ReadGFloating (g : GFLOATING);

> ReadHFloating (h : HFLOATING);

> WriteDFloating (d : DFLOATING; n : CARDINAL);

> WriteGFloating (g : GFLOATING; n : CARDINAL);

> WriteHFloating (h : HFLOATING; n : CARDINAL);

The IBM PC Logitech compiler contains the following procedures:

ReadWrd (VAR w: WORD);

Read a WORD value from the input, which **cannot** be the terminal. WORDs cannot be read from the terminal. Done is TRUE if the read was successful.

WriteWrd (w: WORD);

Write a WORD value to output, which **must** be a file. WORDs cannot be written to the terminal.

D:4 MathLib0

D:4:1 Procedures

arctan (x: REAL): REAL;

Return the arctangent of x in radians.

cos (x: REAL): REAL;

Return the cosine of x.

entier (x: REAL): INTEGER;

Return the integer representation (of type INTEGER) of the integral part of x.

```
exp ( x: REAL ): REAL;
```

Return e^x where e is approximately 2.718281828.

Return e^x where e is approximately 2.718281828.

```
ln ( x: REAL ): REAL;
```

Return the natural logarithm of x. x must be nonnegative.

```
real ( x: INTEGER ): REAL;
```

Convert the integer value stored in x to its representation as type REAL.

```
sin ( x: REAL ): REAL;
```

Return the sine of x.

```
sqrt ( x: REAL ): REAL;
```

Return the square root of x. x must be nonnegative.

D:5 Processes

D:5:1 Types

SIGNAL

Variables of this type must be initialized by the procedure Init before being used in calls to the procedures SEND and WAIT.

D:5:2 Procedures

Awaited (s : SIGNAL): BOOLEAN;

Test whether any process is waiting for the signal s.

Init (VAR s: SIGNAL)

Initialize the signal s.

SEND (VAR s : SIGNAL)

Send the signal s.

StartProcess (P : PROC; n: CARDINAL);

Allocate a memory area of size n for the procedure P and transfer control to P.

WAIT (VAR s : SIGNAL)

Suspend the calling process until the signal s is sent.

D:6 RealInOut

D:6:1 Variables

Done

Similar to Done in InOut.

D:6:2 Procedures

ReadReal (VAR x: REAL);

Read a real number.

WriteReal (x: REAL; n: CARDINAL);

Write a real number in scientific notation in a field of width n.

WriteRealOct (x: REAL);

Write a real number in scientific notation in a field of width n using base 8.

D:7 Storage

D:7:1 Procedures

ALLOCATE (VAR a: ADDRESS; size: CARDINAL);

Allocate a memory area of size size, and place the address of that memory area into a.

```
DEALLOCATE ( VAR a: ADDRESS; size: CARDINAL );
```

Return the memory area at the location whose address is stored in a. Size indicates the number of locations in the area.

```
Available ( size: CARDINAL ) : BOOLEAN;
```

Return TRUE if a memory area of size size is available; otherwise, FALSE is returned.

D:7:2 Variations

The IBM PC Logitech Modula-2 compiler also has the following procedures for the heap:

```
InstallHeap;
```

Install a dynamic heap.

```
RemoveHeap;
```

Remove the dynamic heap.

D:8 SYSTEM

D:8:1 Types

WORD

A memory unit, normally two or more bytes in length, that can be individually addressed.

ADDRESS

Formally defined as

TYPE ADDRESS = POINTER TO WORD

which can contain the address of any word in memory.

PROCESS

Identifies an executable procedure for the support of coroutines.

D:8:2 Procedures

ADR (x: AnyType): ADDRESS;

Return the address of any data object x.

SIZE (VAR v: AnyType): CARDINAL;

Return the number of memory locations occupied by the data object v.

TSIZE (AnyType): CARDINAL;

Return the number of locations of memory allocated to any variable of type AnyType.

TSIZE (AnyType, T1, T2, ...): CARDINAL;

Return the number of locations of memory allocated to the record of type AnyType with variant tags T1, T2, and so forth.

NEWPROCESS (P:PROC; A:ADDRESS; n:CARDINAL;
                                  VAR p:PROCESS);

P is a parameterless procedure that will become a coroutine; A is the address of the workspace reserved for P; n is the size of the workspace in words; and p is assigned the value of the start of P and used by the procedure TRANSFER to maintain the status of P as a coroutine.

TRANSFER (VAR p, q: PROCESS);

Suspend the process p; record the point where p was suspended so that it can be resumed later; and transfer to process q to continue execution at the point where p was suspended.

D:8:3 Variations

Practically all implementations of Modula-2 have extensive variations to provide low-level support to a variety of features. In some cases there are two systems modules, named SYSTEM and System. The VAX/VMS Logitech/Hamburg compiler contains the following types:

BYTE	1 byte
SHORTWORD	2 bytes
WORD	4 bytes
QUADWORD	8 bytes
OCTAWORD	16 bytes
F_FLOATING	REAL
G_FLOATING	64-bit floating point number
D_FLOATING	64-bit floating point number
H_FLOATING	128-bit floating point number

The following procedure is also included:

REGISTER (num : CARDINAL) : CARDINAL ;

Return the contents of the register identified by num.

The Modula-2/86 Logitech compiler also includes the type BYTE (= 1 byte) and a large collection of procedures to support the 8086/88 microprocessor and MS-DOS.

D:9 Terminal

This module provides I/O support at a level below the support given by InOut.

D:9:1 Procedures

Read (VAR ch : CHAR);

Read a character into ch.

BusyRead (VAR ch : CHAR);

Return the value 0C in ch if no character was read; otherwise, it returns the character that was read in ch.

```
ReadAgain;
```

The last character that was read will be read again when Read is called.

```
Write ( ch : CHAR );
```

```
WriteLn;
```

```
WriteString ( s : ARRAY OF CHAR );
```

D:10 TextIO

TextIO is a standard module accompanying several implementations of Modula-2, most notably the VAX/VMS Hamburg/Logitech compiler. It is similar to InOut in that most of the procedures have the same names. It is different in that InOut only supports one input text file and one output text file at a time, whereas TextIO supports several. Also, InOut has two file reassignment procedures, OpenInput and OpenOutput, which assume that any program calling them executes in an interactive environment. They both require a response from the keyboard when they execute. TextIO has four file reassignment procedures, two of which are self-contained and do not require an interaction with the keyboard to perform a file reassignment. These two are the procedures OpenIn and OpenOut.

D:10:1 Constants

EOL

End-of-line indicator.

D:10:2 Types

file

Hidden type.

D:10:3 Variables

Done

> In several procedures this variable of type BOOLEAN is set to TRUE if the operation is successful; otherwise, it is set to FALSE.

termCH

> Contains the character that terminated the last call to ReadString, ReadInt, or ReadCard.

D:10:4 Procedures

CloseInput (f : file);

> Close the input file f.

CloseOutput (f : file);

> Close the output file f.

OpenInput (f : file; defext: ARRAY OF CHAR);

> Accept a file name from the terminal and open the file f for input. If the file name entered ends with a period, the contents of defext (default extension) are appended to the name. If OpenInput is successful, Done is set to TRUE.

OpenOutput (f : file; defext: ARRAY OF CHAR);

> Accept a file name from the terminal and open the file f for output. If the file name entered ends with a period, the contents of defext (default extension) are appended to the name. If OpenOutput is successful, Done is set to TRUE.

Read (f : file; VAR ch: CHAR);

> Read the next character from the file f into ch. Done is TRUE unless the end of file is encountered.

ReadCard (f : file; VAR x: CARDINAL);

Read an unsigned decimal number into x from the file f. Done is set to TRUE if successful, and termCH contains the terminating character.

ReadInt (f : file; VAR x: INTEGER);

Read an integer value from the file f into x. Done is set to TRUE if successful, and termCH contains the terminating character.

ReadString (f : file; VAR s: ARRAY OF CHAR);

Read a string from the file f. Leading blanks are accepted but not placed into s. All characters following leading blanks until another blank or control character is entered are placed into s. If s is not large enough, the input is truncated. termCH contains the character that terminated the input.

Write (f : file; ch: CHAR);

Write ch to the file f.

WriteLn (f : file);

Terminate the output line to the file f.

WriteString (f : file; s: ARRAY OF CHAR);

Write the array s, a string of characters, to the file f.

WriteInt (f : file; x: INTEGER; n: CARDINAL);

Write the integer x, right justified, in a field of n characters to the file f. If x is negative, the output includes a minus sign. If more than n characters are needed, the field is expanded beyond size n. Leading blanks are used to pad the field if fewer than n characters are needed to print x.

WriteCard (f : file; x,n: CARDINAL);

Write the cardinal number in x, similarly to WriteInt, to the file f.

```
WriteOct ( f : file; x,n: CARDINAL );
```

Similar to WriteCard except the number is printed in base 8 rather than base 10.

```
WriteHex ( f : file; x,n: CARDINAL );
```

Similar to WriteOct except the number is printed in base 16.

D:10:5 Variations

The following I/O procedures are defined to work with data types that are specifically declared for the VAX/VMS Hamburg/Logitech compiler.

```
ReadDFloating ( f : file; d : DFLOATING );

ReadGFloating ( f : file; g : GFLOATING );

ReadHFloating ( f : file; h : HFLOATING );

WriteDFloating ( f : file; d : DFLOATING; n : CARDINAL );

WriteGFloating ( f : file; g : GFLOATING; n : CARDINAL );

WriteHFloating ( f : file; h : HFLOATING; n : CARDINAL );
```

E Modula-2 Error Messages

The following collection of error messages is typical for several popular Modula-2 implementations:

```
0   Illegal character in source
1   Illegal symbol
2   Constant out of range
3   Open comment at end of file
4   String terminator not on this line
5   Too many errors
6   String too long
7   Too many identifiers (identifier table full)
8   Too many identifiers (hash table full)

20  Identifier expected
21  Integer constant expected
22  ']' expected
23  ';' expected
24  Block name at the end does not match
25  Error in block
26  ':=' expected
27  Error in expression
28  THEN expected
29  Error in LOOP statement
30  Constant must not be CARDINAL
31  Error in REPEAT statement
32  UNTIL expected
33  Error in WHILE statement
34  DO expected
35  Error in CASE statement
36  OF expected
37  ':' expected
```

38   BEGIN expected
39   Error in WITH statement
40   END expected
41   ')' expected
42   Error in constant
43   '=' expected
44   Error in TYPE declaration
45   '(' expected
46   MODULE expected
47   QUALIFIED expected
48   Error in factor
49   Error in simple type
50   ',' expected
51   Error in formal type
52   Error in statement sequence
53   '.' expected
54   Export at global level not allowed
55   Body of definition module not allowed
56   TO expected
57   Nested module in definition module not allowed
58   '}' expected
59   '..' expected
60   Error in FOR statement
61   IMPORT expected

66   DEFINITION expected

70   Identifier specified twice in importlist
71   Identifier not exported from qualified module
72   Identifier declared twice
73   Identifier not declared
74   Type not declared
75   Identifier already declared in module environment
76
77   Too many nesting levels
78   Value of absolute address must be of type CARDINAL
79   Scope table overflow in compiler
80   Illegal priority
81   Definition module belonging to implementation not found
82   Structure not allowed for implementation or hidden type
83   Procedure implementation different from definition
84   Not all defined procedures or hidden types implemented
85   Name conflict of exported object or enumeration constant in environment
86   Incompatible versions of symbolic modules
87   Illegal parameter passing mechanism for this type
88   Function type is not scalar or basic type
89
90   Pointer-referenced type not declared
91   Tag field type expected

92   Incompatible type of variant constant
93   Constant used twice
94   Arithmetic error in evaluation of constant expression
95   Incorrect range
96   Range only with scalar type
97   Type incompatible constructor element
98   Element value out of bound
99   Set type identifier expected
100 Structured type too large
101 Undeclared identifier in export list of the module
102 Range not belonging to base type
103 Wrong class of identifier
104 No such module name found
105 Module name expected
106 Scalar type expected
107 Set too large
108 Type must not be INTEGER or CARDINAL
109 Scalar or subrange type expected
110 Case label out of bounds
111 Illegal export from program module
112 Code block for modules not allowed

120 Incompatible types in conversion
121 This type is not expected
122 Variable expected
123 Incorrect constant
124 No procedure found for substitution
125 Unsatisfactory parameters of substituted procedure
126 Set constant out of range
127 Error in standard procedure parameters
128 Type incompatibility
129 Type identifier expected
130 Type impossible to index
131 Field not belonging to a record variable
132 Too many parameters
133
134 Reference not to a variable
135 Illegal parameter substitution
136 Constant expected
137 Expected parameter
138 BOOLEAN type expected
139 Scalar types expected
140 Operation with incompatible type
141 Only global procedure of function allowed in expression
142 Incompatible element type
143 Type incompatible operands
144 No selectors allowed in expression
145 Only function call allowed in expression
146 Arrow not belonging to a pointer variable

147   Standard function or procedure must not be assigned
148   Constant not allowed as variant
149   SET type expected
150   Illegal substitution to WORD parameter
151   EXIT only in LOOP
152   RETURN only in PROCEDURE
153   Expression expected
154   Expression not allowed
155   Type of function expected
156   Integer constant expected
157   Procedure call expected
158   Identifier not exported from qualifying module
159   Code buffer overflow
160   Illegal value for code
161   Call of procedure with lower priority not allowed

200   Compiler error
201   Implementation restriction
202   Implementation restriction: FOR step too large
203   Implementation restriction: Boolean expression too long
204   Implementation restriction: Expression stack overflow
205   Implementation restriction: Procedure too long
206   Implementation restriction: Packed element used for VAR parameter
207   Implementation restriction: Illegal type conversion
220   Not further specified error
221   Division by zero
222   Index out of range or conversion error
223   Case label defined twice

300   See 222
301   See 221

303   See 223

400   Expression too complicated: Register overflow

402   Expression too complicated: Branch too long
403   Expression too complicated: Jump table overflow
404   Toomany globals, externals, and calls: Linker table overflow
405   See 205
406   Compiler error: Assertion failed
407   Compiler error: Internal confusion

994   Too many nested procedures
995   See 202
996   CASE label too large
997   Illegal parameter substitution

References

Anderson, Terry L. "A Review of Seven Modula-2 Compilers." **Journal of Pascal, Ada & Modula-2**, 3:2 (March/April 1984), p.38.

Bielak, R. "The VMS Modula-2 Compiler Reviewed." **Journal of Pascal, Ada & Modula-2**, 3:6 (November/December 1984), p.29.

Bingham, L. et. al. **Modula-2 Handbook**. Modula Research Institute, Provo, Utah, 1983.

Coar, D. "Pascal, Ada, and Modula-2." **Byte**, 9:8 (August 1984), p.215.

DeMarco, T. "Special Report: Modula-2." **Journal of Pascal & Ada**, 1:3 (September/October 1982), p.31.

Dotzel, G., and K. Moritzen. "Modula-2 and Its Environment." **Journal of Pascal, Ada & Modula-2**, 3:4 (July/August 1984), p.42.

Eckhardt, H., et. al. **VAX-11 Modula-2 User's Guide**. Universitaet Hamburg, West Germany, 1983.

Eldred, E. "Volition Systems' Modula-2." **Byte**, 9:6 (June 1984), p.353.

Greenfield, S. "An Introduction to Modula-2." **Journal of Pascal, Ada & Modula-2**, 3:3 (May/June 1984), p.36.

Gutknetcht, J. "System Programming in Modula-2: Mouse and Bitmap Display." Tech. Rep. 56. **Institut fur Informatik**, ETH, Zurich, 1983.

Gutknecht, J. "Tutorial on Modula-2." **Byte**, 9:8 (August 1984), p.157.

Hoppe, J. "Some Problems with the Specification of Standard Modules." **Modula-2 News** (October 1984).

Jacobi, C. "Code Generation and the Lilith Architecture." Diss ETH No. 7195. **Swiss Federal Institute of Technology**, Zurich, 1982.

Johnson, M. C., and A. Munro. "Pascal's Design Flaws: Modula-2 Solutions and Pascal Patches." **Byte**, 9:3 (March 1984), p.371.

Joyce, E. "The Making of Modula-2." **PC Magazine**, 3:7 (April 3, 1984), p.177.

337

Joyce, E. "A $40 Invitation to Modula-2." **PC Magazine**, 3:7 (April 3, 1984), p.182.

Joyce, E. "Modula-2 for Pascal Programmers." **PC Magazine**, 3:7 (April 3, 1984), p.193.

Kernighan, B. "Why Pascal Is Not My Favorite Programming Language." Computer Science Technical Report No. 100. **Bell Laboratories** (July 18, 1981).

McAlhany, E., and M. Campbell. "Modula-2 and Ada: A Comparison of Four Features." **Journal of Pascal, Ada & Modula-2**, 3:4 (July/August 1984), p.37.

McCormack, J., and R. Gleaves. "Modula-2. A Worthy Successor to Pascal." **Byte**, 9:4 (April 1983), p.385.

Moffat, D. V. "Some Concerns About Modula-2." **ACM SIGPLAN Notices**, 19:12 (December 1984), p.41.

Muller, R. "Differences Between Modula-2 and Pascal." **ACM SIGPLAN Notices**, 19:3 (March 1984), p.66.

Ogilvie, J. W. "A Pattern Matcher in Modula-2." **Journal of Pascal, Ada & Modula-2**, 3:6 (November/December 1984), p.34.

Ohran, R. "Lilith and Modula-2." **Byte**, 9:8 (August 1984), p.181.

Paul, R. J. "An Introduction to Modula-2." **Byte**, 9:8 (August 1984), p.195.

Pitt, J. "What's New with Modula-2?" **PC Magazine**, 3:7 (April 3, 1984), p.187.

Powell, M. L. "A Portable Optimizing Compiler for Modula-2." ACM 1984 Compiler Construction Conference. **ACM SIGPLAN Notices**, 19:6 (June 1984), p.310.

Powell, M. L. "Modula-2: Good News and Bad News." **Proc. IEEE COMPCON Spring 1984** (February 1984).

Pratt, T. W. **Programming Language, Design and Implementation**, 2nd Edition, Prentice-Hall, Englewood Cliffs, N.J., 1984.

Sewry, D. A. "Modula-2 and the Monitor Concept." **ACM SIGPLAN Notices**, 19:11 (November 1984), p.33.

Sewry, D. A. "Modula-2 Process Facilities." **ACM SIGPLAN Notices**, 19:11 (November 1984), p.23.

Shammas, Namir. "Modula-2: No Strings Attached." **Journal of Pascal, Ada & Modula-2**, 3:1 (March/April 1984), p.44.

Sincovec, R. F., and R. S. Wiener. **Software Engineering with Modula-2 and Ada**. Wiley, New York, 1984.

Spector, D. "Ambiguities and Insecurities in Modula-2." **ACM SIGPLAN Notices**, 17:8 (August 1982), p.43.

Sumner, R. T., and R. E. Gleaves. "Modula-2: A Solution to Pascal's Problems." **ACM SIGPLAN Notices**, 17:9 (September 1982), p.28.

Wiener, R., and R. Sincovec. **Software Engineering in Modula-2 and Ada**. Wiley, New York, 1984.

Wiener, R. "A Generic Sorting Module in Modula-2." **ACM SIGPLAN Notices**, 19:3 (March 1984), p.66.

Wiener, R., and R. Sincovec. "Modular Software Construction and Object-Oriented Design Using Modula-2." **Journal of Pascal, Ada & Modula-2**, 3:3 (May/June 1984), p.41.

Wiener, R., and G. Ford. **Software Development with Modula-2**. Wiley, New York, 1985.

Wirth, N. "Modula: A Language for Modular Programming." **Software Practice and Experience**, 7 (1977), p.3.

Wirth, N. "Design and Implementation of Modula." **Software Practice and Experience**, 7 (1977), p.67.

Wirth, N. "Modula-2." Report No. 36. **Institut fur Informatik**, ETH, Zurich, 1980.

Wirth, N. "Lilith: A Personal Computer for the Software Engineer." **Proceedings 5th Intl. Conf. of Software Engineering** (March 1981), p.2.

Wirth, N. "The Personal Computer Lilith." Report 40. **Swiss Federal Institute**, Zurich, 1981.

Wirth, N. **Programming in Modula-2**, 2nd (Corrected Edition). Springer-Verlag, Berlin, 1982.

Wirth, N. "History and Goals of Modula-2." **Byte**, 9:8 (August 1984), p.145.

Wirth, N. "Revisions and Amendments to Modula-2." **Modula-2 News** (October 1984).

Wittie, L. D., and A. J. Frank. "A Portable Modula-2 Operating System: SAM2S." **1984 National Computer Conference**, July 1984, p.283.

Zehnder, C. A. "Database Techniques for Professional Workstations." Tech. Rep. 55. **Institut fur Informatik**, ETH, Zurich, 1983.

Index

ABS, 164
Abstract data type, 199
Abstract type, 213, 230
Abstraction
  data, 181
Actual parameter, 128, 129
Actual Parameters, 60
Ada, 6
Additive Operator, 21
Additive operator, 24
ADDRESS, 177, 262, 263, 264
Addressing
  hard, 265
ADR, 178, 264
ALGOL-60, 2
ALGOL-68, 3
ALGOL-W, 2
ALLOCATE, 179, 204, 205
Allocation
  dynamic, 15
AND, 13, 24, 27, 44
Arctan, 175
Arithmetic expression, 23
Arithmetic operator, 12, 23
Arithmetic overflow, 43
ARRAY, 83
Array, 82, 115
  element of, 82
  index of, 82
  multidimensional, 112
  open parameter, 130
Array Type, 83
ASCII, 44, 90
Assignment operator, 12, 22
Assignment Statement, 22, 58
Available, 179
AVL tree, 255

Base conversion
  from cardinal, 87
  to cardinal, 89
Binary digit, 36, 262
Binary tree, 236, 237
Birthday Problem, 182
Bit, 36, 47, 48, 262
BITSET, 47, 104
Block, 56, 58, 188
BOOLEAN, 24, 31, 41, 42
Boolean operator, 12, 24, 44
Border-crossing problem, 253
Bubble sort, 92
BY, 77
BYTE, 178, 264, 282
Byte, 262

Call
  by address, 129
  by value, 129
  function, 139
  procedure, 118, 139
  recursive, 139
CAP, 47, 158
CARDINAL, 18, 31, 36
CASE, 67, 68, 95
Case Label List, 68, 99
Case Labels, 68, 99
Case Statement, 68
CHAR, 31, 44, 46, 47
Characteristic, 40
Child node, 236
CHR, 46, 164
CloseInput, 171
CloseOutput, 171
Comments, 29
Communication, 188

Compilation Unit, 9
Complex arithmetic, 97, 205
Component, 94, 96
  of a record, 94, 96
Concordance listing, 246
Concurrent programming, 265, 283, 287
CONST, 32
Constant, 15, 31, 32
Constant Declaration, 33
Constant Expression, 33
Constant Factor, 33
Constant Term, 33
Coroutines, 265, 283, 287, 288
cos, 175
Counting Clause, 77

Data abstraction, 4, 5, 181, 195, 199, 213
Data object, 15, 31
  constant, 15
  digraph, 246
  dynamic, 31, 203
  graph, 246
  list, 210
  queue, 228
  stack, 220
  static, 31
  tree, 236
  variable, 15
Data structure, 203
DEALLOCATE, 179, 204, 205
DEC, 47, 53, 161
Declaration, 32, 188
Definition Module, 193, 194
Definition module, 9, 167, 180, 193
Delimiter, 10, 12, 28
Dequeue, 229
Dereferencing operator, 12, 27, 205
Designator, 22, 84
Difference, 26, 49, 104
Digit, 14
Digits, 12
Digraph, 236, 246
Directed graph, 236, 246
Discrete simulation, 182, 187
DISPOSE, 179, 204, 253
DIV, 13, 23, 27
DO, 72, 76, 96
Done, 62, 74, 171

Dynamic allocation, 15, 97, 179, 204, 253
Dynamic data objects, 203
Dynamic storage allocation, 204

EBCDIC, 51
ELSE, 65, 68, 95
ELSIF, 66
Empty set, 48
END, 63, 68, 72, 76, 78, 95, 96, 118
Enqueue, 229
Entier, 176
Enumeration, 51, 52, 53
EOL, 62, 171
Error-correcting code, 106
EXCL, 162
EXIT, 80
Exp, 175
Export Statement, 194
Expression, 20
Expression List, 60

Factor, 21
FALSE, 24, 41
Field, 94, 96
  of a record, 94, 96
Field List, 95
Field List Sequence, 95
File
  object, 193
  processing, 97
  symbol, 193
  text, 279
Files, 175, 316
FileSystem, 171, 175, 316
FLOAT, 40, 165
Floating point representation, 38, 40
FOR, 76
For Statement, 77
Formal parameter, 128, 129
Formal Parameters, 129
Formal Type, 129
Formal Type List, 155
Function, 133, 134
  ABS, 164
  ADR, 178, 264
  BOOLEAN, 163
  CAP, 47, 158
  CARDINAL, 163

CHR, 46, 164
FLOAT, 40, 165
HIGH, 131, 161
INTEGER, 163
MAX, 162
MIN, 162
MOD, 23
ODD, 164
ORD, 46, 161, 164
pointer valued, 206
REAL, 163
recursion, 137
SIZE, 178, 264
TRUNC, 40, 165
TSIZE, 178, 263, 264
type conversion, 40, 163
type transfer, 37, 161, 163, 262
VAL, 161, 164

Generic, 273
    stack, 274
    structure, 274
Global variable, 128, 130
Graph, 203, 236, 246
    directed, 236, 246

HALT, 161
Hamming error-correcting code, 106
Hard addressing, 265
Heap, 204
Hexidecimal Digit, 17
Hidden type, 181, 195, 212, 230, 234, 286
Hiding detail, 166, 170, 187
HIGH, 131, 132, 161

IBM PC, 46, 167, 177, 270
Identifier, 14
Identifier, 10, 12, 13
    locality of, 125
    qualified, 14
    scope of, 125
    standard, 14
Identifier List, 35
IF, 63
If Statement, 64
IMPLEMENTATION, 9, 196
Implementation module, 9, 167, 180, 196
Implementation Module, 9
IMPORT, 58

Import Statement, 59, 183, 194
IN, 13, 50, 106
INC, 47, 53, 161
INCL, 162
Infinite loop, 72
Infix form, 223
Infix notation, 223
Information hiding, 234
InOut, 61, 168, 170, 174, 321
Integer, 16, 17, 31, 36
Intersection, 26, 49, 104
Invariant record, 94

Kernighan, B., 3
Key, 215

Leaf node, 236
Letters, 12
Lexical symbol, 10, 12
Library module, 180, 189, 192, 197
Lilith, 4, 5, 167
List, 203, 210
    one-way circular, 231
    one-way grounded, 211
    two-way grounded, 219
Literal, 16
Literal, 10, 12
    boolean, 41
    character, 18
    integer, 17
    real, 18
    set, 104
    string, 18
ln, 175
Local module, 180, 187
Local variable, 128
Locality of identifier, 125
LONGCARD, 264
LOOP, 78
Loop
    infinite, 72
Loop Statement, 78
Low-level access, 4, 5
Low-level programming, 262

Mantissa, 39
MathLib0, 175, 325
Matrix, 113
MAX, 162

Memory, 262
Memory management, 178
Mesa, 5
MIN, 162
MOD, 13, 23, 27
Modula, 5
Modula-2, 4
    revised definition, 101, 102, 162, 167, 177,
        194, 264
Modularization, 117
MODULE, 9
Module, 9, 166, 180
    definition, 9, 167, 180, 193
    export, 167
    Files, 175, 316
    FileSystem, 171, 173, 175, 318
    implementation, 9, 167, 180, 196
    import, 167
    initialization, 181
    InOut, 61, 170, 174, 321
    library, 180, 189, 192, 197
    local, 180, 187
    MathLib0, 175, 325
    Processes, 288, 326
    program, 180
    RealInOut, 173, 178, 327
    separate compilation, 166
    Storage, 179, 204, 327
    SYSTEM, 171, 177, 262, 328
    Terminal, 171, 173, 331
    TextIO, 174, 331
Module Declaration, 188
Multidimensional array, 112
Multiplicative Operator, 21
Multiplicative operator, 24

n-ary tree, 240
Natural order tree traversal, 245
Nesting procedures, 120
NEW, 179, 204, 253
NEWPROCESS, 177, 265, 286
NIL, 204, 211
Nonterminal node, 236
NOT, 13, 24, 27, 44
Notation
    infix, 223
    postfix, 223
    reverse Polish, 223
Number, 16

Number
    complex, 97
    hexadecimal, 17
    octal, 17
    ordinal, 17

Object file, 193
Octal Digit, 14
ODD, 164
OF, 68, 83, 95
One-way circular list, 231
One-way grounded list, 211
Open array parameter, 5, 130
OpenInput, 171
OpenOutput, 171
Operator
    additive, 24, 27
    arithmetic, 12, 23
    assignment, 12, 22, 27
    boolean, 12, 24, 44
    dereferencing, 12, 27, 205
    multiplicative, 24, 27
    precedence, 27, 223
    relational, 12, 25, 27, 41
    set, 12, 26, 49, 104
    set inclusion, 106
OR, 13, 24, 27, 44
ORD, 46, 161, 164
Overflow
    arithmetic, 43
Own variable, 4, 5, 128, 166, 181

Parameter, 125
    actual, 128, 129
    association by address, 129
    association by value, 129
    formal, 128, 129
    open array, 5, 130
    procedure as a, 128, 154
Parameter List, 129
Parent node, 236
Parity, 106
Pascal, 2
    UCSD, 2, 4
PL/360, 2
Pointer, 203, 211
POINTER TO, 177
Pointer Type, 204
Pointer type, 177, 234

Pop, 220
Postfix notation, 223
PROC, 155
PROCEDURE, 118, 155
Procedure, 58, 118
  ALLOCATE, 204, 205
  allocation, 128
  as a parameter, 154
  call, 118, 120
  DEALLOCATE, 204, 205
  deallocation, 128
  DEC, 47, 53, 161
  directly nested, 120
  DISPOSE, 179, 204, 253
  EXCL, 162
  function, 133, 134
  HALT, 161
  INC, 47, 53, 161
  INCL, 162
  nesting, 120
  NEW, 179, 204, 253
  NEWPROCESS, 177, 286
  recursion, 137
  side effect, 130, 135
  standard, 15, 158
  TRANSFER, 177, 286
  with parameter, 125
Procedure Call, 60
Procedure Declaration, 118
Procedure Heading, 118, 129
Procedure reference, 118
Procedure type, 154, 155
PROCESS, 177, 265, 286
Processes, 288, 326
Program
  module, 9
  source, 7
Program Module, 10, 180
Programming, 1
  concurrent, 283, 287
  low-level, 262
  system, 262
Pseudomodule
  SYSTEM, 262
Push, 220

QUALIFIED, 169, 194
Qualified Identifier, 14
Queue, 203, 228

Random number generator, 182
Read, 172
ReadCard, 61, 172
ReadInt, 172
ReadString, 172
ReadWrd, 172
Real, 17, 18, 31, 38, 176
RealInOut, 173, 178, 327
RECORD, 94, 115
Record
  component of, 94, 96
  field of, 94
  invariant, 94
  tag field of, 100
  variant, 99, 253
  variant tag component, 254
Record Type, 95
Recursion, 137, 216, 220
Relation, 20
Relational operator, 12, 25, 41
REPEAT, 74
Repeat Statement, 74
Representation
  floating point, 40
Reserved word, 10, 12, 13
RETURN, 134
Reverse Polish notation, 223
Root, 236

Scale Factor, 17, 18, 40
Scope of identifier, 125
Scope of variable, 130
Separate compilation, 4, 5, 166
Sequential logic, 4, 5, 44
Set, 105
SET, 104
Set, 16, 104
  difference, 26, 49, 104
  empty, 48
  inclusion, 106
  intersection, 26, 49, 104
  membership, 26
  operations, 162
  qualifier, 105
  subset relation, 106
  symmetric difference, 26, 49, 104
  union, 26, 49, 104
Set operator, 12, 26, 49, 104
Set Type, 104

Side effect
   procedure, 130, 135
Simple Constant Expression, 33
Simple Expression, 20
Simple Type, 52
Simula, 5
Simulation
   discrete, 182, 187
`sin`, 175
`SIZE`, 178, 264, 265
Sorting, 92, 116
   bubble, 92
Source program, 7
`sqrt`, 175
Stack, 203, 220
   generic, 274
   pop operation, 220
   push operation, 220
Standard identifier
   for type transfer, 164
Standard procedure, 15, 158
Statement, 56, 59
   `CASE`, 67
   decision, 25, 63
   `EXIT`, 80
   `FOR`, 76
   `IF`, 63
   `LOOP`, 78
   looping, 25, 71
   `REPEAT`, 74
   `RETURN`, 134
   `WHILE`, 72
   `WITH`, 96
Statement Sequence, 56, 58
`Storage`, 179, 273, 327
Storage allocation
   dynamic, 179, 204
Stream, 279
String, 17, 18, 47
   implementation of, 143
Structure
   generic, 274
Structured data type
   array, 82
   record, 94
Structured type, 112
Subrange, 51, 52, 53
Subset, 106
Symbol file, 193

Symmetric difference, 26, 49, 104
Syntax diagram, 7 (also see appendix B)
   Actual Parameters, 60
   Additive Operator, 21
   Array Type, 83
   Assignment Statement, 22
   Block, 58, 188
   Case, 68
   Case Label List, 68, 99
   Case Labels, 68, 99
   Case Statement, 68
   Communication, 188
   Compilation Unit, 9
   Constant Declaration, 33
   Constant Expression, 33
   Constant Factor, 33
   Constant Term, 33
   Counting Clause, 77
   Declaration, 32, 188
   Definition Module, 194
   Designator, 22, 84
   Digit, 14
   Enumeration, 52
   Export Statement, 194
   Expression, 20
   Expression List, 60
   Factor, 21
   Field List, 95
   Field List Sequence, 95
   For Statement, 77
   Formal Parameters, 129
   Formal Type, 129
   Formal Type List, 155
   Hexadecimal Digit, 17
   Identifier, 14
   Identifier List, 35
   If Statement, 64
   Implementation Module, 9
   Import Statement, 59, 183, 194
   Integer, 16
   Literal, 16
   Loop Statement, 78
   Module Declaration, 188
   Multiplicative Operator, 21
   Number, 16
   Octal Digit, 14
   Parameter List, 129
   Pointer Type, 204
   Procedure Call, 60

Procedure Declaration, 118
Procedure Heading, 118, 129
Procedure Type, 155
Program Module, 10
Qualified Identifier, 14
Real, 17
Record Type, 95
Relation, 20
Repeat Statement, 74
Scale Factor, 17
Set, 105
Set Type, 104
Simple Constant Expression, 33
Simple Expression, 20
Simple Type, 52
Statement, 59
Statement Sequence, 58
String, 17
Subrange, 52
Term, 21
Type, 35, 52
Type Declaration, 52
Variable Declaration, 35, 269
Variable List, 269
Variant, 99
While Statement, 72
With Statement, 97
SYSTEM, 171, 177, 262, 273, 286, 328
System's life cycle, 1
Systems programming, 262

Tag
    component of a variant record, 254
Tag component, 100
Tag field, 100
Term, 21
TermCH, 171
Terminal, 171, 331
Terminal node, 236
TextIO, 174, 331
THEN, 63
TO, 77
Top
    of stack, 220
Tower-of-Hanoi Problem, 140
TRANSFER, 177, 265, 286
Tree, 203, 236
    binary, 236, 237
    n-ary, 240

natural order traversal, 245
    root of, 236
TRUE, 24, 41
TRUNC, 40, 165
TSIZE, 178, 263, 264, 265
Two-way grounded list, 219
TYPE, 34, 52
Type, 35
Type, 14, 51
    abstract, 199, 213, 230
    ADDRESS, 177, 263
    BITSET, 47, 104
    BOOLEAN, 41, 42
    BYTE, 178, 264, 282
    CARDINAL, 18
    CHAR, 44, 46, 47
    elementary, 31
    enumeration, 51
    hidden, 181, 195, 212, 230, 286
    INTEGER, 17
    LONGCARD, 264
    pointer, 234
    POINTER TO, 177
    predefined, 15
    PROC, 155
    procedure, 154
    PROCESS, 286
    REAL, 18, 38
    SET, 104
    structured, 31, 82, 94, 112
    subrange, 51, 53
    unstructured, 31, 51
    WORD, 177, 178, 263, 282
Type conversion, 40, 163, 164
Type Declaration, 52
Type transfer, 37, 161, 163, 262

Union, 26, 49, 104
UNTIL, 74

VAL, 161, 164
VAR, 34, 128
Variable, 15, 31, 34
    global, 128, 130
    local, 128
    own, 4, 128, 166, 181
    scope of, 130
Variable Declaration, 35, 269
Variable List, 269

Variant, 99
Variant record, 99, 253
VAX, 173, 177, 178
Venn diagram, 106

WHILE, 72
While Statement, 72
Wirth, N., 2, 4, 136, 173, 288
WITH, 96
With Statement, 97

WORD, 177, 178, 263, 282
Write, 172
WriteCard, 61, 172
WriteHex, 172
WriteInt, 172
WriteLn, 61, 172
WriteOct, 172
WriteString, 61, 172
WriteWrd, 172